MW01071260

Private Debt

Founded in 1807, John Wiley & Sons is the oldest independent publishing company in the United States. With offices in North America, Europe, Australia, and Asia, Wiley is globally committed to developing and marketing print and electronic products and services for our customers' professional and personal knowledge and understanding.

The Wiley Finance series contains books written specifically for finance and investment professionals as well as sophisticated individual investors and their financial advisors. Book topics range from portfolio management to e-commerce, risk management, financial engineering, valuation and financial instrument analysis, as well as much more.

For a list of available titles, visit our website at www.wileyfinance.com.

Private Debt

Yield, Safety and the Emergence of Alternative Lending

Second Edition

STEPHEN L. NESBITT

WILEY

Library of Congress Cataloging-in-Publication Data:

Names: Nesbitt, Stephen L., 1953- author.
Title: Private debt : yield, safety, and the emergence of alternative
    lending / Stephen L. Nesbitt.
Description: Second Edition. | Hoboken, New Jersey. : Wiley, [2023] |
    Series: Wiley finance | Revised edition of the author's Private debt, [2019]
Identifiers: LCCN 2022051297 (print) | LCCN 2022051298 (ebook) | ISBN
    9781119944393 (cloth) | ISBN 9781119944416 (adobe pdf) | ISBN
    9781119944409 (epub)
Subjects: LCSH: Investments. | Small business—Finance. | Bank loans.
Classification: LCC HG4521 .N427 2023 (print) | LCC HG4521 (ebook) | DDC
    658.15/2—dc23/eng/20221024
LC record available at https://lccn.loc.gov/2022051297
LC ebook record available at https://lccn.loc.gov/2022051298

Cover Design: Wiley
Cover Image: © s_maria/Shutterstock

SKY10042146_020123

Contents

Introduction

The timing of this second edition is not accidental. The global economic and financial markets are experiencing tremendous volatility, perhaps even a paradigm shift, and investors are beginning to question the traditional 60–40 asset mix and buy-on-the-dip strategies that have served them well in the past. For the first six months of 2022 the 60–40 asset mix is down almost 20%, a drawdown only matched by periods of depression (1932), financial crisis (2008), or stagflation (1974). At the same time, inflation is on a tear, exceeding 9% annualized for the same six months.

Making matters worse, government bonds, which have served as the asset "anchor to windward" for decades, have seemingly lost that position in the currently inflationary environment as interest rates rise. Even Treasury Inflation Protection Securities (TIPS) have struggled despite their inflation hedging characteristics as the increase in real yields have caused TIPS returns to fall 9% for the first six months of 2022, almost equal to the −13% loss for ten-year Treasuries.

An early reversal in the current inflationary environment appears unlikely. The cure for inflation is unfortunately stagflation, with the Federal Reserve's new aggressive interest rate hikes likely to push the US economy into recession.

This economic reordering puts investors in a tough spot. Even after the recent 20% price decline, stocks remain expensive with price-earnings ratios equal to 19 times earnings. By comparison, stock price-earnings ratios averaged nine times earnings during the 1970s stagflation period. Unfortunately, stocks may still be expensive even after their recent bear market decline.

Treasury bond yields now exceed 3%, but these higher levels may still be unacceptable to investors when inflation rates are closer to 10% than zero, and inflation expectations equal 4% over the next two years and 3% over the next 10 years. Historically, Treasury bonds yield 1.5% in excess of inflation, a yield that had offered investors a reasonable 1.5% inflation-adjusted or real return. A return to this historical bond pricing regime would make Treasury bonds vulnerable to further price declines of 10–15% to restore investor demand.

With an outlook for both stocks and bonds in question, it is not surprising that investors are looking for alternatives to the 60–40 mix.

One obvious 60–40 replacement is cash. Holding cash short term may make a lot of sense for some investors, particularly those who have short-term time horizons or potentially large financial obligations. But holding cash is a lose-a-little strategy. Over time, holding cash earns a return that matches inflation but no more. There is no wealth creation, just wealth preservation. Of course, if investors can successfully market time by holding cash until stocks and bonds reach their lows and then buy the 60–40 portfolio, then they could achieve both preservation and wealth creation. Unfortunately, market timing has proven to be almost impossible to succeed at with investors more often losing money at it rather than making money. While holding cash may appear the safe thing to do, investors more often than not sell low, buy high in their cash decisions, suffering losses over time.

The first edition of *Private Debt*, published in 2019, was intended to introduce investors to a relatively brand-new asset class, one that offered high yield in an otherwise low interest rate world. Since that time, private debt has become perhaps the fastest growing investment class globally. This second edition documents that growth and success, but more importantly it presents an investment case why private debt may be an ideal investment in the newly uncertain inflationary world ahead. This investment case rests primarily on the floating-rate nature of middle market corporate loans, which protects investor wealth against inflation and, second, the additional yield spread that allows for wealth creation. These "all-weather" wealth preservation and wealth creation characteristics will likely continue to make private debt one of the fastest growing alternative asset classes.

The focus of this book, like the first edition, is on lending to middle market companies, primarily in the US. Corporate lending had traditionally been the business of commercial banks, but the global financial crisis and ensuing regulatory backlash created an opportunity for nonbank private asset managers to replace bankers as primary lenders to a large swath of middle market businesses. The economic recovery, albeit slow, found many middle market companies looking for debt capital for growth or refinancing. With banks in retrenchment, these companies found asset managers to be willing lenders. Lacking the deposit capital available to banks, the new direct lenders in turn have sought capital from institutional investors hungry for yields closer to 10% than the 1 to 3% available from traditional sources.

Though estimates vary, the size of the corporate direct loan market in the US today is estimated to be $1 trillion, up from $400 billion in 2019, a 2.5-fold increase. The increase is a product of both supply and demand. Corporate borrowing continues its trend toward private lenders, primarily specialized asset managers, preferring the speed, flexibility, and size of capital that asset managers bring relative to banks. Demand from capital providers has also grown as investors, primarily institutional but also retail, have become increasingly comfortable with the risks associated with direct lending that go along with the higher yields.

Chapters 1–6 collectively describe US middle market corporate direct lending, addressing the three characteristics that broadly define any asset class: return, risk, and liquidity. Private debt, including middle market corporate loans, has long been a mystery to investors for lack of credible historical data. The findings in this book would not be possible without a research effort launched in 2015 to construct a database and index for direct middle market corporate loans and published in a major investment journal.[1] That research covering return and risk is updated through March 31, 2022, in this second edition along with a new chapter addressing liquidity. The recent economic downturn associated with the COVID crisis has been a useful stress test for the resilience of direct lending to go along with the 2008 Financial Crisis covered in the first edition.

Chapter 7 is new, focusing in on the relationship between movements in interest rates and middle market loan returns. Unlike traditional investment-grade bonds, whose price goes down as rates rise, middle market loans provide a hedge against rising rates.

As with the first edition, Chapter 8 argues that fixed income as an asset class is more appropriately divided into two separate asset classes: an interest rate (Treasuries) asset class and a credit asset class. Instead of stock and fixed income allocations, investors should think in terms of three asset classes: stock, credit, and interest rate allocations. Our recommendation for separation five years ago has now gained broad acceptance among institutional investors.

Chapter 9 is also new. The demand for direct loans among investors has increasingly focused on senior only loans and less on second lien loans and mezzanine bonds. Since the first edition an index inclusive only of first lien and unitranche direct loans has been developed with results covered in Chapter 9. Later in Chapter 27 another index focused on just venture lending is introduced.

Chapter 10 provides a foundation for the three-asset view by theoretically splitting fixed income into separate credit and interest rate components using option pricing models developed 50 years ago by Robert Merton,

---

[1]Stephen L. Nesbitt, "The Investment Opportunity in U.S. Middle Market Direct Lending," *The Journal of Alternative Investments* (Summer 2017).

Fisher Black, and Stephen Cox. Their concept that any credit instrument can be modeled as a risk-free rate plus a put option forms the basis for sensitivity analysis and simulation to better understand the behavior of yield, return, and risk for various types of direct corporate loans and the value of covenants.

Chapter 10 is particularly useful in setting up Chapter 11. Investors first looking at direct lending are surprised by, and suspicious of, their higher yields. Chapter 11 provides an explanation for the high yields in direct loans by dissecting them into six components, each associated with a distinct risk factor potentially found in loans, and each offering an extra yield, or risk premium, as compensation for the specific risk factor. This yield architecture provides investors with a method for understanding and comparing absolute yields.

Chapter 12 takes a closer look at covenants, a real concern in 2021 and early 2022 when covenants were stripped from new loans in "covenant-lite" deals. The theoretical presentation in Chapter 10 includes an application of the Black-Cox model that gives a formulation for measuring the opportunity cost of covenant-lite in yield-equivalent units. Under one set of assumptions, for example, the Black-Cox model values a covenant package as being worth 1% in yield. Chapter 12 provides an inventory of what comprises a typical loan agreement, including the elements of a full covenant package. Its purpose is to provide the reader a practical knowledge of the types of covenants in a loan agreement that are covered from a theoretical perspective in Chapter 10.

Investments that go terribly wrong generally have too much leverage or involve fraud. Many investors in direct corporate loans apply some leverage to enhance return. Chapter 13 examines the impact of leverage on portfolio return and risk and provides guidance to investors on what leverage level might be appropriate. Unlike traditional stock or bond portfolios, where return and risk characteristics are similar among managers, direct lending offers investors many knobs that can materially differentiate one portfolio from another.

Chapters 14–17 discuss alternative forms for investing in direct corporate loans and some of the practicalities. Chapter 14 is new and highlights the current trend to offer alternative investments to retail investors. BDCs in Chapter 15 and a new Chapter 16 covering interval funds and tender funds together present popular investment vehicles, whereby individuals can access direct loans for personal investment.

Chapters 17–20 address a range of practical questions about direct loan investing, including manager selection, loan valuation, fees, and portfolio construction.

Having covered what direct lending portfolios might look like and how they work, Chapters 21 and 22 together show how institutional investors can use the data and findings covered in previous chapters to validate long-term allocations to direct corporate loans within existing diversified portfolios using standard asset allocation technology. Chapter 22 provides examples of optimized portfolios showing that allocations to direct lending, both unlevered and levered, enhance risk-adjusted return.

Chapter 23 is also new and addresses how direct lending and other asset classes might perform during a stagflation scenario. Having managed investments during the last stagflationary period, this author is keenly aware of the potential destruction of capital that might result if a similar scenario unfolds.

Chapters 24–26 each have a narrow focus. Chapter 24 is more technical in nature but important to direct lending as it is to all floating rate financial contracts. It discusses the shift from Libor to SOFR that is underway.

The research focus contained in this book is on direct corporate lending in the US middle market. But the same financial events that created the direct lending market in the US also occurred in Europe, though to different degrees. Chapter 25 provides an overview of the direct lending market in Europe with comparisons to the US market. Unlike Europe, direct lending in Asia is in its early development stages. Chapter 26 reverses the perspective from lender to borrower and identifies what characteristics a middle market corporate borrower looks for in a lender.

The book concludes with a view of direct corporate lending as part of a larger private debt market. Direct lending should be viewed as a core component with breadth of opportunity and characteristics that should make investors comfortable with it as a long-term investment. Other private debt investments tend to be smaller in market size and might be viewed as enhanced lending with higher return potential but higher risk. Chapter 27 provides short descriptions of 10 types of private debt outside direct lending that might be considered as complementary investments to a dedicated private debt allocation.

Together these chapters are intended to provide readers with a strong foundation for understanding private debt. But a real risk is that the reader gets lost or frustrated among all the data and analysis found within these chapters. That would be a shame because private debt is perhaps the easiest of alternative asset classes to understand, captured by a simple equation:

$$Private\ Debt\ Return = Income \pm Realized\ Gains(Losses)$$
$$\pm Unrealized\ Gains(Losses) - Fees$$

The components of this equation are fairly simple to understand and the content of the chapters ahead will be tied back to it to help the reader with a lifeline should it be necessary.

The first edition successfully introduced direct lending and private debt to an audience that mostly was unfamiliar with the subject. Perhaps the tremendous growth and acceptance of private debt over the subsequent five years was modestly influenced by that first edition. This second edition is intended not only to refresh many of the numbers that have become stale but also to demonstrate that, as predicted, direct lending continues to perform as expected and should perform well in the face of the many challenges ahead.

List of Exhibits

Acknowledgments

There are many individuals at Cliffwater to thank, but especially Josh Belvedere, Steven Harvey, Philip Hasbrouck, Stanley Liu, Joaquin Lujan, Eli Sokolov, Jeff Topor, and Mark Williams whose collective expertise contributed significantly to Chapter 27.

Special thanks goes to the team at John Wiley & Sons: Bill Fallon, executive editor; Samantha Enders, assistant editor; Purvi Patel, production managing editor; Samantha Wu, cover specialist. Thanks also to Susan Geraghty at 1000 Books and Julie Kerr.

CHAPTER 1

Overview of US Middle Market Corporate Direct Lending

This book focuses on the investment opportunity in US middle market corporate direct lending (or direct loans), a large and rapidly growing segment of the global private debt market. Direct loans are illiquid (non-traded) loans made to US middle market companies, generally with annual EBITDA ranging from $10 million to $100 million. These middle market corporate borrowers are of an equivalent size to those companies found in the Russell 2000 Index of medium and small stocks but, in aggregate, they represent a much larger part of the US economy compared to the Index. The US corporate middle market includes nearly 200,000 individual businesses representing one-third of private sector GDP and employing approximately 50 million people.[1]

Exhibit 1.1 illustrates where direct corporate lending fits within the multiple sources of long-term debt financing provided to US companies as of March 31, 2022. Long-term debt financing to US companies totaled approximately $12.6 trillion. By comparison, equity financing to US companies totaled approximately $24 trillion.

Traded, investment-grade bonds represent almost one-half of corporate debt financing, but this debt is issued by the largest US companies. High-yield (non-investment grade) bonds and bank loans represent almost one-half of investment-grade bond issuance. These companies are also larger, with EBITDA over $100 million where scale allows them to access the traded broker markets. Bank commercial lending, the market with which direct lenders compete, is $2.6 trillion in size.

The size of the direct lending US middle market loans is estimated to equal $1.0 trillion as of March 31, 2022. While small compared to traditional sources of corporate financing, the direct loan market has significant

---

[1]National Center for the Middle Market.

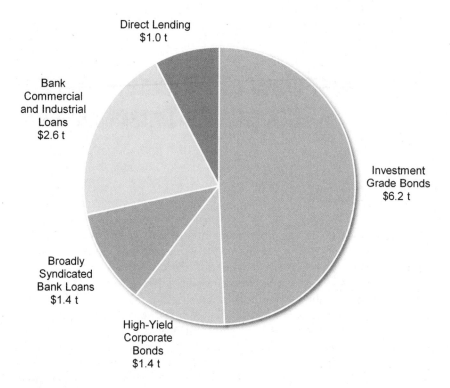

EXHIBIT 1.1   Breakdown of the $12.6 trillion US corporate debt market.
Source: Bloomberg, Federal Reserve Bank, Cliffwater.

potential for growth if it can continue to claim market share from the bank commercial and industrial (C&I) loan business. In fact, direct lending has grown 250% from its $400 billion size in 2019. That is well in excess of the roughly 40% growth across the other debt categories.

THE RISE OF NONBANK LENDING

Commercial banks have been the traditional lenders to US middle market companies. The Federal Reserve reports that US banks hold roughly $2.6 trillion in C&I loans on their balance sheets, which is likely mostly composed of middle market business loans. Banks also make loans to larger companies that are not held on their balance sheets. Instead, these loans are sold and syndicated across many investors, which are subsequently traded as private transactions in the secondary market. These traded loans are also referred to as broadly syndicated loans (BSLs), also known as "leveraged loans." The size of the leveraged loan market is roughly $1.4 trillion, or just over one-half the size of bank C&I loans. These larger traded bank loans have become very popular among institutional and retail investors through pooled accounts, mutual funds, and ETFs, providing a yield advantage to investment-grade bonds while maintaining daily liquidity.

Loans to middle market companies are too small for general syndication and therefore are held by the originating bank, sometimes with a few co-investors. The investment opportunity in middle market loans principally came about as an outcome of the 2008–2009 global financial crisis (GFC), and the years following, when increased capital requirements and tighter regulation on corporate lending made holding middle market corporate loans more expensive and restrictive. As banks decreased their lending activity, nonbank lenders took their place to address the continued demand for debt financing from corporate borrowers.

Direct loans are typically originated and held by asset managers, which get their capital from private investors rather than bank deposits. Asset managers are regulated by the Securities and Exchange Commission and are not subject to the same investment restrictions placed on banks. Investors are primarily institutional rather than retail, representing insurance companies, pension funds, endowments, and foundations. Retail investors have had access to direct loans mainly through publicly traded business development companies (BDCs), which are discussed in Chapter 15.

There are approximately 250 asset managers in the US that invest in direct middle market corporate loans, up from 180 in 2019. Many of them began direct lending during and soon after the GFC and recruited experienced credit professionals from banks that either went into bankruptcy (Bear Sterns, Lehman Brothers) or had their activities sharply curtailed. Important also were the financial problems faced by GE Capital, the financing arm of General Electric, during the GFC. GE Capital, through its subsidiary Antares, was at one point the largest US nonbank lender. The subsequent exodus of credit and deal professionals provided significant intellectual capital to the nascent nonbank lending industry.

While banks continue to hold a key advantage over asset managers by having a low cost of funds (i.e., bank deposits), this is offset by higher capital requirements, which ties up shareholder equity, and restrictions on the type of business loans that can be made by banks and the amount of leverage they can offer to borrowers. While these regulations may ease over time, a less likely prospect with a Democratic administration, the loss of talent during and after the GFC, and subsequent weakening of banks' relationships with borrowers, makes this a daunting prospect.

Finally, the growth of nonbank lending has also been helped by a new type of corporate borrower, the private equity sponsor. Private equity has seen steady growth since it began in the early 1980s but its role in the US economy has picked up significantly since the GFC, particularly in the middle market. These private equity–sponsored companies are professionally managed, use debt strategically in financing, and require timeliness, consistency, and flexibility from lenders, as well as attractive pricing. The advent of direct lending by professional asset managers has given private equity sponsors a preferred source of financing. Currently roughly 75% of direct loans are backed by private equity sponsors.

DIRECT LENDING INVESTORS

Investor interest in middle market direct lending has been driven by several factors. First and foremost are their attractive yields, ranging from 6% for the least risky senior loans to 12% for riskier subordinated loans. These yields compare with 2–3% for liquid investment grade bonds, as represented by the Bloomberg Aggregate Bond Index, a widely used investment grade bond index, and 4–5% for broadly syndicated loans, as represented by the Morningstar LSTA US Leveraged Loan 100 Index, an index used to track the broadly syndicated loan market.

Investors are also attracted to direct loans because coupon payments to lenders (investors) are tied to changes in interest rates and have relatively short maturities (typically five- to seven-year terms, which are typically refinanced well before the end of the loan term). The floating rate feature is particularly important in periods of rising interest rates. Interest rates for direct loans are set by a short-term "base rate" or "reference rate" like three-month Libor, US Treasury bills, or now SOFR, plus a fixed spread to compensate for longer-term default risk and illiquidity. Direct loan investors will see their yields increase as interest rates rise through quarterly adjustments to their base rate. In many respects, rising interest rates are beneficial for direct loan investors.

Conversely, most traditional bond funds primarily hold fixed rate securities, whose yields do not adjust to rising interest rates. Instead, rising rates cause bond prices to fall, in line with the duration of the bonds. A typical bond mutual fund has a five-year duration, a measure of average bond life. In this example, if interest rates for bonds with a five-year weighted average duration rise one percentage point, the bond fund will experience a 5% decline in value (five-year duration multiplied by 1% interest rate increase), offsetting any benefit from increased yield. Direct loans have only a three-month duration, and a one percentage point increase in rates will have only a temporary 0.25% (25 basis point) price decline. The direct loan yield will reset at the next calendar quarter and its value will return to par.

Direct loans generally have a shorter life than their five- to seven-year maturities suggest, which can be both good and bad. The average life of a direct loan has averaged approximately three years, much shorter than their stated maturity due to their being refinanced due to corporate actions, such as acquisition of the borrower by another company or prepayment by the borrower to get a lower interest rate. The good news is that direct loans are not as illiquid as their maturity suggests. At a three-year effective life, one-third of the loans pay off every year, which makes their liquidity profile attractive compared to private equity funds, whose effective life is seven to nine years on average.

However, if prepayments result from the borrower refinancing at a lower interest spread, then the lender is potentially worse off in terms of future yield, which causes the price of the loan to decline. Most loan documents include prepayment penalties, which go to the lender (investor) to make them whole for giving up the higher coupon, but these do not always provide sufficient compensation for the foregone income.

Most US middle market direct corporate loans are backed by the operational cash flow and assets of the borrower. Companies generally borrow from one lender whose security in case of default is all borrower assets but for trade payables and employee claims. The lender is said to have a senior, first lien claim in default. Some companies have additional lenders whose claims in default come after the senior lenders have been paid off. These are subordinated, second lien lenders who receive additional interest income for the greater risk of loss they take.

DIRECT LENDING ILLUSTRATION

Exhibit 1.2 illustrates a balance sheet of a middle market company with $40 million in EBITDA. The company is worth $360 million, or nine times (9×) EBITDA. Companies generally have a small amount of revolving credit for working capital purposes. "Revolvers" enable the borrowing company the right to draw capital as needed, paying an interest rate on amounts drawn as well as a fee on undrawn capital. These can be direct loans provided by an asset manager but, since they entail a high degree of servicing relative to the interest rates charged, are sometimes provided by a bank.

Most debt capital in our example is provided by a senior, first lien direct loan equal to $160 million, which equals 4× EBITDA. This direct loan has first claim on assets in bankruptcy excepting trade receivables, which would satisfy any revolver amount outstanding.

The company also has a $40 million second lien loan in place equal to 1× EBITDA but subordinated to the first lien and revolver debt. Historically, banks provided the senior first lien loan and nonregulated, nonbank institutional investors provided the subordinated second lien loan. Direct lending has increasingly left the nonbank asset manager to provide all debt financing, perhaps with the sole exception of the revolver, for middle market companies.

Companies can also have "unitranche" loans in place that combine first and second lien loans into one. Unitranche loans have become very popular in recent years as borrowers seek a single source of debt financing.

Finally, equity financing equal to $160 million provides the remaining capital that completes this company's balance sheet. Equity has historically been provided by the owner operator but increasingly it is the private equity sponsor who provides equity capital and who also puts in place professional managers to run the business.

The type of lending illustrated in Exhibit 1.2 is often referred to as leveraged finance because the amount of debt represents a higher multiple (leverage) of EBITDA than might be typical of investment-grade debt of a large multinational company. Rating agencies typically assign a non-investment

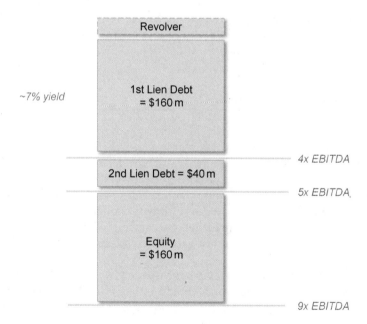

EXHIBIT 1.2 Capital structure of $40 million EBITDA company.

grade rating to direct loans. This is due to the higher debt leverage multiple, the relatively small size of the borrower, and the private ownership of the company, as opposed to public listing. Consequently, direct loan performance is more closely correlated to non-investment grade "junk" bonds, or broadly syndicated bank loans, rather than investment-grade corporate bonds found in indexes like the Bloomberg Aggregate Bond Index.

With this overview as an introduction, Chapter 2 provides a detailed description of the historical investment characteristics of US middle market direct loans.

The Historical Performance of US Middle Market Direct Loans

A prerequisite for institutional asset class standing is the presence of an index. No index for middle market loans existed until the Cliffwater Direct Lending Index was developed in 2015. It now has become the industry standard measure for middle market performance.

THE CLIFFWATER DIRECT LENDING INDEX (CDLI)

Most asset classes become institutionalized only after a long maturation period that permits discovery of both return and risk. That discovery process also involves the establishment of a database of unbiased information on the asset. For example, the CRSP database served that early role in the study of stock performance, as did the Capital International database for international stocks and the Salomon Brothers database for corporate bonds.

A major challenge for investors considering US middle market direct lending has been the lack of data on which to understand long-term return and risk. Bank C&I loans or direct loans held by insurance companies might be valuable sources of information, but these records are proprietary and not kept in a form that is conducive to the rigorous performance analysis available for other asset classes. As a result, investors who have engaged in direct lending have relied primarily on the attractive yields available on current private corporate loans and the performance records of a few asset managers who have engaged in middle market direct lending over an extended period of time. Currently investors might collect and compare performance records of direct lending managers, but these records suffer from being self-reported with inconsistencies in loan valuation, asset quality, use of leverage, and time period.

Fortunately, a significant and rapidly growing segment of the direct lending market consists of loans originated and held by BDCs where quarterly

SEC disclosures provide a vast amount of loan (asset) information, including listings of individual loans and quarterly valuations conducted by independent valuation firms. The information provided is comprehensive enough to calculate quarterly performance measures for direct loans that include income return, price return, and total return. It is from these SEC disclosures going back to 2004 that a corporate direct loan database has been constructed by Cliffwater LLC, together with a performance index called the Cliffwater Direct Lending Index (CDLI). As of March 31, 2022, the CDLI represented over $224 billion in direct loan assets covering 8,000+ loans from 111 individual public and private BDCs managed by the largest direct lending asset managers.

The loans captured by the direct loan database and the Cliffwater Direct Lending Index are a significant subset of the direct lending universe (~25%) and, importantly, represent loans that are originated and held to maximize risk-adjusted return to shareholders/investors.

The following describes the construction of the Cliffwater Direct Lending Index:

1. *Index Base Date*: September 30, 2004
2. *Index Launch Date*: September 30, 2015
3. *Data Universe*: All underlying assets held by private and public BDCs that satisfy certain eligibility requirements
4. *Index Reporting Cycle*: All index returns and characteristics are reported with a 2.5 month lag to allow sufficient time for release of SEC filings
5. *BDC Eligibility*:
   a. SEC regulated as a BDC under the Investment Company Act of 1940
   b. At least 75% of total assets represented by direct loans as of the calendar quarter-end
   c. Release SEC 10-K and 10-Q filings within 75 calendar days following the calendar quarter-end
   d. Eligibility reviewed at quarterly eligibility dates (75 calendar days following the calendar quarter-end)
6. *Weighting*: Asset-weighted by reported "fair value"
7. *Rebalancing*: As of calendar quarter-end
8. *Reported Quarterly Index Characteristics*: total asset return, income return, realized gains(losses), unrealized gains(losses), and total assets
9. *Location*: www.CliffwaterDirectLendingIndex.com

The CDLI is consistent with other private asset indexes in its quarterly reporting cycle, fair value asset valuation, and asset weighting. The loans are valued quarterly following SFAS 157 guidance. Returns are unlevered and gross of both management and administrative fees.

Theoretically, the CDLI is investable indirectly through public or private BDC share purchases. However, the primary CDLI return series excludes the application of leverage and imposition of fees, both management and administrative, which for some institutional investors can be negotiated based on objectives and size of investment. The CDLI return series should be useful to potential investors as a building block on which to customize returns series for expected fees and desired leverage. Later in this chapter are pro forma net-of-fee returns using the CDLI return series and leverage.

Importantly, SEC filing and transparency requirements eliminate common biases of survivorship and self-selection found in other industry universe and index benchmarks. And finally, loan assets in the CDLI are managed for total return largely by independent asset managers, unlike similar assets within insurance companies where statutory and other regulatory requirements can result in non-performance objectives.

US MIDDLE MARKET DIRECT LOAN PERFORMANCE

Exhibit 2.1 provides Cliffwater Direct Lending Index (CDLI) returns from its September 30, 2004, inception through March 31, 2022. All returns are based on quarterly data and are gross of fees and expenses.

Total returns are divided into the three major components investors use to assess performance for credit driven securities: income, unrealized gains (losses), and realized gains (losses). Income return is composed of contractual interest payments and, to a lesser degree, price discounts direct lenders might receive when they originate loans. Unrealized gains (losses) represent

| | | | Trailing Periods ending March 31, 2022 | | | |
		Q1 2022	Last 4 Qtrs	Last 5 Years*	Last 10 Years*	Sep 2004 Inception*
	Income	1.93%	8.67%	9.75%	10.46%	10.79%
plus	Net Realized Gains (Losses)	0.03%	0.49%	−1.23%	−0.97%	−1.08%
plus	Net Unrealized Gains (Losses)	−0.19%	1.85%	0.18%	0.01%	−0.19%
equals	**Total Return****	**1.76%**	**11.17%**	**8.63%**	**9.43%**	**9.46%**

*Annualized return.
**Return subcomponents may not add exactly to total return due to compounding effects.

EXHIBIT 2.1   Cliffwater Direct Lending Index performance.

change in loan values as determined by valuation agents and are generally a reflection of movement in overall market spreads or change in assessment of specific loan credit risk, akin to a loan loss reserve. Finally, realized (gains) losses are predominately losses and are the product of loan specific defaults and recoveries, which result in a write-down of loan principal.

Exhibit 2.2 plots the performance of the Cliffwater Direct Lending Index and its components. Visualizing performance in this way helps our understanding of what generates returns and what detracts from performance over time.

The heavy line in Exhibit 2.2 plots the cumulative (growth of $1.00) CDLI return, consisting of gross yield (top diagonal line) plus net realized gains/losses and plus net unrealized gains/losses (dashed line). The vertical axis uses a log scale. A log scale is useful for plotting cumulative returns over long periods of time because a constant rate of return produces a straight line. For example, the CDLI income return over the 17.50-year period appears as a straight line. This suggests that direct lending income (yield) has remained relatively constant over the period. Casual inspection also shows that direct lending income return drives total return over time, reduced periodically by net realized and unrealized losses. For the entire CDLI history, the direct loans in the Index returned 9.46%, annualized, with current income equal to 10.79%; unrealized losses equal to −0.19%, and realized losses equal

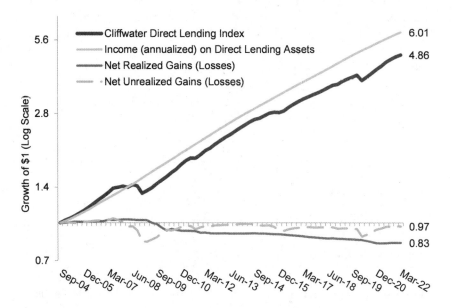

EXHIBIT 2.2   Components of direct lending returns, September 2004 to March 2022.

to –1.08%. These returns are consistent with the investment thesis underlying most fixed income strategies that investors should try to maximize yield but subject to preventing losses (realized and unrealized) in loan principal.

YIELD ON DIRECT LOANS

Exhibit 2.3 shows rolling four-quarter income return (yield) on direct CDLI loan assets. Beginning 2004, income has been fairly stable within the US middle market with income ranging roughly between 8% and 12% and averaging 10.79%. Higher income is associated with periods of recession while lower income is associated with periods of economic expansion.

A useful yield comparison is between middle market direct loans (CDLI) and three-month Treasury bills, plotted at the bottom of Exhibit 2.3. Because middle market loans are floating rate, equal to a fixed yield spread on top of a variable or floating short-term "reference rate," and because often-used reference rates like Libor and SOFR are closely linked to T-bill yields, the difference between middle market yields and T-bill yields is a good measure of the yield premium from middle market loans associated with their unique risks. That historical yield premium equals 9.67%, the

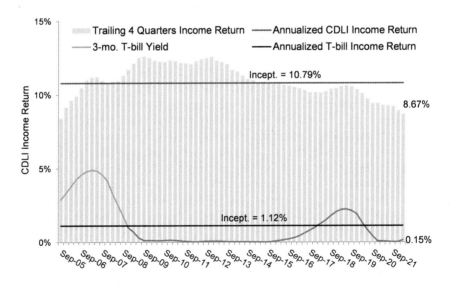

EXHIBIT 2.3 Direct loan income as percentage of loan asset value, rolling four quarters.
Source: Cliffwater, Bloomberg.

difference between the 10.79% historical average yield for middle market loans and the 1.12% historical average yield for three-month T-bills. On March 31, 2022, the premium equaled 8.52%, the difference between an 8.67% middle market loan yield and a 0.15% T-bill yield, down from the 9.67% long-term average. This yield spread decline is likely attributable to the growth of senior secured loans within the middle market at the expense of subordinated loans, a trend taken up later.

Not all income from middle market loans is traditional interest (coupon) income. Asset managers who originate corporate direct loans also receive fees for arranging and servicing the loans. These fees come in the form of discounts at origination of the loan. A typical example might be a loan that pays the lender $100 in principal value at maturity in five years, but the lender advances the borrower only $98 in financing. The lender receives a 2% discount ($100 minus $98) for arranging the loan. Principal value remains at $100 while net asset value at origination is set at $98. Accounting treatment for the $2 discount, called the original issue discount or OID, can vary with some reporting OID as income at origination but most amortizing the discount over the life of the loan. Understanding the accounting treatment of OID can be important because income can appear to spike during time periods of high origination or prepayments.

OID income generation for direct loans can be identified in the statement of cash flows in BDC quarterly SEC filings, which reports the dollar value associated with amortization of discounts. Over the five years ending March 2022 during which current CDLI total income return averaged 9.75% per year, origination income or OID contributed 0.40% (40 basis points) per year. Expressed differently, OID has represented 4% of the income associated with middle market direct loans. With direct loans averaging a five-year maturity at origination, the 0.40% annual amortized OID yield would be equivalent to a 2.0% average discount to principal value at origination.

Another less well understood source of income for some middle market loans is payment-in-kind, or PIK income. Instead of quarterly cash interest payments, PIK income represents a quarterly noncash increase in principal. PIK income is generally associated with subordinated debt or lower quality borrowers that may have limited free cash flow in the short term or, more recently, loans to high-quality growth companies with strong earnings potential but limited near-term cash flow generation. Like OID, PIK income is also found in the statement of cash flows in quarterly SEC filings. Over the last five years during which current CDLI total income return averaged 9.75%, PIK income contributed 0.62% (62 basis points) per year.

The proportions of income attributable to OID and PIK are potentially important statistics in measuring the risk of underlying loans. The presence

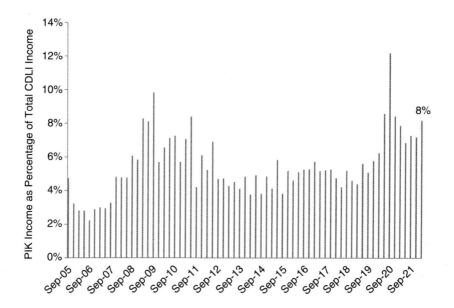

EXHIBIT 2.4   PIK as a percentage of total income in middle market direct loans.

of OID lowers risk because cash income is paid faster than the interest accrual. However, the presence of PIK increases risk because cash income is postponed, increasing both the potential for credit losses and the interest rate risk inherent in the loan by increasing loan's duration.

Exhibit 2.4 reports quarterly PIK income as a percentage of total CDLI income. Note that PIK is a higher percentage of total income during and around stress periods, including the GFC (2008), the oil crisis (2016), and the COVID crisis (2020).

NET GAINS (LOSSES)

While the CDLI income return component largely drives long-term total return, net gains (losses) can significantly affect returns over shorter time periods and can be very important in differentiating individual manager (lender) performance.

Net gains (losses) are defined as the periodic change in loan valuation. It is the equivalent of price change for traded securities. Net gains (losses) are frequently divided into two components, realized and unrealized.

Realized gains (losses) represent the component of valuation change that reflects completed transactions. In the case of a portfolio of loans, such as the CDLI, realized gains (losses) mostly come in the form of realized losses generated by write-downs of loan principal that result from borrower default. The amount of the write-down depends on the value of the post-default collateral or new principal amount.

Unrealized gains (losses) represent the component of valuation change that is sourced by a change in market price or, in the case of a portfolio of loans, such as the CDLI, a change in fair value not attributable to a transaction.[1]

It is instructive to review the mechanisms by which gains and losses for direct loans typically are generated, as well as the linkage between realized and unrealized gains and losses.

- Loan values are established quarterly based on a fair value assessment as to what the loan is worth. Fair value takes account of the probability and size of future loan impairments based on individual loan circumstances.
- Price changes in the broader traded credit markets, including high-yield bonds and bank loans, help guide expectations for future loan impairments and fair values.
- Quarterly changes in fair value create unrealized net gains (losses), which cause fair value to differ from cost (par) value. Most likely, fair value will be below cost value to reflect some probability of impairment.[2]
- Unrealized losses from reductions in fair value usually occur in advance of actual loan impairments as the certainty of loss increases as default approaches.
- A subsequent default event triggers a realized loss that is a permanent reduction in the cost (par) value of the loan.

---

[1]ASC 820 (previously FAS 157) defines *fair value* as "the price that would be received to sell an asset or paid to transfer a liability in an orderly transaction between market participants at the measurement date." Assets with a value that cannot be determined by observable measures, which would include the direct loans in the CDLI, are considered Level 3 assets (illiquid) and where valuation models are used to determine fair value. Best practice is to use an outside valuation firm to independently set or recommend fair value.

[2]An exception might be venture debt, when equity and warrants are offered by borrowers as enhancements.

- The realized loss (from a default or restructuring) replaces the existing unrealized loss through an offsetting unrealized gain. The new unrealized gain equals the prior unrealized loan loss if the default event and realized loss was correctly anticipated.
- Over time, investors observe a buildup in net realized losses, as defaults accumulate. These realized losses are comparable to loss rates[3] reported by rating agencies and banks for high-yield bonds and bank loans.
- Unrealized losses will generally build in the early stages of a credit downturn and reverse in the later stages as realized losses from defaults replace them.

This background should help put the realized losses and unrealized gains reported for the CDLI over the quarter and trailing year in better context.

NET REALIZED GAINS (LOSSES)

Exhibit 2.5 shows rolling four-quarter and cumulative realized gains (losses) for all direct CDLI loans. Unlike current income, realized gains (losses) for direct loans are not consistent and positive but episodic and mostly negative, corresponding (with some lag) to the general US business cycle or industry-specific events. For the entire 17.5-year period, cumulative realized losses equaled −17.28%, or −1.08% annualized.

Direct loans in the CDLI experienced modest realized gains over the brief period prior to the 2008 GFC. These gains were largely associated with equity and warrants that sometimes come with direct loans, particularly pre-2008 when most direct loans were subordinated, had lower yields, but came with more equity participation. This was also a period following the 2000–2002 recession when the equity markets were experiencing a sharp rebound. In the current direct lending environment, where lending is senior in orientation with little equity participation, the occurrence of net realized gains for direct lending generally will be less likely.

The second period covering the GFC is of great interest because it is a period that investors now use to stress test different asset classes. Also, because direct lending is a newer asset class, it is the first time period that can be used to study likely maximum loss scenarios.

---

[3]Default and recovery rates are more frequently reported for high-yield bonds and loans. The credit loss rate is equal to the default rate multiplied by one minus the recovery rate.

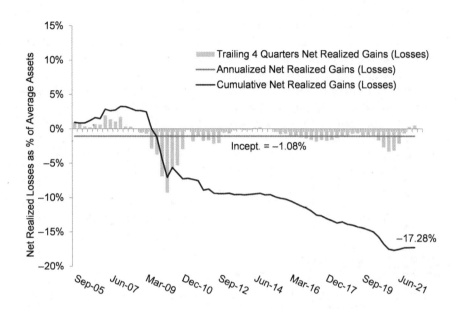

EXHIBIT 2.5 Net *realized* gains (losses) as percentage of loan assets, rolling four quarters and cumulative returns.

Cumulative realized losses for direct loans caused by the GFC totaled –10.20%, covering the years 2008, 2009, and 2010. Realized losses are not confined to 2008 because defaults in 2009 and 2010 likely result from financial impairments that occurred in 2008.

The third period extends from 2011 to 2015, when realized losses continued to ebb with the final three years, 2013 to 2015, reflecting an unusual period of almost no realized losses. But for the euro crisis early during this period, it was a time period marked by slow but steady US business expansion and a climbing stock market.

The fourth period begins in 2016 with the oil crisis and a continuing period of retail disruption. Realized losses were slightly above the historical average and began to slow again with the pickup in the economy in the three years 2017 through 2019.

The 2020–2021 COVID crisis represents the fifth period and a second major stress test for the markets generally and direct loans post-GFC. Realized losses totaled –3.53% over the five-quarter period starting January 1, 2020, and running through March 31, 2021, and equaled a little more than one-third of the realized losses experienced during the GFC. Of course, the COVID crisis was very short and unusual in many ways, just as the GFC was perhaps unique in its severity.

A look at the CDLI data shows that realized losses from defaults come in waves. Unlike the steady source of income that comes from direct loans, credit losses are episodic and appear highly correlated with the business cycle. The unfortunate news is that turns in the business cycle are almost impossible to predict, though investors seem to spend an inordinate amount of energy trying to predict them. There are two more reliable ways to reduce realized losses. The first is to invest in senior loans, but the cost of that strategy is lower yield, which may be greater than the higher realized losses the investor would otherwise incur. The second method is to select a skilled lender (asset manager) who has strong underwriting capabilities and can sense when market risk may be higher or lower and adjust strategy appropriately. There is evidence that credit underwriting skill persists, which is covered in Chapter 17.

NET UNREALIZED GAINS (LOSSES)

Unrealized gains (losses) measure changes in loan asset value that come about not by actual transactions or write-downs but by changes in the value of loans given by a market or third-party valuation agent. Since middle market direct loans are seldom traded and instead held to maturity, periodic changes in loan value that create unrealized gains (losses) are determined by the lender itself or third-party valuation agents. This type of valuation is referred to in accounting as fair value, and guidance for determining fair value is given by accounting standard AFAS 157.

AFAS 157 places assets for valuation purposes into Levels 1, 2, and 3. Level 1 assets are exchange traded where a market price is available at the end of each day. Public stocks are an example. Level 2 assets are traded through broker/dealer markets with prices determined when a transaction occurs or when a price (broker quote) is requested. Level 3 assets are valued based on the lender's valuation policy, which incorporates quantitative models and qualitative insight in determining fair value for each loan. These lender valuations incorporate overall market credit spreads and loan specific credit outlooks. In fact, in their quarterly reporting, most BDCs provide an assessment of creditworthiness by categorizing loans into varying default risk categories. Most direct loans are Level 3 assets.

Valuation involving Level 3 assets, such as direct loans, is most often performed quarterly. Changes in valuation give rise to quarterly unrealized gains (losses) that theoretically harbinger expected but uncertain future credit losses. Unrealized losses for direct loans can be viewed in the same way that banks create and periodically change reserves against future realized losses from loan defaults.

The practice of pricing through lender valuations versus independent third-party valuations varies and often depends on the needs of investors. Best practice is to have all loans valued quarterly by third-party valuation firms. But this can be expensive and unnecessary if the information generated has little use, as it would in a private fund or partnership that does not trade or its investors are captive. More likely, fair value is determined only once a year by a third-party valuation firm, either by valuation of all loans once a year or valuing one-quarter of the portfolio at every quarter-end. At those times when loans are not being independently valued, the lender itself is valuing the loans based on methodologies similar to what the third-party valuation firm would otherwise use.

Exhibit 2.6 shows rolling four-quarter and cumulative unrealized gains (losses) for all direct loans in the Cliffwater Direct Lending Index.

Long-term cumulative returns for unrealized gains (losses) should average close to 0% because, as discussed previously, unrealized losses will either convert to net realized losses on a credit default and recovery, or they will be reversed when principal is fully repaid. The cumulative net unrealized gain (loss) line in Exhibit 2.6 is consistent with this expectation.

For example, unrealized losses expanded in the 2007–2008, 2013–2014, and 2019–2020 periods, anticipating rising realized losses ahead. When

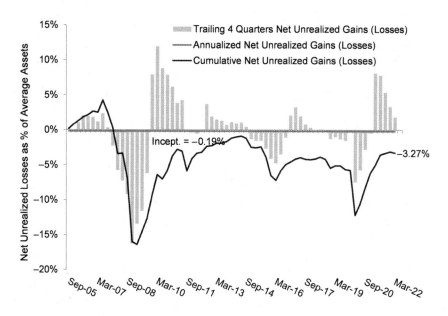

EXHIBIT 2.6 Net *unrealized* gains (losses) as percentage of loan assets, rolling four quarters and cumulative returns.

loans are subsequently written down it creates a realized loss but also potentially an unrealized gain if the realized loss was previously anticipated in a prior period by recognizing an unrealized loss. Two accounting entries equal in dollar value, a realized loss plus an unrealized gain, convert an unrealized loss into a realized loss.

TOTAL RETURN

Exhibit 2.7 combines income, realized gains (losses), and unrealized gains (losses) into a single total return. As with the components, total return reported in the exhibit represents rolling four-quarter periods.

Rolling four quarter CDLI total returns in Exhibit 2.7 have been high and fairly consistent, averaging 9.88% for the entire 17.5-year history of the Index. The exception occurred during the GFC when the worst four-quarter (one-year) period was calendar 2008 when the CDLI total return equaled −6.50%. Component returns for the same one-year period were 11.72% (income), −2.89% (realized losses), and −16.25% (unrealized losses).

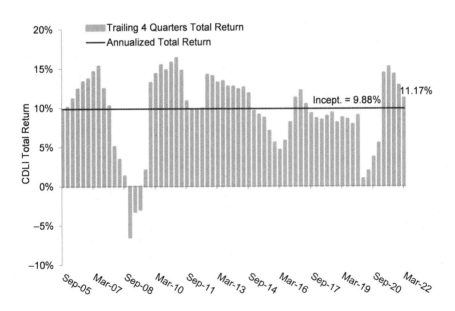

EXHIBIT 2.7   Direct loan total return as percentage of loan asset value, rolling four-quarter returns.

A first cut at filling out the private return equation using CDLI as the performance benchmark and its return components covering 17.5 years would be as follows:

$$Private\ Debt\ Return = Income \pm Realized\ Gains(Losses)$$
$$\pm\,Unrealized\ Gains(Losses) - Fees$$

$$Private\ Debt\ Return^4 = 9.46\% \approx 10.79\% - 1.08\% - 0.19\% - Fees$$

---

[4]Component returns do not add exactly to total return due to compounding effects.

CHAPTER 3

Performance Comparisons to Other Asset Classes

Little has changed with respect to basic asset allocation theory over the last 55 years since Harry Markovitz introduced portfolio optimization based on asset return, risk, and correlation. In practice, however, there are many more asset class choices available to investors today, and newer asset classes like direct lending are only successful to the extent that they have differentiating investment features compared to other asset classes. A high current yield is the most obvious differentiating feature, but for institutional investors this is not enough to warrant consideration. Direct loans must also demonstrate attractive return and risk characteristics that justify their inclusion into a diversified portfolio of assets. This chapter provides a comparative analysis of return and risk across the major asset classes that direct loans might compete with for inclusion into a diversified portfolio.

Exhibits 3.1, 3.2, and 3.3 compare direct lending performance, measured by the Cliffwater Direct Lending Index, with the most commonly used public and private asset classes.

Full definitions for the individual indexes are provided in the Glossary but note here that all index returns are before fees except for private equity, represented by the Cambridge Associates US Buyout Benchmark whose returns only report net of all fees, including carried interest. Asset class return and risk measures cover the same 17.25-year period ending December 2021. The starting date is chosen because it reflects the start date for the Cliffwater Direct Lending Index (CDLI) and the end date corresponds to the last date all return data is available, with private equity returns being the most delayed. All calculations are based on quarterly returns to be consistent across asset classes. Finally, only US asset classes are included because the comparison is meant to gauge return and risk within a single market, without currency and country-specific impacts.

Return Correlations

	Return*	Risk*	Return/Risk Ratio	Max Draw-down	Stock Beta**	Russell 3000	ML T-Bills	Bloom Aggr	Mstr LSTA 100	Bloom High Yield	CDLI	NPI	CIA Buyout
Russell 3000	11.08%	16.58%	0.67	-46%	1.00	1.00	-0.12	-0.20	0.71	0.79	0.70	0.17	0.80
Merrill Lynch 0–3 Month T-Bill	1.31%	0.82%	1.59	0%	-0.01	-0.12	1.00	0.14	-0.14	-0.15	-0.10	0.22	0.01
Bloomberg US Aggregate	4.00%	3.31%	1.21	-3%	-0.04	-0.20	0.14	1.00	-0.16	0.00	-0.29	-0.18	-0.27
Morningstar LSTA US Lev Loan 100	4.47%	9.54%	0.47	-29%	0.41	0.71	-0.14	-0.16	1.00	0.94	0.75	-0.04	0.59
Bloomberg High Yield	7.25%	10.56%	0.69	-27%	0.50	0.79	-0.15	0.00	0.94	1.00	0.75	-0.08	0.65
Cliffwater Direct Lending Index	9.50%	3.63%	2.61	-8%	0.15	0.70	-0.10	-0.29	0.75	0.75	1.00	0.36	0.81
NCREIF Property (Real Estate)	8.62%	5.09%	1.69	-24%	0.05	0.17	0.22	-0.18	-0.04	-0.08	0.36	1.00	0.46
Cambridge (CIA) US Buyout	15.26%	10.05%	1.52	-28%	0.48	0.80	0.01	-0.27	0.59	0.64	0.81	0.46	1.00

* Annualized.
** Russell 3000 used to measure stock beta.

EXHIBIT 3.1 Asset class return and risk, September 2004 to December 2021.

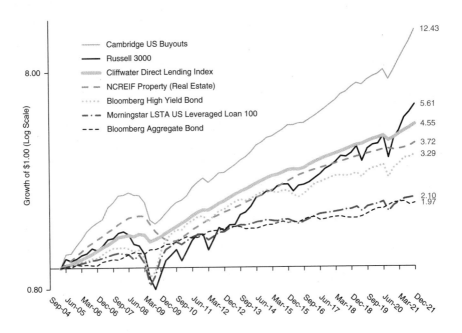

EXHIBIT 3.2   Asset class cumulative returns (growth of $1.00), September 2004 to December 2021.

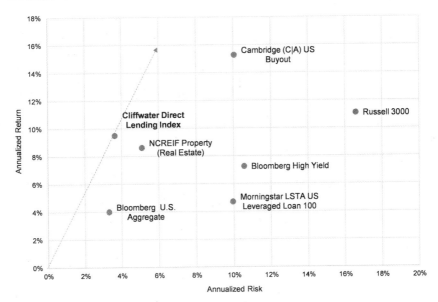

EXHIBIT 3.3   Asset class return versus risk, September 2004 to December 2021.

Asset classes are grouped by type in Exhibit 3.1. The Russell 3000 Index, which includes large and middle market companies, represents the performance of the US public equity market. Next, two measures of investment-grade fixed income are provided. The Merrill Lynch 0–3 Month T-Bill Index represents short-term rates, and the Bloomberg Aggregate Bond Index represents the most popular benchmark for fixed income portfolios and the index most commonly used for passive fixed income investing. Two measures of traded non-investment grade credit are provided. The Morningstar LSTA US Leveraged Loan 100 Index measures the performance of broadly syndicated bank loans and is the most common index currently used to benchmark direct loan and other private debt strategies. The Bloomberg High Yield Bond Index is the most common index used to benchmark high-yield bond portfolios. Like direct lending, high-yield bonds are non-investment grade, but they are actively traded and have fixed, not floating, rate coupons. Last, Exhibit 3.1 shows two other private asset classes in addition to the CDLI. NCREIF (National Council on Real Estate Investment Fiduciaries) measures the quarterly performance of institutional real estate equity. Its construction is very similar to that used for the CDLI. Finally, the Cambridge Associates US Buyout Benchmark measures performance of private partnerships that invest in private US companies, not private equity companies themselves. Again, Cambridge Associates US Buyout Benchmark is net of fees while the other indexes are reported gross of fees.

RETURN

The asset class returns shown in Exhibit 3.1 are consistent with expectations. Equities are expected to outperform other asset classes over long time periods, as private and public equities do in Exhibit 3.1. US buyouts, measured by the Cambridge Associates US Buyout Benchmark, was the best-performing asset class with a 15.26% annualized return, which was 4.18% above the 11.08% annualized return for the Russell 3000 Index return of public US equities. The 4.18% difference between private and public equity compares favorably with the 3.00% per annum excess return for private equity over public equity targeted by most institutional investors.

Direct lending, measured by the CDLI, returned an annualized 9.50% and outperformed the other asset classes listed except for private and public equity, which it trailed by 4.76% and 1.58%, respectively. The outperformance by the Cambridge Associates US Buyout Benchmark should be expected because it represents capital that has less seniority than direct loans in the corporate capital structure and therefore should have a higher return (see Exhibit 1.2). Given that the private equity returns are net of fees and the CDLI is gross of fees, the difference would be closer to 6–7% if the CDLI were adjusted for likely fees and expenses. This estimated net-of-fee difference in private equity and private debt returns is in line with under-writing of sponsored equity and debt financing.

The 9.50% CDLI return outperformed the NCREIF Property Index (NPI) of institutional commercial real estate equity return of 8.62% for the measurement period, which is of note because both indexes have common construction methodologies and similar ASC 820 oversight in asset valuation. Also, both asset classes share the common role of stable income, lower risk, and inflation protection within diversified institutional portfolios.

Another important comparison is between the annualized 9.50% CDLI return and the 4.47% Morningstar LSTA US Leveraged Loan 100 Index return. This 5.03% annualized difference is approximately equal to the historical yield spread between the two indexes and represents a reasonable expectation for an illiquidity premium for private floating rate non-investment grade loans over equivalent publicly traded loans. Adjusted for fees, the estimated difference is closer to 3.53%, because direct lending investors pay roughly 1.5% more for a direct loan portfolio compared to a portfolio of bank leveraged loans. Many direct lending investors are bench-marking their direct lending portfolio returns to a 1–2% spread over the Morningstar LSTA US Leveraged Loan 100 Index. The historical returns in Exhibit 3.1 suggest this might be a somewhat conservative benchmark.

At first glance, the 7.25% annualized return for the Bloomberg High Yield Bond Index looks attractive both because its return is closer to the 9.50% CDLI return and it far exceeds the 4.70% return on the Morning-star LSTA US Leveraged Loan 100 Index. However, both comparisons are misleading because (1) high-yield bonds are fixed rate, not floating rate, and (2) high-yield bonds generally have lower seniority, sitting in a company's capital structure below senior secured debt.

The high-yield bond return can be adjusted for the fixed/floating difference by subtracting the spread between the Bloomberg 3–5 Year US Treasury return of 3.19%, whose duration is similar to that of high-yield bonds, and the Merrill Lynch 0–3 Month T-Bill return of 1.31%. The 1.88% difference is what needs to be subtracted from the 7.25% Bloomberg High Yield Bond Index return to get an equivalent floating rate return for high-yield bonds equal to 5.37%, annualized, and a return that would be equivalent to buying high-yield bonds but adding a fixed/floating interest rate swap.

Before fees and using the equivalent duration high-yield bond return, the three floating rate credit indexes returned 9.50%, 5.37%, and 4.70% for direct loans, high-yield bonds, and leveraged loans, respectively, over the 17.25-year measurement period. Adjusting for estimated fees equal to 1.90%, 0.65%, and 0.65% for direct loans, high-yield bonds, and leveraged loans, respectively, after-fee and floating-rate equivalent returns for these three asset classes would equal 7.60%, 4.72%, and 4.05%, respectively.[1] The 0.67% spread between public high-yield bonds and leveraged bank loans is attributable to the subordinated credit position of most high-yield bonds, which should entail a higher credit spread compared to leveraged bank loans.

Finally, the 9.50% CDLI return compares very favorably to the 4.00% return for the popular Bloomberg Aggregate Bond Index, composed of all investment-grade public US debt. A similar 1.88% downward adjustment to the 4.00% return is warranted to make it a floating-rate equivalent return. Assuming the same 1.90% fee for direct lending and a 0.04% fee for an index tracking investment grade bond index, there is a net 5.52% difference (= 9.50% − 1.90% − 4.00% + 1.88% + 0.04%) between direct-lending and investment-grade fixed income returns. Future chapters will show that calculated net 5.52% return premium would seem to be an attractive investor reward for allocating assets to direct lending.

Exhibit 3.2 provides a graphical representation of asset class returns. As in Exhibit 2.2, cumulative returns in Exhibit 3.2 are plotted on a log scale so that a constant return appears as a straight line and drawdowns are scaled by return, not dollar loss.

The strong performance for private equity (Cambridge US Buyout Index) is striking from Exhibit 3.2 with a hypothetical $1.00 invested on September 30, 2004, growing to $11.86 by December 31, 2021. In comparison to public equity (Russell 3000 Index), the performance difference is shown to be quite wide, with a dollar of public equity growing to $5.61 after 17.25 years, less than one-half profits produced by private equity.

The performance shown for the CDLI is not as strong as it is for private equity, nor should it be, but in a comparison with equivalent public securities, measured by the Morningstar LSTA US Leveraged Loan 100 Index, the CDLI displays consistent and widening separation, with a dollar growing to $4.55 after 17.25 years compared to $2.10 for the Morningstar LSTA US Leveraged Loan 100 Index. Like private equity, private debt more than doubled the profits over the time period examined compared to public debt.

RISK

Historical standard deviation of return in the second column and maximum drawdown in the fourth column of Exhibit 3.1 give investors a comparison of the volatility found in direct lending compared to the other asset classes.

---

[1] Direct lending fees based on survey research presented in Chapter 19. High-yield bond and leveraged loan fees are based on reported ETF expense ratios.

Risk values for the public asset classes show little surprise with public equity measuring the highest 16.58% standard deviation; non-investment grade credit through bank loans and high-yield bonds incurring slightly less risk at 9.95% and 10.56%, respectively; and investment grade intermediate maturity bonds represented by the Bloomberg Aggregate Bond Index at a 3.31% risk level.

Standard deviations for private equity, private real estate, and private direct loans equal 10.05%, 5.09%, and 3.63%, respectively. Relative volatility among these three private asset classes is likely consistent with the perceived risk being taken, with private equity the highest risk and private debt the lowest risk. However, the absolute levels of risk from private assets are likely understated due to the use of fair value accounting, which results in a smoothing of asset values. This undoubtedly occurs, but it is difficult to precisely measure its impact on risk and correlation. We address this in more detail in Chapter 18.

Exhibit 3.3 provides a useful depiction that combines return and risk by asset class with return shown by the vertical axis and risk shown in the horizontal axis. The return/risk ratio, reported in Exhibit 3.1, is depicted in Exhibit 3.3 by the dashed line extending from the origin through the asset class plot point. The radius of the dashed line equals the return/risk ratio. The dashed line depicted is for the Cliffwater Direct Lending Index, which has the highest radius value of 2.61. This is an important finding because investors have been searching over the past decade for strong return in combination with safety. Direct lending is increasingly getting recognition for potentially filling that void.

DRAWDOWN

Investors increasingly look at maximum drawdown as another important measure of risk. This return measures the cumulative, unannualized percentage decline in value from peak value to lowest value. Maximum drawdown became an important complement to the more familiar standard deviation risk measure after the 2008–2009 GFC. The standard deviation measure of risk works only if the periodic returns on which the calculation is based are uncorrelated with each other. (They are not serially correlated and follow a random walk.) But that is not how markets behaved in 2008 and 2009. Down months followed down months in a pattern that led a standard deviation risk measure to understate the true risk of loss. As a result, most investment professionals added the maximum drawdown calculation to their risk metrics. The maximum drawdown calculation also avoids the understatement of standard deviation risk caused by serial correlation.

Though it occurred 15 years ago, the near halving of stock values during the GFC hasn't been forgotten. The maximum drawdown for the Russell 3000 Index equaled −46%, transpiring over a six-quarter period from September 30, 2007, through March 31, 2009, and gave rise to a renewed emphasis on risk management strategies. In hindsight, Treasury securities proved to be the best risk mitigator. Treasury indexes, and broader investment-grade bond indexes like the Bloomberg Aggregate Bond Index, which is predominately composed of Treasury and agency bonds and notes, lost little or no value during the GFC, earning risk-off status among chief risk officers. However, as investment professionals discovered, the opportunity cost of holding these securities has been significant, with Treasury yields averaging less than 3%, and sometimes below 2%. Since the GFC, asset allocators have been looking for strategies or asset classes that might better balance return and risk and sit somewhere between stocks and Treasuries in the risk spectrum. The performance of direct loans strongly suggests it might be a good choice to fill that between role.

Make no mistake, direct loans are a risk-on asset class, as the correlations in Exhibit 3.1 demonstrate. The correlation between the CDLI and the Russell 3000 index measures 0.70. R-Squared, the square of the correlation, equals 0.49, meaning that 49% of the volatility of the CDLI is explained by the volatility of the Russell 3000 index. In other words, direct loan returns are heavily influenced by the ups and downs of stocks. Why direct loans have a strong correlation to stocks is answered from a theoretical perspective in Chapter 10.

However, direct loan fair values do not display the same high volatility as stocks. While directionally influenced by stocks, direct loan values have a Treasury-like 3.5% standard deviation. The CDLI beta to the Russell 3000 Index, which is the product of relative standard deviation and correlation, measures 0.15 and would be considered a strong portfolio diversifier by most risk management standards.

DIRECT LENDING AND THE GFC STRESS TEST

Exhibit 3.4 provides comparative asset class performance beginning September 31, 2007, marking the beginning of Q4 2007 when an economic recession began, through the GFC, and ending March 31, 2011, when asset classes had mostly recovered to precrisis values.

Investment grade bonds, measured by the Bloomberg Aggregate Bond Index, was the only risk-off asset class that escaped the GFC, as Exhibit 3.4 shows. All other asset classes suffered losses of varying amounts. Direct lending, measured by CDLI, was down a modest 5% from September 2007 while

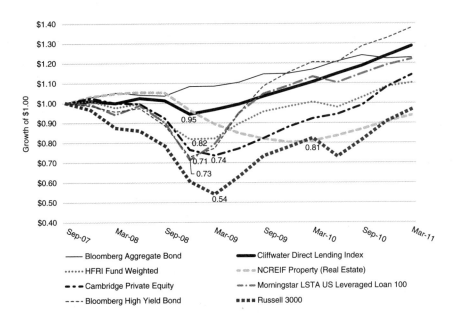

EXHIBIT 3.4 Asset class cumulative total returns through the GFC, September 2007 to March 2011.

losses in all other asset classes were severe, ranging from an 18% loss for hedge funds (HFRI Fund Weighted Index) to a 46% loss for public equities. Also noteworthy is the low 5% loss for direct lending compared to public debt losses of 27% for leveraged loans and 29% for high-yield bonds.

Equity real estate, measured by the NPI, is an interesting case. It too suffered a significant 19% loss ($0.81) during the GFC, but its lowest point came two to three quarters after the other asset classes. The lagged experience for real estate is discussed further in Chapter 18 covering valuation, but note here that real estate values are notoriously sticky, which causes returns to be smoothed through serial correlation.

Exhibit 3.5 contains a similar analysis but defines the drawdown period separately for each asset class with the starting date defined as the quarter-end when the asset class experienced its highest value (rather than the singular September 2007 date used in Exhibit 3.4) through the quarter-end date when the asset class reaches its lowest value.

The severity of the GFC market decline hit traditional risk-oriented asset classes the hardest with stocks, leveraged loans, and high-yield bonds suffering the largest losses. Private equity and private real estate lost about one-quarter of their value. Even hedge funds incurred significant –19%

Asset Class Index	Beginning Date	Max Drawdown	Quarters to Recovery
Bloomberg US Aggregate	3/31/2008	–1%	1
Cliffwater Direct Lending Index	6/30/2008	–8%	4
HFRI Fund Weighted (hedge funds)	12/31/2007	–19%	7
NCREIF Property (real estate)	6/30/2008	–24%	12
Cambridge US Buyout	12/31/2007	–25%	9
Bloomberg High Yield	9/30/2007	–27%	8
Morningstar LSTA US Leveraged Loan 100	9/30/2007	–30%	8
Russell 3000	9/30/2007	–46%	18

EXHIBIT 3.5 Asset class max drawdown and recovery period during the GFC.

losses despite being regarded at the time as protection against market downturns. Direct lending experienced a modest –8% drawdown compared to the other asset classes, largely attributable to its high cash yield that significantly mitigated losses. Also noteworthy is the short four-quarter recovery for direct lending compared to the other asset classes. Private equity and private real estate required 9 and 12 quarters, respectively, to recover completely from the GFC. The relatively long 12-quarter recovery period for real estate is also consistent with the notion of sticky valuations mentioned previously.

Exhibit 3.6 examines the drawdown experience of direct lending in more detail by examining the income, realized gain (loss), and unrealized gain (loss) components of the CDLI. The time period chosen differs slightly from previous exhibits, starting at June 2008, the beginning of the CDLI drawdown, and ending on December 2010 when CDLI realized losses reached their highest level.

For the CDLI, high current interest income provided a strong buffer against losses. At the June 2008 start of its drawdown, the yield on the CDLI equaled 9.90% and subsequently increased during the drawdown period, reaching a 11.27% December 2008 high. Loan valuations were adjusted downward in the third and fourth quarters of 2008, creating unrealized losses peaking at –14% ($0.86) in March 2009. The –8% drawdown through December 2008, cited in Exhibit 3.5, came six months after the

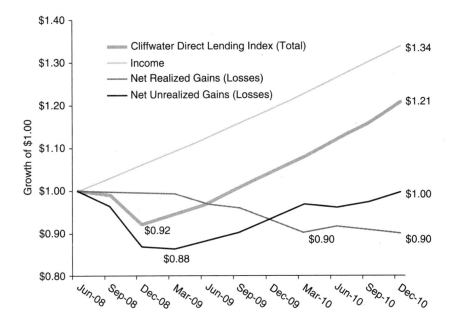

EXHIBIT 3.6 Direct lending performance attribution during/after the GFC, June 2008 to December 2010.

drawdown began and was a combination of positive current income being more than offset by downward adjustments to loan fair values (unrealized losses). Note that realized losses did not contribute to the −8% CDLI maximum drawdown. Realized losses came gradually in subsequent quarters and totaled −10% ($0.90) when they bottomed in December 2010. Unrealized losses were gradually replaced by realized losses until December 2010 when cumulative unrealized losses were again zero ($1.00).

An important observation about the behavior of direct loans during the GFC is that the fair value accounting process worked. In fact, one could argue that the process worked too well (i.e., was too conservative). In the end, the −14% in *unrealized* losses imposed on direct loans in the second half of 2008 exceeded the −10% in total *realized* losses or actual principal impairments that ended two years later in December 2010. If one can think of unrealized losses as loan loss reserves, those doing independent valuations on loans overestimated future impairments by −4%. In the end, the 2008 GFC was not only a stress test on direct loan performance but also a stress test on the process used to determine loan values.

A study by Cambridge Associates indirectly supports the drawdown analysis reflected in the CDLI performance.[2] Using a limited, but institutional-quality sample set, the author estimates realized losses for a portfolio of senior loans through the GFC with outcomes very similar to those reported by the CDLI. Unfortunately, the study does not provide yield and unrealized losses, but its reporting of loss experience provides the confirming evidence of the loss research presented.

Examination of the GFC shows that direct lending can perform well in the context of risky assets. But every crisis is different and the next one will likely find direct lending potentially vulnerable to lower yield, covenant-lite, and higher EBITDA leverage conditions. However, the direct lending market today is more senior-driven, populated with better-skilled lenders, with a more diversified set of borrowers than existed before the last crisis. It will be different the next time but not by much.

DIRECT LENDING AND THE COVID STRESS TEST

Every recession is different and the COVID crisis clearly demonstrated that. But in many respects, asset class behavior was like the GFC except it was less severe and of shorter duration, lasting one year. In statistical parlance, the GFC was a 3-sigma event while COVID was a 1.5-sigma event.

Exhibits 3.7 and 3.8 display COVID-related losses across asset classes.

Not surprising, the investment-grade Bloomberg Aggregate Index return was never impaired, just as during the GFC. Neither was real estate, but this is likely due to the valuation lag found in real estate and the quick recovery that vacated the need for the subsequent write-downs found during the GFC. Direct lending, measured by the Cliffwater Direct Lending Index, suffered only a modest –5% ($0.952) drawdown while private equity, hedge funds, high-yield bonds, and leveraged loans experienced low teen losses. As during the GFC, public equities had the largest drawdown.

Exhibit 3.9 shows that the components of the CDLI return during COVID followed the same pattern found during the GFC. A strong income return moderated losses, which during the drawdown were driven almost entirely by 7% ($0.93) in unrealized losses. Only in subsequent quarters were 3% ($0.97) in losses realized, and far less than the 7% anticipated by early unrealized valuation markdowns. And again, as described previously, as losses are realized, unrealized losses are reversed.

---

[2]"Stress and Losses Among Middle-Market Senior and Unitranche Loans," Tod Trabocco, Cambridge Associates.

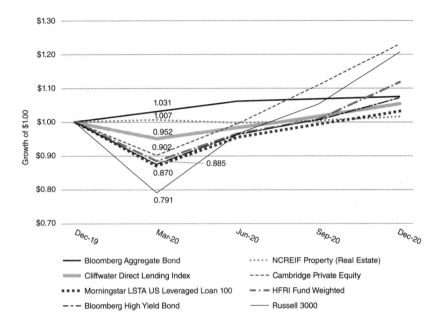

EXHIBIT 3.7 Asset class cumulative total returns through the COVID crisis, December 2019 to December 2020.

Asset Class Index	Beginning Date	Max Drawdown	Quarters to Recovery
Bloomberg US Aggregate	12/31/2019	NA	NA
NCREIF Property (real estate)	12/31/2019	NA	NA
Cliffwater Direct Lending Index	12/31/2019	–5%	2
Cambridge US Buyout	12/31/2019	–10%	2
HFRI Fund Weighted (hedge funds)	12/31/2019	–11%	2
Bloomberg High Yield	12/31/2019	–13%	2
Morningstar LSTA US Leveraged Loan 100	12/31/2019	–13%	3
Russell 3000	12/31/2019	–21%	2

EXHIBIT 3.8 Asset class max drawdown and recovery period during the COVID crisis.

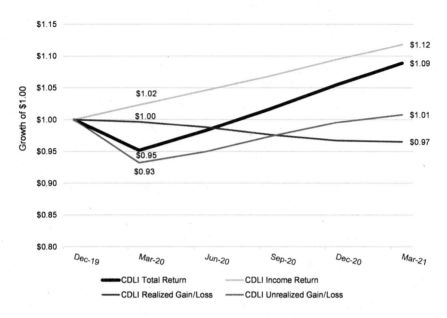

EXHIBIT 3.9   Direct lending performance attribution during/after the COVID crisis, December 2019 to December 2020.

Summarizing, direct lending is driven by income and realized losses, which can take time to unfold. Unrealized losses represent the primary source of direct lending volatility but are muted because income is the primary source of return. Historically, direct lending as measured by CDLI has demonstrated not only a very competitive return against all asset classes but also low volatility that produces the highest return-to-risk ratio across asset classes.

CHAPTER 4

Current Yield or Yield to Maturity?

Yield is one of the most basic of financial measures and one that strongly influences investor behavior. This is especially true for fixed income where return is driven almost entirely by coupon income. Direct corporate loans also fall into this description. Other asset classes that distribute most or all their earnings, from whatever source, also rely on yield to inform investors about investment attractiveness. These include REITs and MLPs. While yield at first seems the most intuitive of concepts, investors find that it can take on unexpected complexity when applied in practice. Since direct lending returns depend almost entirely on their yield, understanding how yields are calculated is especially important.

There are two basic yield calculation methods: current yield and yield-to-maturity.

CURRENT YIELD

In previous chapters references to direct lending yield have used the current yield method. Current yield is calculated as the most recent quarter's interest income divided by average assets over the quarter. Assets are defined by their fair value in the current yield calculation, not their cost or principal value. For example, CDLI interest income during the 2022 first quarter totaled $4.2 billion on a fair value of assets that averaged $214.8 billion. Dividing income by assets gives a quarterly yield equal to 1.96%. We multiply the 1.96% quarterly yield by 4 to get a 7.82% annualized current yield.

YIELD-TO-THREE-YEAR TAKEOUT

Total return fixed income investors often think of yield through the lens of yield to maturity or yield to worst, reflecting current income plus amortization of the difference between principal amount at maturity (or call date) and the fair value of the security. In other words, the yield-to-maturity (worst) calculation includes the amortization of unrealized gains and losses into its definition of yield.

The yield-to-maturity calculation is the more common method for expressing fixed income yield, but an underlying assumption is that principal value will be paid at maturity. This may not be true if the amortization of unrealized loss that is factored into the yield-to-maturity calculation is based on expected future credit losses. If it is, the yield-to-maturity calculation is assuming no credit impairment and represents the maximum return the loan could achieve. Current yield, however, assumes that current asset fair value is what will be realized on maturity.

Both current yield and yield to maturity are used throughout this book. Current yield is the preferred calculation because of the view that current unrealized losses, equal to the difference between fair value and principal value, are expected future credit losses and should not enhance yield as it does in the yield-to-maturity calculation. Loan yield-to-maturity is also shown in many examples because it may be more appropriate when making yield comparisons to other asset classes or where a measure of yield that is gross of credit losses is called for.

Unlike current yield, the calculation for yield-to-maturity explicitly incorporates a maturity date, or date when loan proceeds are repaid. While most direct loans have a five-year stated maturity, refinancings, prepayments, and corporate actions have historically reduced their average or effective life to approximately three years. As such, a yield-to-three-year takeout calculation is used for direct loans. When fair value is less than principal value, the difference, unrealized losses, is effectively amortized over a three-year horizon and added to current yield. In the less frequent case when fair value exceeds principal value, unrealized gains are amortized over a three-year horizon and subtracted from current yield.

A yield-to-three-year takeout calculation for the CDLI requires both principal and fair value. We calculate these values by aggregating individual loan principal and fair values reported quarterly in financial statements. Exhibits 4.1 and 4.2 illustrate how differences between fair value and principal value create differences between current yield and yield-to-three-year takeout for the CDLI.

Loan fair value generally remains below principal or par value due to expectations for future defaults. The few instances where fair value climbs above principal value are when credit conditions for loans have improved to an extent that default expectations are below what was expected at loan origination. The pattern of fair versus principal value shown in Exhibit 4.1 shows that when it comes to the fair value of non-investment grade loans, potential downside exceeds potential upside.

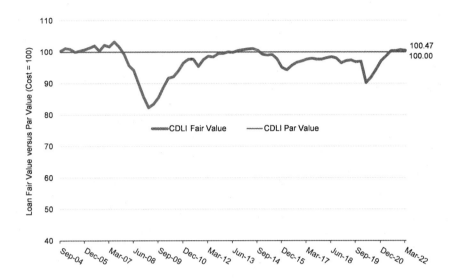

EXHIBIT 4.1 Direct loan fair value versus par (principal) value.

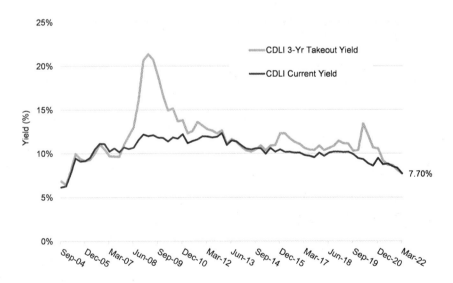

EXHIBIT 4.2 Current yield and yield-to-three-year takeout for the Cliffwater Direct Lending Index.

Exhibit 4.2 compares current yield and yield-to-three-year takeout for the CDLI. Whenever loan fair value dips below principal value, as shown in Exhibit 4.1, the yield-to-three-year takeout (yield to maturity) for direct loans exceeds the current yield. The difference is the amortization of the fair value discount over a three-year assumed effective loan maturity. This difference was very significant in 2008 when the CDLI yield-to-three-year takeout exceeded 20% while CDLI current yield climbed to just 12%. A more recent yield divergence occurred during the 2016 oil crisis when the energy sector entered recession and fair values for oil and gas loans were reduced. Current yields were modestly affected, but yield-to-three-year takeout jumped again under the calculation assumption that the fair value discount would be eliminated in three years.

High-yield bonds and broadly syndicated loans (also called *leveraged loans*) are the closest to US middle market corporate direct loans from an investment perspective. All three expose investors to significant credit risk but compensate investors by offering higher yield. Consequently, yield comparisons among the three are relevant.

The most quoted yield for high-yield bonds is yield to worst, a measure akin to yield-to-three-year takeout because it also amortizes differences between current price and par value over the expected life of the bond. Exhibit 4.3 provides a yield comparison of direct loans (represented by the

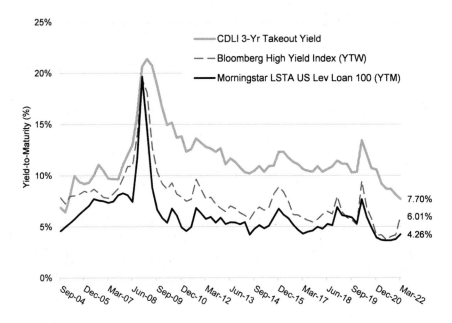

EXHIBIT 4.3   Yields for direct loans (CDLI), high-yield bonds, and leveraged loans.

CDLI yield-to-three-year takeout), high-yield bonds (represented by the Bloomberg High Yield Bond Index yield to worst) and leveraged loans (represented by the Morningstar LSTA US Leveraged Loan 100 Index yield to maturity). These yield definitions provide the best apples-to-apples comparison across the three credit driven asset classes.

The top line in Exhibit 4.3 plots the yield-to-three-year takeout for the CDLI. The middle, dashed line plots the yield to worst for the Bloomberg High Yield Bond Index. The lowest yield line plots the yield to maturity for the Morningstar LSTA US Leveraged Loan 100 Index, composed of the 100 most liquid syndicated bank loans. These apples-to-apples yields for direct loans, high-yield bonds, and leveraged loans follow a very similar pattern, suggesting that underlying corporate credit conditions over time are affecting all three markets in a similar way. It also shows that investors in the private direct loan market have earned yields significantly higher than investors in publicly traded high-yield bonds and leveraged loans.

The average yields for the entire 17.5-year period reported in Exhibit 4.3 were 11.63%, 7.74%, and 6.15% for the CDLI, Bloomberg High Yield Bond Index, and Morningstar LSTA US Leveraged Loan 100 Index, respectively. These spreads have varied somewhat over time but there is a consistent and large spread in favor of middle market direct loans, represented by the CDLI. Note also that yields for high-yield bonds generally are above those for leveraged loans, but to a much lesser degree. The higher bond yields are due to their lower (subordinated) quality generally and their fixed rate character, which will give them a higher yield compared to leveraged loans as long as the yield curve is positive.

This historical yield record gives middle market direct loans a 3.89% average yield spread over high-yield bonds and a 5.48% average yield spread over leveraged loans.

In Chapter 5 we compare credit losses across the three credit asset classes.

Comparative Credit Loss Rates

Credit-oriented fixed income instruments like US middle market direct loans achieve their long-term returns by capturing high yields without offsetting principal impairments by way of realized losses. Chapter 1 stated a 10.79% income return (yield) for US middle market direct loans and a –1.08% annual realized loss since the start of the CDLI in September 2004. Chapter 4 showed that levels of direct lending income (yield) were consistently and significantly above yields on more familiar and more liquid high-yield bonds and leveraged loans, even when differences in fees are accounted for. An important question in this comparison is whether there is a difference in credit losses between the –1.08% found for US middle market loans and credit losses for high-yield bonds and leveraged loans. In other words, is the roughly 3.5–4.5% after-fee yield spread partially compensating direct loan investors for higher credit losses in middle market loans? The answer is no.

Exhibit 5.1 reports calendar year default, recovery, and loss statistics for high-yield bonds, leveraged loans, the CDLI, and US bank C&I loans from 2005 through 2021.

Credit loss equals the product of default ratio and one minus the recovery rate. Data on default and recovery rates are readily available on publicly traded securities from bankers and rating agencies. But because direct middle market corporate loans are privately negotiated and held to maturity, there is no database that tracks these statistics in the same way as for high-yield bonds and leveraged loans. However, realized credit loss rates are available through public filings, and those statistics are used to calculate CDLI realized losses, which largely represent credit losses. US bank credit losses on their business commercial loans are also provided as a comparison. Default and recovery rate information on bank business loans are also not available. Banks report charge-off rates for their loan portfolio that are similar to realized credit losses for nonbank middle market direct loans.

	High-Yield Bonds[a]			Leveraged Loans[a]			CDU Middle Market Debt[b]	US Bank Commercial & Industrial Business Loans[c]
	Default Ratio	Recovery Rate	Credit Loss	Default Ratio	Recovery Rate	Credit Loss	Credit Loss**	Charge-Off Rate
2005	2.8%	56%	1.23%	3.0%	84%	0.48%	−0.89%	1.01%
2006	0.9%	55%	0.41%	0.5%	84%	0.08%	−0.63%	1.27%
2007	0.4%	55%	0.18%	0.2%	69%	0.06%	−1.74%	2.25%
2008	2.3%	27%	1.68%	3.7%	58%	1.55%	0.59%	5.03%
2009	10.3%	36%	6.59%	12.8%	61%	4.99%	6.91%	9.37%
2010	0.8%	41%	0.47%	1.8%	71%	0.52%	2.96%	6.01%
2011	1.7%	49%	0.87%	0.4%	67%	0.13%	1.78%	2.85%
2012	1.3%	53%	0.61%	1.4%	55%	0.63%	0.60%	1.73%
2013	0.7%	53%	0.33%	1.7%	69%	0.53%	0.19%	1.06%
2014	2.9%	48%	1.51%	4.3%	73%	1.16%	−0.01%	0.81%
2015	1.8%	25%	1.35%	1.7%	48%	0.88%	0.70%	1.20%
2016	3.6%	31%	2.48%	1.5%	63%	0.56%	1.41%	1.65%
2017	1.3%	52%	0.61%	1.8%	62%	0.70%	1.75%	1.38%
2018	1.8%	40%	1.08%	1.7%	62%	0.66%	0.93%	1.11%
2019	2.6%	26%	1.95%	1.6%	48%	0.85%	0.87%	1.65%
2020	6.2%	22%	4.84%	4.0%	48%	2.08%	3.30%	1.82%
2021	0.3%	47%	0.16%	0.5%	52%	0.24%	−0.27%	0.60%
Inception	2.4%	37%	1.54%	2.5%	62%	0.94%	1.07%	2.38%
Last 10 Yrs	2.2%	34%	1.48%	2.0%	59%	0.83%	0.94%	1.30%

EXHIBIT 5.1 Credit loss comparison, 2005 to 2021.

[a]*Source:* JPMorgan Markets.

[b]*Source:* Cliffwater Direct Lending Index (Realized Credit Losses).

[c]*Source:* Federal Reserve (Fred: CORBLACBS).

Exhibit 5.1 shows that the 1.07% average credit loss rate from US middle market direct loans over the 2005 to 2021 period is very close to the 0.94% loss rate for leveraged loans and below both the 1.54% loss rate for high-yield bonds and the 2.38% loss rate for bank C&I loans. Also, credit losses follow the same pattern over time with the highest loss rates occurring during the GFC and COVID crisis.

On their face, these comparative loss rates are not surprising. Direct loans have much more in common with leveraged bank loans than high-yield bonds. Direct loans and leveraged bank loans are primarily floating rate, intermediate-term, senior secured loans. High-yield bonds are fixed rate, longer-term subordinated debt so an investor would expect to experience higher credit losses, primarily through lower recovery rates. That characteristic is also visible from the data in Exhibit 5.1.

The charge-offs on bank C&I loans are about 1% higher on average compared to the other credit loss rates. Most of the higher losses are attributed to the three-year GFC period 2008–2010 when C&I losses totaled 20% compared to 10% for the other credit types. For the last ten years, C&I losses averaged 1.30% and have been more consistent with the other corporate credits, as Exhibit 5.1 shows. Bank reporting is not sufficient to explain fully their higher GFC losses, but it is likely that business loans at the time had greater real estate exposure, and lending standards were more relaxed leading up to the GFC.

NONACCRUALS AND IMPLIED RECOVERIES FOR MIDDLE MARKET CORPORATE LOANS

Reported default and recovery rates, the two components of loss rates, are flow statistics, meaning they express quantities per unit of time. In the case of defaults and recoveries, the typical time period reported for high-yield bonds and leveraged loans is monthly. Since loss rates are a product of defaults and recoveries, they too are available monthly. These same statistics are not available for middle market corporate direct loans. Loss rates are available, but only on a quarterly basis.

Fortunately, something similar to default and recovery rates are reported and available for the CDLI. These are loans on nonaccrual status, meaning loans that are no longer current in paying interest income and would be considered in default. This nonaccrual default statistic is different from what is reported for high-yield bonds and leveraged loans in that it is a stock statistic, not a flow statistic. Stock statistics represent quantities accumulated over time rather than for a subperiod (monthly or quarterly) of time. As a result, direct loan nonaccruals levels should exceed default rates as long as it takes over a quarter for recoveries to be realized.

Exhibit 5.2 reports CDLI nonaccrual loans (left axis) both at cost (par) value and at fair value, as a percentage of all CDLI loans at cost (par) value. The cost value of loans on nonaccrual have averaged 2.31% of total loan assets over the 14.75-year period shown. Like default rates, nonaccruals peak during periods of recession, most notably during the GFC and COVID subperiods, but also during the 2015–2016 oil crisis. Note that the 2.31% average nonaccrual stock level is not dissimilar from the 2.50% average default flow rate for leveraged loans. These stock and flow numbers would be similar if loans on nonaccrual took about one year to complete a work-out of some sort, a plausible assumption.

Also shown in Exhibit 5.2 (right axis) is the implied recovery rate, equal to the fair value of loans on nonaccrual divided by the cost (par) value of those same loans. Implied recovery rates have been fairly consistent over the measurement period, averaging 48% as measured in Exhibit 5.2 (right axis). It is this implied recovery rate that should be compared to the actual historical recovery rates for high-yield bonds (37%) and leveraged loans (62%) reported in Exhibit 5.1. The 48% implied recovery rate for direct loans, falling between recovery rates for high-yield bonds and leveraged loans, seems reasonable given that CDLI direct loan composition over the measurement period has averaged 55% senior loans (the quality of lever-aged loans) and 45% subordinated loans (the quality of high-yield bonds).

The loss rates examined in this chapter show that the higher yields for middle market loans when compared to more liquid high-yield bonds and leveraged loans, reported in Chapter 4, are not offset by a finding of higher loss rates. In fact, the 1.07% average annual loss rate for middle market direct loans is low, only 0.13% above the average loss rate for leveraged loans and 0.47% less than the average loss rate for high-yield bonds. This is an important finding because middle market borrowers are generally smaller than the larger corporate borrowers that finance in the public mar-kets by issuing leveraged loans or high-yield bonds. Larger companies are often thought to be safer, which is inconsistent with our findings. Why this

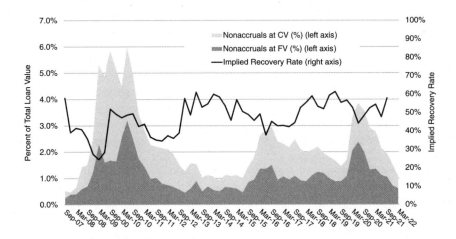

EXHIBIT 5.2   CDLI nonaccruals and recovery rates, September 2007 to March 2022.

is so will be discussed in the chapters ahead but unlike the large borrowers accessing the public markets for financing, middle market loans are much more likely to have protective covenants and the borrowing companies are more likely owned by private equity firms (sponsor backed) with better alignment of interest with lenders should companies get in financial trouble.

Chapter 6 examines the cash flow characteristics of middle market direct loans. If loss rate differences don't explain the higher yields for direct loans, perhaps a lack of liquidity is responsible. After all, these directly originated loans are generally held to maturity.

How Liquid Are Direct Loans?

For some investors, an attractive feature of US middle market direct loans is an effective life that is shorter than their typical five- to seven-year maturity. Understanding effective life is useful for measuring overall portfolio liquidity, which in turn can help investors in setting commitment levels to direct lending portfolios, and help managers who must balance cash flows from direct loan assets with potential investor withdrawals or manage financing when direct loan assets are leveraged at the portfolio level.

US middle market direct corporate loans have historically had an effective life that averages 3.09 years, based on data underlying the CDLI covering the period from September 2004 through March 2022. However, unlike many of the investment characteristics for direct lending that show stability, the measurement of effective life has varied considerably over time, from a low of 2.09 years (September 2013) to a high of 6.95 years (September 2009). And, unfortunately but predictably, the effective life in direct lending varies inversely with general conditions of market liquidity. In other words, direct loan liquidity declines when credit conditions deteriorate.

A significant benefit of investing in US middle market direct loans is their comparatively high cash flow from principal repayment, which is a by-product of a short effective life and high current income. The CDLI database shows principal-related cash flow averages approximately one-third of total assets annually. Interest income has averaged over one-tenth of total assets, bringing the combined average annual cash flow from direct loans to more than 40% of loan value, even when PIK (payment-in-kind) income is stripped out. At this high level of cash flow, direct loans become a very fungible asset that provides asset allocators the flexibility they generally want to rebalance overall portfolios. The high cash flow from direct loans also serves to reduce the uncertainty in periodic loan valuation as a loan's value will quickly converge to par if its current value is discounted.

Exhibit 6.1 reports principal cash flow from loan maturities, prepayments, and some asset sales in the CDLI as a percentage of total investments at cost for the period from September 2005 through March

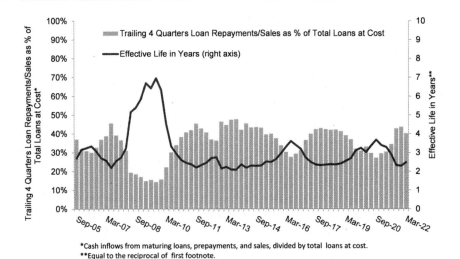

*Cash inflows from maturing loans, prepayments, and sales, divided by total loans at cost.
**Equal to the reciprocal of first footnote.

EXHIBIT 6.1   Liquidity measurement for US middle market direct loan assets.

2022. Measurements reflect trailing four-quarter (one-year) periods. Also included in Exhibit 6.1 is the effective life, which is calculated by taking the reciprocal of the principal-related cash flow percentage. For example, a portfolio with 33 1/3% of loans repaid or sold every year will turn over once every three years.

Principal-related cash flow from portfolios of direct loans average 32.4% annually for the entire 16.75-year measurement period shown in Exhibit 6.1. Alternatively, direct loans can be thought of as having an average 3.09-year effective life. Combined with interest income that averaged 10.8%, compounded annually, over the same period, direct loan portfolios generated 43.2% (32.4% plus 10.8%) on average in combined annual cash flow. On their face, these are impressive metrics for investors with short-term cash flow requirements or investors wanting vintage (time) diversification without having to hold back allocations over several years as is common for private equity.

However, the CDLI data also shows that principal-related cash flow from direct loan assets is correlated to the credit cycle. As credit conditions tighten, borrowers are less able to refinance or repay outstanding debt. Conversely, when credit conditions ease, borrowers are better able to refinance loans and can prepay outstanding debt, shortening the average life. Principal-related cash flow dropped more than one-half its long-term average during the GFC, to 14.5% of loan assets for the four quarters ending September 2009, raising the effective life to 6.9 years. Principal-related cash flow dipped again during the 2015–2016 energy downturn, to 27.5% of loan assets, raising effective life to 3.6 years, and more recently dipped to 27.2% during the 2020 COVID crisis, raising effective life to 3.7 years.

Interest income from direct loan portfolios, however, show modest gains during periods of market stress. For example, during the GFC when principal-related cash flow dropped to 13.9%, cash flow from loan income reached a 12.6% peak level for the same time period, compared to 10.79% for the entire measurement period. This is likely explained by lenders requiring higher interest payments on newly originated loans or loan extensions to incentivize them to alter loan terms when credit risk increases. Together, the combined principal and income cash flow from direct loans fell to a 26.8% low, as a percentage of cost (par) during the GFC, compared to 46.2% combined annualized cash flow over the entire measurement period.

Understanding the liquidity of direct loans is important for many reasons. The first is time diversification, which is also referred to as vintage diversification in private fund investing. Ideally, and in the absence of any tactical market views, investors would prefer to invest, and reinvest, equal dollar or percentage amounts in each calendar year to effectively dollar average their entry price. While this discipline has been known and largely practiced for decades in private equity, investors have been known to allocate excessive amounts of capital during peak valuations both because total assets are inflated (at least in hindsight) and distributions from private equity is high as general partners sell portfolio companies at high multiples and return capital to investors. The net result is that private equity investments become concentrated in higher priced vintage years rather than being equally distributed.

Vintage diversification is also important in direct lending but to a lesser extent because of the shorter duration of the assets. With the strong cash flow characteristics described in Exhibit 6.1 vintage diversification can be achieved by averaging investor capital over a two- to three-year period rather than the five-year period allocation period generally favored by private equity investors. The importance of vintage diversification for direct lending is also mitigated by the lower periodic volatility in direct lending returns. Departures from the vintage discipline can produce worse outcomes for private equity when compared to direct lending. Nonetheless, investors in direct lending should pay attention to the vintage weighting, particularly if they use leverage, which will increase return volatility in direct lending and hence the downside risk in departing from vintage diversification.

These first chapters have hopefully provided a basic understanding of US middle market direct corporate loans and their investment characteristics. The chapters that follow are meant to shift from details about direct loans and instead provide a top-down perspective on credit risk within an overall portfolio allocation. Unlike most other asset classes, credit opportunities come in many shapes and sizes with varying expectations for return, risk, and liquidity. A framework for how much to allocate to credit and specific types of credit opportunities is useful at this juncture.

CHAPTER **7**

Middle Market Loans as a Hedge Against Rising Interest Rates

Chapter 3 reported the relative strong performance of middle market loans during recession-induced stock market declines. Middle market loan return drawdowns were shown to be mild by comparison to other asset classes and short-lived, as measured by the CDLI.

Today, investors are focused on unexpected increases in interest rates, a phenomenon not seen since the stagflation period of the 1970s when inflation and interest rates climbed to double-digit levels and stayed there for almost ten years. They should be concerned. As of this writing, CPI inflation is hovering at a 9.00% annualized rate, as shown in Exhibit 7.1, while short-term interest rates remain low at 1.21%. Real interest rates, equal to the difference between nominal interest rates and inflation, are at record −7.79% lows.

High inflation virtually requires interest rates to go higher to keep monetary policy neutral. If not, current negative real interest rates will spur additional inflation. Consequently, interest rate increases are on the way; how much and when remains uncertain.

In the current environment investors should reevaluate allocations to fixed rate securities, the most popular being represented by the Bloomberg Aggregate Bond Index, composed of all investment-grade US fixed income securities. This index, and the portfolios/ETFs that track it, have benefited from more than 20 years of declining interest rates. That tailwind appears over for the foreseeable future. One natural substitute is middle market direct loans both because their floating-rate yield increases with the general level of interest rates, and, as covered in Chapter 6, their short three-year effective maturity and high coupon income create generous liquidity to reinvest cash flow at the highest current rates.

Ideally, data on the performance of middle market loans during the inflationary 1970s would be useful to demonstrate their resilience during rising interest rates. Unfortunately, that information does not exist.

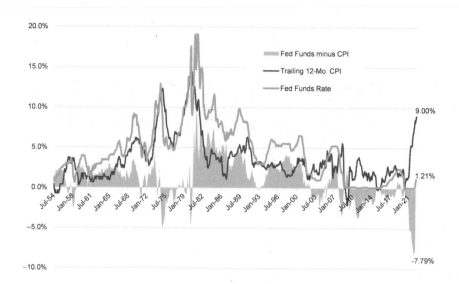

EXHIBIT 7.1 US short-term interest rates versus inflation, August 1954 to June 2022.
Source: FRED.

Even traded leveraged loan index data goes back only to 2000. Instead, Exhibits 7.2 and 7.3 examine return data for the CDLI and the Bloomberg Aggregate Bond Index against the backdrop of changes in ten-year Treasury rates going back to 2004, when CDLI data became first available.

Exhibit 7.2 plots 72 quarterly CDLI and Bloomberg Aggregate Bond Index returns (*y*-axis) against the quarterly change in ten-year Treasury yields (*x*-axis). As expected, Bloomberg Aggregate Bond Index returns are negatively related to increases in ten-year Treasury yields as suggested by the pattern of triangle symbols and regression line. The regression has a 0.71 R-squared, which means 71% of the Bloomberg's quarterly return is explained by changes in ten-year yields, a measurement consistent with the tight proximity of individual data points to the regression line. The regression equation shown means that for every 1% positive change in ten-year Treasury yield, the Bloomberg Aggregate Bond Index return falls −3.10%.

CDLI returns, by contrast, experience quite the opposite result when ten-year Treasury yields change. The dots representing quarterly CDLI returns are positively sloped, meaning that CDLI returns increase during periods of rising ten-year Treasury yields. The regression line has a much lower 0.32 R-squared, which means that only 32% of the CDLI quarterly return is explained by changes in ten-year yields. Visual inspection of the scatterplot for the CDLI shows a much looser connection of CDLI returns

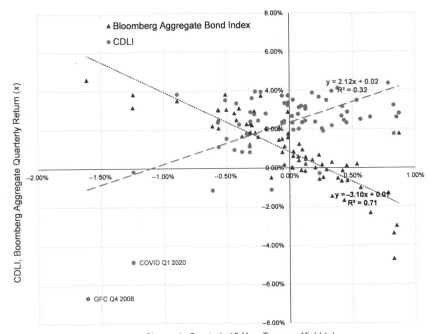

EXHIBIT 7.2 Impact of interest rate changes on Bloomberg Aggregate Bond Index and CDLI, Q4 2004 to Q1 2022.

Quarterly Periods	Average 10-Year Yield Change	Bloomberg Aggregate Bond Index Return	Cliffwater Direct Lending Index Return (CDLI)	CDLI Return *minus* Bloomberg Aggregate Return
Rising Interest Rates	0.33%	−0.35%	2.78%	3.13%
Falling Interest Rates	−0.40%	2.26%	1.80%	−0.46%

EXHIBIT 7.3 Impact of interest rate changes on Bloomberg Aggregate Bond Index and CDLI, Q4 2004 to Q1 2022.

with interest rate changes. This is not surprising since credit risk and other factors play a more important role in generating CDLI returns unlike the Bloomberg Aggregate Bond Index, where interest rate risk is virtually the only driver of return. A preview of the impact of credit risk on CDLI returns can be seen in the two CDLI plot points labeled COVID Q1 2020 and GFC Q4 2008. Both plot points depart significantly from the regression line. The two departures should be interpreted as another noninterest rate factor influencing those quarterly returns. That additional factor is a dramatic increase in perceived credit risk during those two unique quarters, a subject discussed in Chapter 8.

The regression equation for the CDLI means that for every 1% positive change in ten-year Treasury yield, the CDLI return increases by 2.12%. The positive slope for CDLI is likely overstated, influenced by the two highly negative COVID and GFC data points. Conceptually, interest rate changes and middle market loan returns should impact one another positively, in a one-to-one manner given the floating rate nature of loans. If the two COVID and GFC data points are eliminated from the graph, the 2.12% slope changes to 0.89%, approximately equal to what would be expected.

The table in Exhibit 7.3 provides a second depiction of investment grade and middle market loan returns as interest rates change.

Time periods are divided into two subsets. The first subset consists of all quarters when ten-year Treasury yields rose quarter over quarter. The second subset consists of all quarters when ten-year Treasury yields fell quarter over quarter. Shown in the table for each subset are the average change in yield, the average Bloomberg Aggregate Bond Index return, the average CDLI return, and the difference in average returns between the CDLI and Bloomberg Aggregate Bond Index.

The rising rate environment, represented in the first row, clearly favors investing in floating rate middle market loans with a 3.13% average quarterly return difference, while the falling rate environment, represented in the second row, slightly favors investment grade bonds with a 0.46% return advantage over the CDLI. Assuming an environment of anything other than declining rates, middle market loans provide a significant return advantage over investment-grade bonds.

The relationship between investment-grade bonds and middle market loan returns and interest rates is similar if changes in short-term Libor replaces ten-year Treasury bonds as the measure of interest rate changes. A rising Libor is associated with positive and higher CDLI returns and negative and lower Bloomberg Aggregate Bond Index returns.

In summary, inflation rates are well above historical norms as well as Fed targets, which will likely cause interest rates to rise significantly. Middle market loans, represented by the CDLI, are likely to produce positive and improving returns in such an environment as their floating rate yields increase. Fixed-rate investment-grade bonds, however, will suffer low and likely negative returns given their high interest rate sensitivity.

CHAPTER 8

Credit as a Separate Asset Class

This chapter presents the case for credit and private debt more broadly as an asset class to be considered as part of any asset allocation study.

WHAT IS AN ASSET CLASS?

An asset class is defined as a group of securities that share similar characteristics or common risk factors. Further, academics and practitioners limit asset class status to securities that by their nature produce a significant and persistent return above cash precisely because their associated risks can't be diversified away.[1] Equities, fixed income, and cash[2] have traditionally been identified as the three primary investor asset classes. However, by this definition securities like physical commodities, currencies, and hedge funds would not achieve asset class status.

Credit meets the traditional asset class definition because its primary risk—the probability of borrower default—can't be diversified away, and consequently the market provides investors significant returns above riskless cash as a reward. Exhibit 8.1 provides historical returns and risks for investing in equity, US Treasuries (i.e., interest rate risk), and three categories of liquid corporate credit.[3]

The analysis in Exhibit 8.1 includes only liquid asset classes and begins December 31, 1999. Prior to 2008, institutional credit portfolios consisted primarily of allocations to traded non-investment grade high-yield bonds and/or leveraged loans (a.k.a. bank loans, broadly syndicated loans) with perhaps modest and infrequent investments in private debt.

---

[1]Non-diversifiable risks are also known as systematic or beta risks.

[2]Cash is included as an asset class, representing the risk-free rate of return.

[3]The January 1, 2000, start date was selected because it is the first date bank loan data is available.

	Interest Rates	Equity	Credit		
			Investment Grade (IG) Corporates	Leveraged Loans	High Yield (HY) Bonds
1 Description	Time value of money	Compensation for uncertain earnings and multiples	Compensation for the probability of principal loss	Compensation for the probability of principal loss	Compensation for the probability of principal loss
2 Measurement	10-Yr. Treasury	Russell 3000 Index	Bloomberg US Corporate Bond Index	Morningstar LSTA US Leveraged Loan Index	Bloomberg High Yield Bond Index
3 Total Return	4.21%	6.51%	5.03%	4.47%	6.17%
4 *minus* duration adjustment[†]	0.00%	0.00%	-2.39%	0.00%	-1.89%
5 *minus 30-day T-bills*[††]	–1.62%	–1.62%	–1.62%	–1.62%	–1.62%
6 Excess Return	2.60%	4.90%	1.03%	2.86%	2.66%
7 Excess Risk	7.20%	14.80%	5.44%	6.55%	10.88%
8 Excess Return/Risk	0.36	0.33	0.19	0.44	0.24

EXHIBIT 8.1 Return and risk for interest rates, equity, and credit, December 31, 1999, to June 30, 2022.

9 Correlations:

	Interest Rates	Equity	Credit		
			Investment Grade (IG) Corporates	Leveraged Loans	High Yield (HY) Bonds
Term Structure	1.00	-0.29	-0.39	-0.34	-0.50
Equity		1.00	0.65	0.55	0.72
Credit (IG)			1.00	0.79	0.87
Credit (BL)				1.00	0.82
Credit (HY)					1.00

All return and risk data is annualized. Risk is calculated as annualized standard deviation of excess return.

†Historical return attributable to Bloomberg Investment Grade and High Yield Bond Index durations, respectively, and calculated by monthly adjustments of the Treasury bond excess returns to equal the same duration as the Investment Grade and High Yield Bond Index durations, respectively.
(*Source:* Bloomberg Index Services Limited.)
††*Source:* ICE BofAML 3 Month T-Bill Index.

EXHIBIT 8.1 (*continued*)

The first two columns in Exhibit 8.1 provide historical return and risk data for interest rate and equity risk. The last three columns show the same data for three different categories of liquid credit investments, with increasing levels of credit risk: investment-grade bonds, leveraged loans, and high-yield bonds. Investment grade bonds represent the lowest credit risk level. Leveraged loans are senior secured debt but considered non-investment grade in quality because interest coverage and debt ratios compare less favorably to investment-grade debt. Finally, high-yield bonds represent primarily subordinated, higher risk debt.

Excess return is shown in row 6 and measures the portion of total return that is solely attributable to the type of beta risk identified by the column. Excess return is also commonly referred to as risk premium and is generally calculated by subtracting the risk-free rate (30-day T-bill return) from total return. However, in the case of investment-grade and high-yield bonds there is an interest rate risk factor as well as a credit risk factor embedded in their total returns. Interest rate risk is stripped out by subtracting Treasury bond returns—in excess of three-month T-bill returns—whose durations equal those of investment-grade and high-yield bonds. This duration adjustment results in lowering returns by –2.39% and –1.89% for investment grade and high-yield bonds, respectively. No duration adjustment is needed for leveraged loans because interest income is based on a short-term floating rate instrument, such as T-bills or Libor, which adjusts every 30 or 90 days, plus an agreed-to yield spread. Such instruments have little or no interest rate duration.

Excess returns for all three credit measures are positive over the measurement period. For leveraged loans and high-yield bonds, their respective 2.86% and 2.66% credit-driven excess returns exceed the 2.60% excess return for the interest rate asset class, represented by ten-year Treasuries. As expected, the excess return is greatest for equities that experienced the highest level of risk.

Also relevant for asset allocation purposes are risk-adjusted excess returns, measured by excess return divided by excess risk. Leveraged loans had the highest excess return/risk ratio, equal to 0.44, followed by interest rates and equity that had excess return/risk ratios equal to 0.36 and 0.31, respectively. The lowest ratios fell to investment grade credit and high-yield bonds, with values equal to 0.19 and 0.24, respectively.

Exhibit 8.1 also reports correlations of excess returns between interest rates, equity, and the three credit categories. Not surprising, the three credit measures have high cross correlations, ranging from 0.79 to 0.82. From an asset allocation perspective, less attractive are the high correlations of the three credit categories with equities, ranging from 0.55 to 0.72, far less attractive as a diversifier when compared to ten-year Treasuries, which have a negative –0.29 correlation to equities. Nonetheless, the correlations between the credit categories and equities are sufficiently low for public credit instruments to deserve an allocation within a diversified portfolio. The allocation question is considered in further detail in Chapter 22.

The growing allocation to credit within portfolios from fractional amounts ten years ago to meaningful allocations today is almost solely the result of private, not public, debt opportunities, anchored by the growth of direct lending. The reason is that absolute and risk-adjusted returns for direct lending, as measured by the CDLI, are multiples of those achieved in public credit as presented in Exhibit 3.1. But direct lending is not the whole story.

PRIVATE DEBT: THE FULL PICTURE

Earlier and later chapters focus on corporate direct lending, which is only part of what most institutional investors define as the private debt asset class, though clearly the largest and arguably the most important. Exhibit 8.2 catalogs multiple types of private debt assets grouped into two subclasses. The eastern hemisphere represents corporate direct lending, which is the largest subsector of private debt, estimated to represent $1 trillion in loan assets.

Direct lending is considered to be a core investment because it best represents the features of private debt: cash-paying, broad diversification across borrowers and industries, floating rate without interest rate risk, principal security with covenant protections, and a fairly short effective loan life that best provides for the opportunity for liquidity. Core private debt, when properly implemented, reflects primarily the beta[4] characteristics of private debt, just as core real estate, fully developed, leased, and diversified represent the beta characteristics of private real estate.

The enhanced private debt strategies represented by the western hemisphere in Exhibit 8.2 are defined in Exhibit 8.3. The list is by no means exhaustive but does represent strategies with significant deployed capital.

The allocations reflected in Exhibit 8.2 are for illustrative purposes only. The chart is intended to identify the subsectors within the private credit opportunity set and not recommended allocations. From a practical perspective it would be difficult to push high allocations to the enhanced strategies, leaving direct lending to represent the largest fraction of a composite credit portfolio allocation.

---

[4]Asset return and risk are often broken down into beta and alpha components where beta represents broad drivers of return represented by an index, like the CDLI, and alpha represents outsized allocations to specific credits, sub-strategies, or industries. Beta-driven returns are a by-product of the asset class while alpha-driven returns are a by-product of decisions made by the manager to earn returns in excess of an index. As a result, alpha-driven returns depend much more on manager selection than beta-driven returns, where returns depend on the collective positions of many managers.

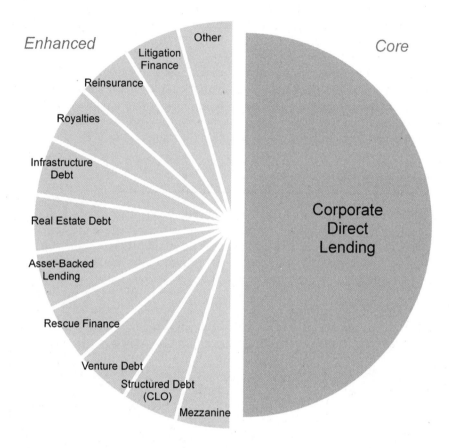

EXHIBIT 8.2 The broader private debt landscape.

Enhanced private debt strategies are expected to achieve higher levels of return, after fees, when compared to direct lending. Historical returns suggest that enhanced lending performance might be expected to produce a 3–5% higher return when compared to direct lending, but outcomes can vary depending on the enhanced debt strategies and managers selected. For example, infrastructure debt has emerged as a private debt opportunity only over the past five to seven years. Unlevered, the net yield on private infrastructure debt is approximately 6%, below that of direct lending. What makes infrastructure debt more interesting to investors is when financing (leverage) is applied or when structured to produce a higher yielding subordinated note. The same is true for commercial real estate debt in general. Unlevered, net yields are not so attractive, but when structured (levered) to

Strategy	General Description	Characteristics
Mezzanine	Directly originated corporate loans subordinate to senior debt. Can be secured by assets or unsecured, but have priority to equity	Focus on total return, combination of cash and PIK income, plus equity warrants
Structured (CLO equity)	Typically, highly levered investments in lower risk credit collateral	High, but risky cash flow
Venture Debt	Loans to venture capital–backed companies that are typically not yet profitable; investments can be a combination of cash and PIK income plus equity/warrants	Private equity–type upside return profile with baseline contractual return from the debt component
Rescue Financing	Senior debt provided to a company in or approaching bankruptcy	High returns but higher risk, short duration, super senior debt; typically not a standalone strategy
Asset-Backed Lending	Lending against or leasing of assets; collateral may include hard assets, such as commoditized equipment or mission critical assets, or financial assets such as trade claims and receivables	Fixed or floating rate, amortization and duration varies by the underlying asset type, underwritten to asset value, not cash flow
Real Estate Debt	Loans collateralized by real estate; typically takes the form of (1) a whole loan with the senior portion syndicated to a bank partner or (2) a mezzanine unsecured loan	Hard asset collateral, higher LTVs (60–90% range versus 50–60% for corporate debt)

EXHIBIT 8.3 Descriptions of enhanced private debt strategies.

(*continued*)

Strategy	General Description	Characteristics
Infrastructure Debt	Senior and mezzanine debt investments backed by infrastructure assets	High-quality hard asset collateral, with long-term contractual cash flows
Royalties	Investments in intellectual property rights with credit-like cash flow characteristics or debt investments to companies collateralized by intellectual property rights	Uncorrelated to credit markets, typically health care, entertainment, or other IP rights
Reinsurance	Investment in insurance-linked notes or catastrophe bonds (CAT bonds) that pay cash income in exchange for payment of claims from earthquake, flooding, and hurricane events	Uncorrelated returns, high fees, and a limited market can cause inconsistent returns
Litigation Finance	Financing, including loans, to law firms or claimants backed by legal fees or awards	Uncorrelated with a wide range of risks and returns (9–30% + gross) depending on strategy
Other	Fund finance, life settlements, marketplace lending (fintech)	

EXHIBIT 8.3   *(continued)*

produce a commercial mortgage-backed security, the yields climb to high single-digit levels. Again, most investors in enhanced lending strategies try to take measured risks to earn returns well above core direct lending returns.

It is also noteworthy that both direct lending and enhanced debt strategies are available in the UK and Europe, but to a lesser degree in Asia, where legal protections for lenders are less certain. In addition, opportunistic credit strategies have surfaced since the GFC. Opportunistic credit strategies have become quite popular and enable managers/funds to allocate tactically across private and public credit strategies to take advantage of the most attractive investments over time.

CHAPTER 9

Senior and Unitranche Direct Lending

The growth in private debt investing is distributed across most credit-driven strategies but the largest beneficiary has been senior and unitranche corporate direct lending. One-stop unitranche loans, which combine traditional senior and second lien loans into a single loan, have seen the greatest growth for their convenience to borrowers and higher yields offered to investors. The market surge toward loan seniority is seen in Exhibit 9.1, where the weighting of the senior lending, as a percentage of the CDLI, has grown from 42% in 2012 to 76% on March 31, 2022.

Several factors explain the market shift to senior direct lending. The first is the transition in middle market lending from banks to asset managers. Bank lending is traditionally senior secured, and its transition to alternative direct lending through independent asset managers has expanded the senior composition of direct middle market loans. The innovation of the unitranche loan has also limited the need for borrowers to find second lien financing.

Equally important is investor demand for a replacement for traditional investment-grade fixed income. While middle market loans are seldom rated, and most likely would be considered non-investment grade if they were, a portfolio of senior or unitranche loans would be much closer in quality to traditional fixed income than second lien loans.

Finally, banks and insurance companies will lend against senior and unitranche loans at attractive rates, but not second lien loans. This effectively gives investors seeking higher yields a choice between holding higher-yield second lien loans or holding senior loans partially financed by borrowing from a bank or insurance company. The use of leverage and financing in middle market lending is taken up in Chapter 13.

The Cliffwater Senior-Only Direct Lending Index (CDLI-S) was created in 2017 to measure the comparative performance of only senior middle market loans. The CDLI-S is a subset of the broader CDLI and includes more than 3,000 senior and unitranche middle market loans held within BDCs. CDLI-S follows the same construction methodology as CDLI but only includes loans held by managers of BDCs that have an investment style

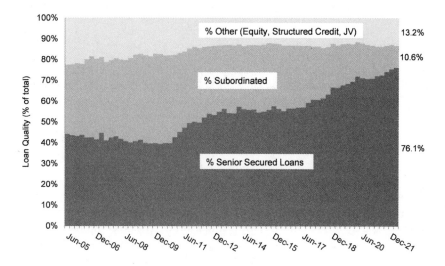

EXHIBIT 9.1 Growth in senior secured direct lending (as percentage of CDLI).

that clearly focuses on senior secured loans. The CDLI-S beginning date is September 30, 2010, compared to September 30, 2004, for the CDLI. The shorter historical series for CDLI-S is attributable to the post-2008 introduction of most senior-only direct lending BDC strategies. As with the CDLI, CDLI-S does not suffer from biases (backfill and survivorship) found in other databases because all source data come from required SEC filings. Exhibit 9.2 provides some key differences between the CDLI and CDLI-S.

Senior loans within the CDLI-S are generally represented by larger, sponsored (private equity–backed) borrowers with a track record of lower realized losses and a lower rate of nonaccrual status. Not surprising, the senior-oriented CDLI-S is composed of higher-quality loans, which is

Descriptor	CDLI-S	CDLI
# loans	3,210	9,475
Total assets	$84 b	$223 b
EBITDA (median)	$79 m	$46 m
Nonaccrual (as % of cost)	0.4%	1.1%
Implied recovery rate	72%	58%
% sponsor	90%	79%
% senior	94%	76%

EXHIBIT 9.2 CDLI, CDLI-S comparison, March 31, 2022.

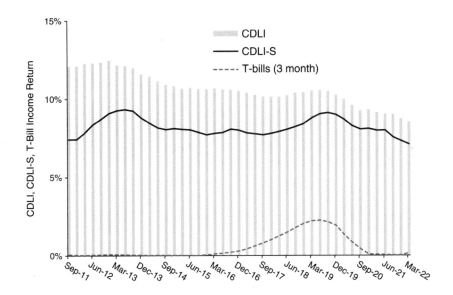

EXHIBIT 9.3 Historical CDLI, CDLI-S, T-Bill yields, September 2010 to March 2022.

reflected in its lower yield when compared to the broader CDLI, as shown in Exhibit 9.3.

The CDLI earned an average but declining yield equal to 10.70% over the 11.5-year period shown in Exhibit 9.3. The CDLI-S average yield equaled 8.14% and was relatively stable. The declining CDLI yield is attributable to the increasing composition of senior loans in the middle market, as shown in Exhibit 9.1. T-bill yields averaged 0.52%, producing a 7.62% yield spread for senior middle market loans. Unitranche loans represent roughly one-half of the senior loans within the CDLI-S.

Senior middle market loans alone earned a 2.54% lower yield compared to the entire set of loans in the CDLI, but lower realized credit losses in the CDLI-S offset almost one-half of the yield difference, as shown in Exhibit 9.4.

While the gross yield difference between the CDLI and CDLI-S equaled 2.54% (10.70% minus 8.14%) over the 11.5-year history of CDLI-S, CDLI suffers higher realized losses equal to –1.06% annualized, compared to just –0.12% for CDLI-S. The 0.94% realized loss difference reduces the net-of-loss yield difference to 1.60%.

Other differences between the CDLI and CDLI-S might matter as well to investors. While long-term unrealized losses are about the same, near zero, for both indexes, the short-term volatility is greater for CDLI.

Index Components	Q1 2022	Last Four Quarters	Last Five Years*	From CDLI-S Inception September 2010
		CDLI-S Returns		
CDLI-S total return**	1.52%	8.44%	7.92%	8.05%
= Income	1.66%	7.45%	8.12%	8.14%
+/– Net realized gains (losses)	0.02%	0.18%	–0.30%	–0.12%
+/– Net unrealized gains (losses)	–0.15%	0.77%	0.11%	–0.02%
		CDLI Returns		
CDLI total return**	1.76%	11.17%	8.63%	9.80%
= Income	1.93%	8.67%	9.75%	10.70%
+/– Net realized gains (losses)	0.03%	0.49%	–1.23%	–1.06%
+/– Net unrealized gains (losses)	–0.19%	1.85%	0.18%	–0.23%

*Annualized return.
**Return subcomponents may not add to total return due to compounding effects.

EXHIBIT 9.4   Comparison of CDLI-S and CDLI performance.

Over the entire measurement period the broader CDLI annualized return standard deviation measured 2.95% compared to 2.43% for CDLI-S. Both risk levels are low, but the difference is significant and produces an identical 3.32 return-to-risk ratio for both indexes.

A final factor that generates interest in CDLI-S is the greater capacity to finance senior and unitranche loans compared to second lien and mezzanine private debt. The low level of volatility in senior secured middle market loans attracts financing for lenders that wish to enhance returns to their investors. The use of financing and leverage is discussed more fully in Chapter 13 but is generally limited to senior secured and unitranche loans.

CHAPTER 10

Loans and the Theory of Credit

Much of the credit research presented thus far has been empirical, using historical data to drive an understanding of credit return and risk. However, credit can also be understood from a theoretical perspective, using option pricing theory to explain and measure credit return and risk. This chapter reviews some basic theoretical underpinnings of credit and ties its conclusions to market behavior.

The chapter begins with a review of the Merton model for pricing corporate debt; shows how it can be applied to calculate credit risk premiums for middle market corporate loans, including sensitivity analysis; estimates credit risk using Monte Carlo simulation; and, finally, tests risk findings against historical risk measures.

This research approach can be helpful in several ways. For example, understanding the Merton model better informs investors of loan pricing and its determinants. Take the tightening of yield spreads for credit securities relative to comparable maturity Treasury securities (also called *spread compression*), for example, which is generally attributable to capital inflows but instead could be explained by a rise in the risk-free rate. Another application is determining return and risk expectations for less familiar debt instruments such as second lien and mezzanine loan structures, which can be estimated through simulation techniques when empirical data are not available.

To better understand the implications of the current covenant-lite trend, an extension of the Merton model, called the Black-Cox model, is considered. The Black-Cox model provides a method for pricing covenants and, in so doing, gives us a way to price (in yield equivalent) the cost of covenant-lite loans. For example, using Black-Cox, we estimate that a trend toward covenant-lite structures reduces return by approximately 1% but that cost varies considerably and directly with the loan-level leverage.

Like CAPM and Black-Scholes, the Merton and Black-Cox models have withstood the test of time but remain imperfect approximations of a complex credit world. Nonetheless, this chapter shows that theoretical guideposts exist to better understand and measure credit-driven investment opportunities and risks.

THE MERTON MODEL

Current corporate credit theory remains almost entirely based on Robert Merton's 1974 adaptation of Black-Scholes option pricing formula to corporate credit.[1] Merton showed that the same formula for pricing stock options could be used for pricing bonds by associating the level of corporate debt with the exercise price of a stock option.

In Merton's world, the corporate lender can be thought of as (1) providing the corporate borrower a fixed amount of debt capital, expecting full repayment at maturity plus interest, plus (2) selling the corporate borrower a put option and receiving a premium, giving the borrower the right to repurchase the debt at maturity for the then value of corporate assets. At maturity, the borrower's put option only has value if the value of corporate assets is less than the value of the corporate debt, and the debt can be settled in full by remaining corporate assets.

In Merton's world, the expected risk of default is fully absorbed by the corporate borrower through the premium cost of the put. Hence, the principal value of the debt becomes technically default-free and the interest rate in (1) is deserving only of the risk-free rate of return to compensate for the time value of money. Hence, the value of corporate debt can be written as:

$$\text{Corporate Debt} = Xe^{-rT} - \text{Put}_0 \qquad (10.1)$$

X = value of debt at maturity

T = time to maturity

r = riskless rate of interest

e^{-rT} = discounted value of a dollar

Put_0 = value of a put option at T on corporate value
at exercise price equal to X

---

[1]Robert C. Merton, "On the Pricing of Corporate Debt: The Risk Structure of Interest Rates," *The Journal of Finance* (May 1974).

The annuitized value of Put_0 in Equation (10.1) can be viewed as the annualized credit risk premium. However, Merton provides a more direct calculation of the credit risk premium in Equation (10.2).

$$\text{Credit Premium} = R - r = -\frac{1}{T} ln\left\{ \Phi\left(h_2\right) + \frac{1}{d}\Phi\left(h_1\right) \right\} \qquad (10.2)$$

R = yield

r = risk-free rate

T = time to maturity

σ = standard deviation of firm assets

Φ = cumulative normal distribution function

$$d = \frac{\text{debt}\left(e^{-rT}\right)}{\text{total assets}} \approx \text{present value of debt to assets} \approx \text{strike price}$$

$$h_2 = -\left[\frac{1}{2}\sigma^2 T + \ln(d)\right] / \sigma\sqrt{T}$$

$$h_1 = -\left[\frac{1}{2}\sigma^2 T - \ln(d)\right] / \sigma\sqrt{T}$$

As expected, equation (2) has the same look as Black-Scholes but here the contents in the brackets represent a weighted average of the current asset coverage ratio ($\frac{1}{d}$) and an asset coverage ratio equal to 1.0, the default point. The weights (h_2, h_1) depend on time to maturity, firm risk, and debt levels. More weight is given to the debt coverage ratio as debt increases. The first term ($\frac{1}{T}$) amortizes the credit premium over the life of the loan.

Exhibit 10.1 applies Merton's formula to a hypothetical middle market corporate loan. We assume a five-year loan, a borrower whose assets (unlevered firm) exhibit a 40% standard deviation, and a 1.75% riskless rate of interest over the life of the loan. Because we also are modeling a private loan, we assume a 2.00% liquidity premium and a 0.5% annualized original issue discount (OID), values that are consistent with research on middle market loans presented in Chapter 11.

Line 3 in Exhibit 10.1 is the investor's required interest rate at varying leverage levels to compensate for time, liquidity, and credit risk. For example, in an efficient market a lender would require a 7.10% yield for a

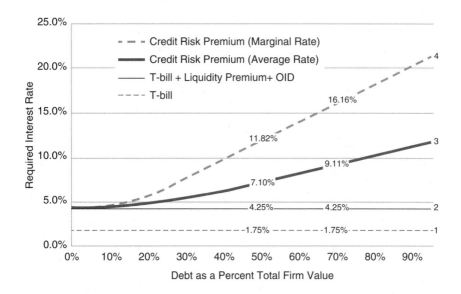

EXHIBIT 10.1 Merton model representation of debt costs and loan-to-value ratios for private debt.

private loan equal to 50% of total firm value. That 7.10% would be composed of a riskless 1.75% for the time value of money, 2.00% for the loss of liquidity, 0.50% for the cost of creating the loan, and 2.85% to compensate for default risk. As expected, yield increases as debt increases. At 70% debt, a level reflective of some unitranche loans, the required yield increases to 9.11%.

The representation of yield in line 3 is an *average* yield because it represents the composite pricing of debt capital from the first dollar (1% of total assets) through the last dollar (i.e., the 1% of debt capital that brings total debt from 49–50%). Theoretically, each incremental dollar of debt brings greater risk and should have a greater yield. *Marginal* yield represents the pricing of incremental debt capital and is shown in line 4. For example, the yield required for the last 1% of debt capital before a cumulative 50% of total assets is reached equals 11.82%. For a unitranche loan seeking 70% debt capital, the last marginal 1% requires a yield equal to 16.16%.

Marginal yields are useful for at least three reasons. First, they inform investors that the high yields they see reported for second lien, subordinated, and mezzanine debt are necessary to compensate for credit risk. For example, the 70% loan-to-value (LTV) 9.11% unitranche loan in Exhibit 10.1 can be divided into a 50% LTV senior loan and a 20% LTV subordinated loan. The senior loan has a 7.10% required yield from Exhibit 10.1. The subordinated loan has a required yield equal to 14.1%. The subordinated debt required yield can be calculated by solving the equation: $9.11\% = x(0.29) + 7.10\%(0.71)$, where x equals the subordinated debt required yield, 9.11% equals the required unitranche yield, 7.10% equals the required senior debt yield, and 0.28 and 0.71 are the debt weightings to junior and senior tranches, respectively. Alternatively, the subordinated debt required yield can be calculated by solving the integral to the equation for line 4 with limits from 50% LTV to 70% LTV.

Second, marginal yields help investors understand the yield differences for varying senior debt structures—that is, super senior, senior, stretch senior, and unitranche—each having differing attachment or detachment points. For example, a 70% unitranche loan that sells a 20% first-out loan participation raises the required yield on its remaining last-out loan by almost two percentage points, from 9.11% to 10.88%.

Third, marginal yields inform as to the importance and pricing of covenants that offer lenders protection against potential adverse marginal use of corporate assets by borrowers, something covered in detail later in this chapter.

It is useful to understand how credit risk premiums react to changes in the value of its three key inputs: firm volatility, the risk-free rate, and time.

FIRM VOLATILITY

Exhibit 10.2 plots the credit risk premium (excluding the Libor and OID premiums in Exhibit 10.1) component of return at firm risk levels of 30%, 40%, and 50%, respectively. Firm volatility levels of 30% and 50% represent approximately one standard deviation from the mean firm volatility.[2]

As Exhibit 10.2 shows, credit risk premiums are quite sensitive to perceived asset volatility. At a 50% debt to firm value level, credit risk premiums can double or halve with a major one standard deviation move in the VIX.

Firm risk is generated primarily from three sources: overall market conditions, firm-specific conditions, and industry conditions. Changes in market conditions would likely set and move credit risk premiums similarly across all loans. Firm-specific conditions, by definition, are unique to

---

[2]The standard deviation of the VIX Index, a measure of equity market risk, equals 8.06% when measured monthly over the 25 years ending March 2022. We estimate that the average beta for middle market companies equals 1.2, so that one standard deviation of market risk applied to middle market companies equals 9.67%. We assume company-specific risk does not change and add (subtract) 10–40% average firm risk.

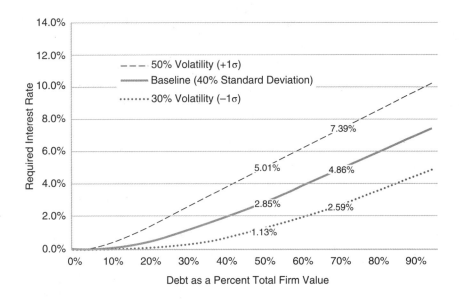

EXHIBIT 10.2   Credit risk premium and firm risk.

individual companies and would move risk premiums singularly. Industry conditions affect the loan pricing of borrowers as a subgroup within the same industry.

Exhibit 10.3 shows firm asset volatility estimates across industry groups based on companies in the Russell 2000 Index covering the 14-year period from 2007 through 2021. Russell 2000 companies were selected as the proxy for middle market companies because they are the closest traded equivalent to middle market companies. Individual firm volatility (standard deviation) is calculated by adjusting firm stock volatility over the measurement period for firm leverage (debt to total assets) over the measurement period. The average volatility for all firms within the same industry is calculated and reported in Exhibit 10.3, ordered from highest volatility industry to lowest volatility industry. Average volatility for all Russell 2000 companies is reported as well.

The disparity in firm volatility by industry coupled with the sensitivity of credit risk premiums to firm volatility suggest that industries should each carry substantially different yields, everything else being equal. For example, the same 49% debt ratio loan should carry a 4.16% risk premium for the average health care borrower but a much lower 2.17% for an information technology company. Not surprisingly, lenders that specialize tend to select the higher volatility industries where the reward from skilled underwriting is potentially greater.

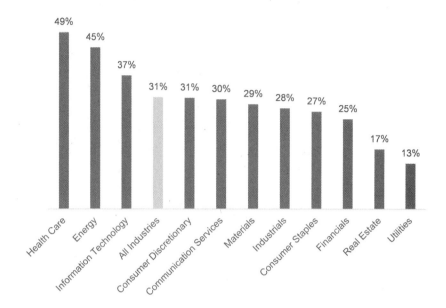

EXHIBIT 10.3 Unlevered firm volatility (standard deviation) by industry group.

Higher yields for smaller borrowers, discussed Chapter 11, may also be partially attributable to differences in expected firm asset volatility. Unlevered asset standard deviations for the 1,000 largest and 1,000 smallest companies in the Russell 2000 Index equal 27% and 38%, respectively. This difference in standard deviation would require smaller borrowers to pay an additional 1.50% yield relative to larger borrowers, a difference consistent with the empirical findings presented for middle market loans in Chapter 11.

RISK-FREE RATE

Exhibit 10.4 shows how the credit risk premium changes with the risk-free rate. Exhibit 10.4 focuses only on the credit risk premium itself and does not include how the risk-free rate directly affects the base rate on floating rate loans.

Credit risk premiums are inversely correlated to the risk-free rate. At a 50% debt to firm value level, the credit risk premium is 3.19% at a 0% T-bill rate and 2.15% at a 5% T-bill rate. A higher risk-free rate lowers the effective strike price of the put sold to borrowers by lenders. The lower

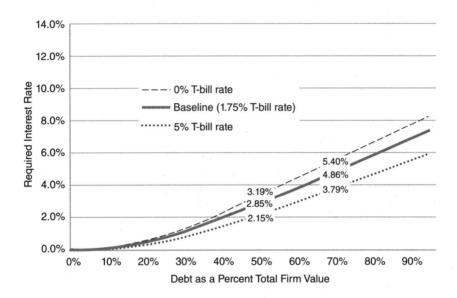

EXHIBIT 10.4   Credit risk premium and the risk-free rate.

strike price makes the put less valuable, lowering the option premium and, therefore, the credit risk premium received by the lender.

As Exhibit 10.4 shows, the impact of rising interest rates on credit spreads is not inconsequential. At the 50% debt level, an increase in the risk-free rate from 0–5% lowers the credit risk premium by 1.04%. At a 70% debt level, the credit risk premium falls by 1.61%. A 20% loan subordinated to a 50% senior loan would see its credit risk premium fall by 3.03%, from 10.92% to 7.89%, from a 0% to 5% T-bill rate change.

The relationship described in Exhibit 10.4 may explain some of the yield spread compression that has been coincident with rising short rates.

TIME TO MATURITY

Exhibit 10.5 describes the relationship between credit spreads and time to maturity. Unlike volatility and the risk-free rate that change credit spreads in the same direction across debt to total firm assets, time to maturity changes direction.

Exhibit 10.5 mostly confirms conventional thought that longer maturity loans are riskier for the lender and require higher spreads. However, at very high debt ratios (60% and above in our example), longer maturity loans are less risky.

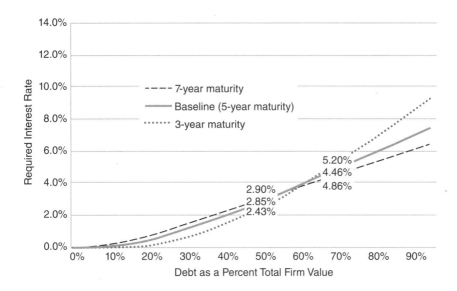

EXHIBIT 10.5 Credit risk premium and time to maturity.

ESTIMATING LOAN RISK

The Merton model is also useful for estimating the risk characteristics of a corporate loan. To demonstrate this, stock returns are simulated, and the Merton formula is applied to show the impact on corporate loan pricing.

Simulation inputs:

(a) Middle market corporate loans with a five-year maturity.
(b) Floating interest rates so the five-year risk-free bond has zero risk (no duration).
(c) Annualized firm-level risk equal to 34%, derived in the following way. We calculate the stock risk of every company in the Russell 2000 small stock index over the last 14 years ending December 31, 2021, finding a 47% average. Since our Merton model requires firm-level volatility, not stock volatility, we convert the 47% stock risk to an estimate of firm level risk by deleveraging using the average 0.27× Russell 2000 debt-to-total assets ratio over the same 14-year period. Deleveraging produces a 34% annualized unlevered risk estimate for the average Russell 2000 company. Russell 2000 companies were selected as a proxy for US middle market companies because their average EBITDA of $77 million is at roughly the

midpoint of the $10 million to $125 million EBITDA range that generally defines the corporate middle market.[3] The difference is that Russell 2000 companies are exchange traded while most middle market borrowers are private companies.

(d) The 34% firm-level risk estimate is divided into two risk sources: market-related risk (beta) and nonmarket idiosyncratic risk. Market risk is assumed to be 20%, equal to the risk of the Russell 2000 Index over the same 14-year period. Knowing that, by definition, market and nonmarket risks are independent of each other, the calculation for the nonmarket risk for the average middle market company equals 39%.[4]

Exhibit 10.6 provides simulation results for three loans. The first represents a senior, first lien loan with a principal value equal to 50% of initial firm assets. The second represents a unitranche loan, intended to incorporate first and second lien loans into one, with a principal value equal to 70% of firm assets. The third loan is second lien with a value equal to 20% of initial firm assets and with lien protection above the 50% asset value. Results are based on 1,000 trials.

Exhibit 10.7 displays the simulation outcomes for the first lien and second lien graphically.

Exhibits 10.6 and 10.7 together provide useful guidance on what to expect in terms of risk from different loan structures. Not surprisingly, risk (standard deviation) increases from 8.54% for a senior loan to 12.04% for a unitranche loan and 24.88% for a second lien loan. However, correlation and R-square with the Russell 2000 Index remain largely unchanged across the three loan types as equity risk represents a roughly constant percentage of total risk. Finally, equity beta increases from 0.19 for a senior loan to 0.27 for a unitranche loan and 0.57 for a second lien loan. Loans do act more like equity further down in the capital structure.

Loans also possess other less desirable risk features. The simulated loan returns feature negative convexity, consistent with the short volatility nature of the short-put feature in Equation (1). However, the negative convexity is not severe and is far less than what is found in hedge fund returns.[5] Loans also display a negative skew, or downside tail, in the distribution of returns. But unlike risk and convexity, skew improves as credit quality declines.

---

[3]Borrowers in the CDLI have a median and average EBITDA equal to $45 million and $62 million, respectively, at March 31, 2022.

[4]$0.39^2 = 0.34^2 + 0.20^2$, assuming zero correlation between market and nonmarket risk.

	First Lien	Unitranche	Second Lien
Loan size	50% of firm assets	70% of firm assets	20% of firm assets
Recourse	All firm assets	All firm assets	Firm assets above 50% first lien
Risk (std. dev.)	8.54%	12.04%	24.88%
Corr. w/ Russell 2000	0.45	0.47	0.48
R-Square	20%	21%	22%
Beta	0.19	0.27	0.57
Convexity	−0.26	−0.30	−0.42
Skew	−1.01	−0.64	−0.23

EXHIBIT 10.6 Simulation results for a hypothetical first lien, unitranche, and second lien loan.

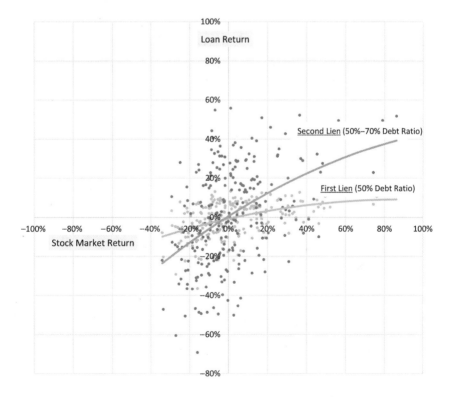

EXHIBIT 10.7 Simulation results for hypothetical first lien and second lien loans.

ESTIMATING LOAN PORTFOLIO RISK

Exhibits 10.8 and 10.9 contain risk characteristics for a portfolio of loans, which is likely of greater interest. We simulate returns for portfolios of senior loans, unitranche loans, and second lien loans, assuming 100 loans in each portfolio. As before, we simulate equity market risk and company-specific risk separately.

Equity market risk affects all loans the same, at least directionally. Conceptually, company-specific risk should be independent with zero correlation across companies. However, we assume the same 0.25 cross correlation for all 100 loans instead of a zero correlation because, in our experience, there are common factors in addition to the market factor that tend to push returns in the same direction. These common factors could include industry, liquidity, and size factors. Our choice of 0.25 is consistent with values found for hedge fund returns after market returns are stripped from total returns. With these assumptions, the nonmarket firm-level risk for a portfolio of loans equals 16% compared to 32% for a single corporate borrower. The simulation results in Exhibits 10.8 and 10.9 are based on 1,000 trials.

Portfolio diversification reduces nonmarket risk, causing higher beta, correlation, and R-square values for loan portfolios in contrast to individual loans. Convexity worsens but skew improves slightly.

	First Lien	Unitranche	Second Lien
Loan size	50% of firm assets	70% of firm assets	20% of firm assets
Recourse	All firm assets	All firm assets	Firm assets above 50% first lien
Risk (std. dev.)	5.67%	8.29%	17.78%
Corr. w/ Russell 2000	0.73	0.74	0.75
R-Square	54%	55%	57%
Beta	0.22	0.32	0.70
Convexity	−0.39	−0.48	−0.80
Skew	−0.81	−0.55	−0.26

EXHIBIT 10.8 Simulation results for hypothetical first lien, unitranche, and second lien 100 loan portfolios.

---

[5]For example, Cliffwater calculates an average convexity value equal to −0.75 for a diversified group of 500 larger hedge funds covering a five-year period ending December 31, 2021.

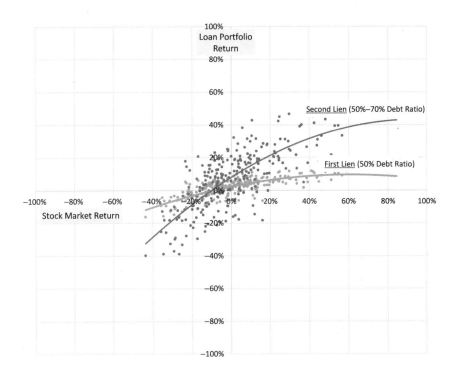

EXHIBIT 10.9 Simulation results for hypothetical first lien and second lien loan portfolios.

TESTING THE MERTON MODEL

The simulated loan portfolio risk estimates contained in Exhibit 10.9 are next compared to risk calculations for actual returns reported for two corporate credit indexes: the Morningstar LSTA US Leveraged Loan 100 Index and the Bloomberg High Yield Bond Index. The first index is composed of traded floating rate bank loans, generally senior in credit standing, while the second index is composed of traded fixed rate corporate bonds, generally subordinated to bank loans. Our risk calculations are based on monthly returns from January 2000 through December 2021.

In addition, because the Bloomberg High Yield Bond Index returns are at a fixed rate, their monthly returns are affected by changes in longer maturity interest rates. By contrast, our simulated returns assume floating rates. To convert the fixed rate Bloomberg High Yield Bond Index to a floating rate, the duration-equivalent monthly Treasury bond return is subtracted from the monthly Index return. The result should be what the Bloomberg

High Yield Bond Index would have returned if the underlying bonds were a floating rate rather than a fixed rate.[6]

Exhibit 10.10 compares the simulated loan portfolio risk characteristics with calculations based on actual index returns.

A comparison of the simulated first lien risk calculations and the Morningstar LSTA US Leveraged Loan 100 Index reveals similarities and differences. Risk values (standard deviations) are very similar as are the betas. Convexity and skew are higher for the Morningstar LSTA US Leveraged Loan 100 Index but that is likely because the Russell 2000 Index itself displayed some of those same characteristics during the measurement period, which probably magnified the Morningstar LSTA US Leveraged Loan 100 Index values.

A comparison of the simulated second lien risk calculations and the duration-adjusted Bloomberg Barclays High Yield Bond Index also includes similarities and differences. Importantly, higher risks and higher betas for subordinated debt are exhibited in both simulated and duration-adjusted actual returns. The biggest difference is the much higher 17.78% risk level for simulated second lien versus 10.88% for the duration-adjusted Bloomberg High Yield Bond Index. This difference is likely due to an inexact match in debt ratios between our hypothetical second lien loan and the actual debt ratio specifications for the Index.

	(Exhibit 10.7) Simulated First Lien	(Exhibit 10.7) Simulated Second Lien	Morningstar LSTA US Leveraged Loan 100 Index	Duration-Adjusted Bloomberg Barclays High Yield Bond Index
Risk (std. dev.)	5.67%	17.78%	6.46%	10.88%
Corr. w/ Russell 2000	0.73	0.75	0.53	0.71
R-Square	54%	57%	28%	50%
Beta	0.22	0.70	0.10	0.38
Convexity	−0.39	−0.80	−0.92	−0.55
Skew	−0.81	−0.26	−2.45	−1.22

EXHIBIT 10.10 Simulated versus actual risk calculations.

---

[6]A monthly Treasury bond return of equal duration to the Bloomberg Barclays High Yield Bond Index is calculated using durations and returns for the five-year maturity Treasury and three-month T-bill.

MERTON MODEL WITH COVENANTS

Easy credit conditions not only result in spread narrowing but also relaxation in loan covenants. An extension of the Merton model by Fisher Black and John Cox[7] (Black-Cox) addresses the value of covenants where the Merton model was covenant free. This is useful for lenders who want to understand the cost of foregoing customary covenants late in a credit cycle.

The Merton model has no provision for bankruptcy prior to loan maturity. Loan covenants vary in type but all act to trigger a default or restructure prior to maturity. By doing so, covenants can protect possible further erosion in firm assets and enhance recoveries. They can also accelerate cash flow to the lender, thereby creating value.

Black-Cox extends the Merton model to include covenants, also using option pricing theory.[8] Covenants are intended to protect the value of firm assets and ultimately can terminate the loan through default before maturity if firm assets fall below loan face value. Ideally, the loan face value becomes a barrier for firm assets after which default is declared in a covenant-tight world. More likely, the look-back nature of covenants results in a barrier that falls below face value, but once the covenant barrier is broken the lender takes the keys and replaces the equity holder.[9] Black-Cox argue that this dynamic mirrors a down-and-in call option given to the lender and can be valued in the same way.

Exhibit 10.11 provides an example of a down-and-in option.

At loan underwriting (time = 0), firm assets are well above face value but take a declining path to equal just 25% of loan value at maturity. Under the Merton model, default would occur at maturity and the lender would recover just 25% of principal.

In the Black-Cox model, loan covenants produce a value barrier giving lenders the opportunity to force borrowers into default before maturity. In our example, covenants allow the lender to force default at time t where recovery equals 70% of principal, saving 45% of value (70% minus 25%). Our example is one of many scenarios that could play out, including some where asset recovery makes early default costly.

---

[7]Fisher Black and John C. Cox, "Valuing Corporate Securities: Some Effects of Bond Indenture Provisions," *The Journal of Finance* (May 1976).

[8]Fisher Black is the same author of Black-Cox and Black-Scholes models.

[9]At barrier breaches, lenders more often extract value from borrowers other than taking the keys, including special payments or yield adjustments, whose potential value can also be represented by Black-Cox.

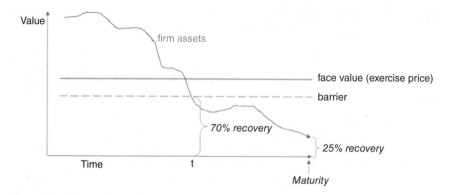

EXHIBIT 10.11 Illustration of down-and-in option.

Conceptually, covenants give the lender the right to buy the firm at an exercise price equal to the face value of the loan once covenant terms have been violated, which is represented by firm assets falling below the barrier value. The representation of loan principal as exercise price means that through default the lender pays for the firm assets by absolving the borrower of principal repayment. This description fits the standard options pricing model except that the option comes into existence and has value only on the condition that firm assets drop through a barrier created by the loan covenants. The Black-Cox model values the down-and-in option, and in so doing, the value of the covenant.

In Exhibit 10.12 we take the example in Exhibit 10.1 but add a covenant package that creates a barrier equal to 60% of the face value of the loan. We select 60% because it approximates the historical average recovery rate on broadly syndicated leveraged loans, which generally come with covenants.

Lines 1 and 2 are repeated from Exhibit 10.1 and show average and marginal loan rates using the Merton model *without* covenants. Lines 3 and 4 are added and represent the average and marginal loan rates using the Black-Cox model *with* covenants. As expected, lender protections from covenants add value to a loan as measured by a down-and-in call option and convert to a lower interest rate required by the lender. For example, a senior loan representing 50% of firm assets would require a 6.56% rate without covenants and a 6.18% rate with covenants. Covenants could be said to be worth an extra 0.38% (6.56% – 6.18%).

Observe that covenants become much more important to the lender as a loan stretches to higher ratios of firm value. At a 70% loan to asset

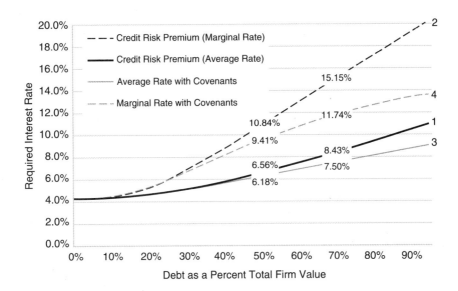

EXHIBIT 10.12 Debt costs with/without covenants (a theoretical representation using the Black-Cox model).

value, the loss of covenant protection requires an additional 0.93% of yield (8.43% – 7.50%), compared to 0.38% for the 50% loan.

Finally, marginal rates without and with covenants are represented by lines 2 and 4, respectively, and point to their critical importance in pricing second lien loans. For example, a second lien loan representing 20% of firm assets with a 50% attachment point would require a yield equal to 13.11% without covenants and 10.80% with covenants, a 2.31% difference.

Understanding the imprint of covenants on loan pricing would seem critical in an environment trending toward covenant-lite because it represents an erosion in expected return not reflected in headline credit spreads.

Covenants also reduce many risk measures for a portfolio of loans. Exhibit 10.13 compares risk statistics for a diversified portfolio of unitranche loans without covenants (see Exhibit 10.8) and with covenants.

Covenants lower risk and beta and improve convexity and skew. What doesn't really change is the correlation and R-Square with stocks. In summary, covenants play an important role in both the pricing (yield) and risk of loan portfolios and can be measured by the Black-Cox model.

	Unitranche Without Covenants	Unitranche With Covenants
Loan size	70% of firm assets	70% of firm assets
Recourse	All firm assets	All firm assets
Risk (std. dev.)	8.29%	6.20%
Corr. w/ Russell 2000	0.74	0.73
R-Square	55%	53%
Beta	0.32	0.24
Convexity	−0.48	−0.11
Skew	−0.55	−0.39

EXHIBIT 10.13 Simulation results for hypothetical unitranche 100 loan portfolio with and without covenants.

The Merton model provides a useful framework for understanding the pricing of corporate loan yield spreads. Coupled with simulation methods, investors can develop useful estimates of return and risk for loans of differing credit seniority, including covariances useful for multi-asset optimization.

The Merton model reveals that credit risk premiums (yields) rise rapidly as loan leverage ratios increase and that expectations of underlying firm risk, whether market, industry, or firm specific, can produce significant differences in risk premiums. Simulation confirms that corporate loans of varying leverage levels all have high correlations with the stock market. However, senior loans display much lower levels of risk compared to subordinated loans.

The Black-Cox model shows how to value loan covenants and measure the impact of covenant-lite structures. A reasonable estimate for the value of covenants is approximately 1% per annum, but that value will increase (decrease) with loan seniority and leverage ratios.

CHAPTER 11

Risk Premiums in US Middle Market Lending

Risk premium is an often-used term in finance to identify factors common to a group of securities where because that group possesses unique risk-generative characteristics that cannot be diversified away, there exists an expected or ex ante return attributable to that common factor. Oddly, while called a risk premium, it is a return premium for taking risk.

It is also worth emphasizing that risk premiums accrue to common factors that are non-diversifiable or can't otherwise be eliminated through diversification. Consequently, risk premiums are considered beta and not alpha. When risk premiums are found in less traditional asset classes or investment strategies they are sometimes referred to as alternative beta.

Most familiar to investors and perhaps the largest risk premium is the equity risk premium. Stock risk can't be diversified away in portfolio construction so investors, being risk averse, demand a premium for holding stocks in a portfolio. A wealth of historical data has verified the existence of a stock risk premium, measuring somewhere between 4% and 6% over long time periods. Another familiar example is the *term structure premium*, reflecting the common factor among long-dated bonds that the risks relating to lending at fixed rates for long periods of time can't be diversified away and deserves a premium return relative to short-term lending. Again, historical studies have attributed 1–2% in premium return to investing in long-dated bonds, unrelated to credit risk.

Modern finance is perhaps currently suffering from risk premium inflation, where investment analysts are mining for and discovering risk premiums in every data set. These efforts have produced, probably prematurely, investment products that "harvest alternative risk premia" that collectively are expected to produce systematic excess return unrelated to the basic stock and bond risk premiums. These second-order risk premiums are undoubtedly much smaller, if they exist at all.

Potential investors in US middle market direct loans frequently question why middle market yield spreads are so high, particularly when the record shows historical credit losses have been about the same as losses found in more liquid broadly syndicated loans and high-yield bonds. Does the "free lunch" label apply to this newly forming institutional asset class or is there something else going on?

Analysis of the direct loan database underlying the CDLI shows that middle market direct lending is a collection of yield spreads, each associated with a different risk factor and each risk factor is non-diversifiable and deserving of a risk premium. This is very unlike investing in stocks, bonds, or liquid credit where there is one dominant factor receiving a risk premium. Instead, direct lending is a collage of risk premiums, each identifiable with consistent excess returns associated with each. Risk premium excess returns primarily take the form of excess income or yield in our analysis.

There are four identifiable risk premiums unique to middle market direct lending with quantifiable yield spreads associated with each one. Exhibit 11.1 reports yield spreads (premiums) available to the four risk factors found within middle market lending. The measurement date is March 31, 2022.

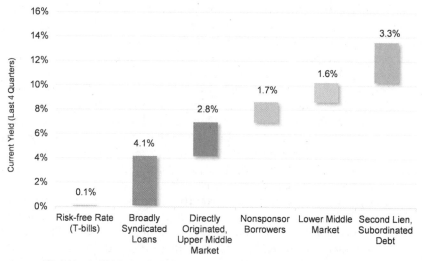

¹Excludes potential deductions for differential credit losses and fees.

EXHIBIT 11.1   Available risk premiums in direct US middle market corporate loans, March 31, 2022.

The left most bar in Exhibit 11.1 represents the 0.1% yield on the risk-free T-bill. The second bar to the right is the excess yield available in broadly syndicated loans (BSLs), measured by the Morningstar LSTA US Leveraged Loan 100 Index, which equaled 4.1% on March 31, 2022. The 4.1% excess yield represents investor compensation for taking pure liquid credit risk in the public market. The four bars to the right identify four additional yield spreads, each associated with a unique risk premium. Yield for all six bars is defined as trailing four-quarter interest income. The four risk premiums and their values at March 31, 2022, are as follows:

1. *Directly originated, upper middle market.* There is a 2.8% yield premium for moving from liquid broadly syndicated bank loans to senior loans backed by upper middle market, sponsor-driven borrowers. This yield premium can be interpreted as a liquidity premium because underlying loan characteristics are most like bank loans except for being privately originated as opposed to bank originated and syndicated to the public market.
2. *Nonsponsored borrowers.* There is a 1.7% yield premium for holding debt of companies not controlled by private equity firms, something that could be interpreted as a governance premium or nonsponsor premium. Nonsponsored borrowers might be viewed as riskier because management behavior, particularly under corporate distress, could be less predictable and costlier to lenders compared to sponsor-backed borrowers.
3. *Lower middle market.* A 1.6% yield premium is found for lending to lower middle market borrowers, companies with annual EBITDA less than $10 million, compared to upper middle market borrowers with EBITDA over $100 million. This could be a size premium often found in other asset classes.
4. *Second lien, subordinated debt.* Not surprisingly, the largest yield premium is associated with the seniority premium. Subordinated loans have a 3.3% higher yield when compared to senior loans within the US middle market.

Exhibit 11.2 displays how the risk-free rate, the credit risk premium, and the four middle market direct loan risk premiums in Exhibit 11.1 have changed over the last 5.5 years.

The four middle market risk premiums have shown some variability over time, but not much. The risk premium with the most volatility is the seniority premium for subordinated loans, which has been as high as 4.2% in June 2016 and as low as 1.8% in December 2018. The higher yield spread fluctuations in the seniority premium are consistent with

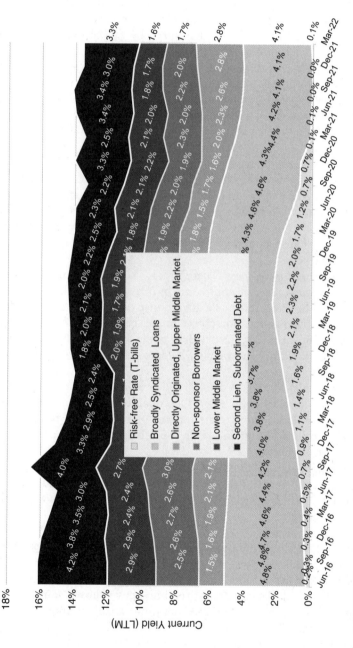

EXHIBIT 11.2 Time-varying middle market loan risk premiums, June 2016 to March 2022.

varying yield spreads for junior and mezzanine debt in the broadly syndicated and structured credit markets and are correlated with the overall business and credit cycles.

Investors are often interested in discovering relative value within asset classes, including private debt. A common approach is to compare current yields or yield spreads against historical values. Historical average values for the premiums (excluding the risk-free rate) in Exhibit 11.2 are broadly syndicated loans (4.2%); directly originated, upper middle market (2.1%); nonsponsored borrowers (2.3%); lower middle market (2.1%); and second lien, subordinated debt (2.9%). Current values can then be compared to these averages to identify opportunities. Applying this simple methodology on March 31, 2022, lending to upper middle market sponsor-backed borrowers, perhaps even in a second lien position, tilts the construction of a portfolio of loans toward a composition that takes advantage of risk premiums that are above historical averages and away from risk premiums that are below historical averages.

Understanding risk premiums is also useful in developing return expectations for direct loans and understanding past performance. Equation 11.1 illustrates how investors can use the risk premiums in combination with direct loan manager portfolio risk exposures.

$$\text{Expected Direct Loan Yield} = \text{Libor} + \text{BSL Spread} + b_1\left(P_1\right)$$
$$+ b_2\left(P_2\right) + b_3\left(P_3\right) + b_4\left(P_4\right) \quad (11.1)$$

$$\text{Libor} = \text{short-term} \left(\text{generally three-mo.}\right) \text{benchmark rate}$$

$$\text{BSL Spread} = \text{broadly syndicated bank loan spread over Libor}$$

$$i = \text{middle market risk factor } 1 \ldots 4$$

$$b_i = \text{loan exposure to middle market risk factor } i$$

$$P_i = \text{risk premium for middle market risk factor } i$$

Take, as example, a conservative manager whose focus is senior, sponsor-based loans across the middle market and the middle market loan risk factors and premiums are the four described in Exhibit 11.1. The manager's beta (b_i) exposure to the first factor, directly originated private corporate loans, equals 1.0, by definition, if the manager stays fully invested in direct loans. Our conservative manager wants the convenience of investing only with sponsor-backed borrowers so the beta exposure to the nonsponsored risk premium equals 0.0. The manager's exposure to the third lower middle market risk premium equals 0.5, because roughly one-half the loans are upper middle market and the other one-half are lower middle market. Finally, our conservative manager by style wants to remain in the senior part of the borrower's capital structure and therefore has a beta exposure to the subordinated risk premium equal to 0.0. Equation 11.2 calculates the expected yield for our conservative manager on March 31, 2022.

$$\text{Manager Yield} = 0.1\% + 4.1\% + 1.00(2.8\%) + 0.00(1.7\%)$$
$$+ 0.50(1.6\%) + 0.00(3.3\%) = 7.8\% \qquad (11.2)$$

The 7.8% expected yield for this conservative manager, gross of fees, leverage, and credit losses, falls 0.9% below the 8.7% gross yield on the CDLI on March 31, 2022, as calculated in equation 11.3.

$$\text{CDLI Yield} = 0.1\% + 4.1\% + 1.00(2.8\%) + 0.21(1.7\%)$$
$$+ 0.50(1.6\%) + 0.20(3.3\%) = 8.7\% \qquad (11.3)$$

The 0.9% yield deficit for the conservative direct loan manager compared to the asset-weighted average manager, who mirrors the CDLI, could be overcome by several factors so that actual total return performance, and risk, is competitive or superior to the average manager. For example, expected credit losses could be lower. A reasonable expectation is for a senior-only manager to have realized credit losses that are 0.50% below the average manager represented by the CDLI based on differences in historical credit losses for senior and subordinated debt.[1] Second, expected fees for a senior-only manager should be about 0.50% lower (including both asset-based and incentive fees) and the nonsponsor focus for our conservative manager should lower fees another 0.10%. The relationship between fees and individual risk factor exposures is covered in Chapter 19. Suffice for now that investors could reasonably expect that a senior-only, nonsponsored lender might offer fees that are 0.60% (0.10% plus 0.50%) below the average direct lending fee. Third, the cost of borrowing to finance leverage should be lower for a senior-only direct lending portfolio. Comparing financing costs for BDCs that invest in only senior debt shows an approximate 0.55% lower cost of financing for senior loan portfolios compared to the overall CDLI. The financing cost comparison is based on a leverage ratio equal to approximately 1.05× net assets. Multiplying the 0.55% in lower borrowing costs with the 1.05× leverage level gives a net savings equal to 0.58%.

The likely net cost savings for our senior-focused direct lending manager equals 1.68%, equal to the 0.50% savings from credit losses, the 0.60% savings on fees, and the 0.58% savings on financing costs. Subtracting the

---

[1] Exhibit 9.4 shows historical credit losses of –0.12% annualized for CDLI-Senior compared to a much higher –1.06% for CDLI.

1.68% in cost savings from the 0.90% deficit in yield spread leaves a 0.78% yield advantage to our senior lender.

There is one other point worth noting. Senior loans have lower levels of PIK income, averaging 5% of total interest income compared to 8% for more diversified portfolios. To the extent that PIK income is not valued as highly as cash, the 0.21% in additional PIK income (out of 8.7%) earned by the average manager might be viewed as a soft difference.

The risk premium model for middle market direct corporate loans described in Exhibit 11.1 is a useful construct in understanding where yield comes from and the risk factors underlying them. This understanding is very important in yield-driven asset classes where investors are often mesmerized by the manager or fund with the highest yield, on the presumption that yield translates into realized return. Differences in fees, realized losses, and financing opportunities are direct mitigating factors that need to be considered when comparing yields, but so also is general risk-taking, and each risk factor likely possesses incremental valuation risk (unrealized losses).

METHODOLOGY

The discovery of risk premiums in middle market loans is based on data collected from public information disclosed by public and private BDCs and from private data sources.

Risk premiums are calculated through a cross-sectional regression where the dependent variable is portfolio yield and the three independent variables are expected/actual share of sponsor/nonsponsor lending (measured by percentage allocations to sponsor or nonsponsor lending), expected/actual portfolio company size (measured by average EBITDA), and loan seniority (measured by percentage allocations to senior or subordinated debt). The independent variables are scaled such that higher values represent higher expected risk (e.g., nonsponsor borrower, smaller borrower, and more junior debt). By design, the intercept term is the yield on larger-sized, sponsor-backed senior loans. The yield on a broadly syndicated loan, measured by the Morningstar LSTA US Leveraged Loan 100 Index yield, is subtracted from the intercept yield to separately capture what is interpreted as the liquidity premium.

The results from the regression's intercept and coefficients are the yield premiums reported in Exhibit 11.1. Each regression coefficient is statistically significant (T-stat >2.0) with an overall regression R-squared equal to 55%.

Ideally, the identified risk premiums would be measured net, not gross, of credit losses. Useful further study would be analysis on the relationship between risk premiums and credit losses, something that is currently challenging because it requires another downward credit cycle, such as the 2008–2010 period when significant realized credit losses last occurred in middle market direct lending.

However, credit losses for two of the risk premiums seem fairly settled. The 2.1% average historical illiquidity premium is not offset by incremental credit losses. Credit losses on the CDLI have not been statistically different from credit losses on broadly syndicated bank loans so the 2.1% yield spread should be viewed as both gross and net of credit losses. By comparison, evidence shows that the 2.9% average yield spread for the seniority premium comes with incremental credit losses. There is plenty of data showing that subordinated debt experiences higher credit losses, primarily through lower recovery rates, when compared to senior debt.

That leaves questions about credit losses for sponsored versus nonsponsored debt and upper- versus lower-middle market debt. The author knows of no published study addressing the sponsor, nonsponsor question. On the matter of upper- versus lower-middle market debt, a 2012 Moody's Analytics RiskCalc 4.0 study examining factors predictive of default found that seven financial variables were predictive of default frequency. The most important was the amount of debt as a percentage of corporate assets. The least important factor was company size, measured by assets. At this time, it seems the relationship between credit losses and nonsponsored borrowers and smaller borrowers remains largely unanswered.

The presence of unique risk premiums in US middle market direct lending will be very important in later chapters on asset managers. While all asset manager lenders have exposure to the illiquidity premium, exposures to a nonsponsor, lower-middle market and subordinated risk factors vary widely. This makes discriminating among asset manager lenders based only on yield very difficult, if not misleading, because of possible differences in risk-taking. Investors often make the mistake of investing with asset managers or in funds with the highest yield. Know that risk-adjusted portfolio yield is an important part of understanding manager performance and selection.

CHAPTER 12

Covenants and the Loan Agreement

L oan agreements generally include legal requirements, or *covenants*, governing borrower behavior through the life of the loan. The loan covenant package theoretically sets the barrier in the Black-Cox model and helps create value for the lender in addition to regular payments of interest. The value created likely takes the form of higher recovery rates should default occur or additional lender income through interest rate resets or fees charged by the lender to waive covenant violations. This report provides an overview of a typical loan agreement and catalogs the more common loan covenants.

Direct loans are governed by lengthy agreements between the borrower and lender, generally structured as follows:

- *Definitions:* Like most financial agreements, direct loan agreements begin with definitions and measures that are at the foundation of the loan agreement. Definitions for over 200 terms are generally found, including calculations for such variables as EBITDA, the base rate, interest spread, fees, and definitions of default.
- *Loan commitment:* This section spells out the size of the loan or loans, drawdown and repayment schedules, payment procedures, and voluntary and involuntary prepayment. It also specifies the terms of payment, including interest calculations, timing, and what constitutes default. Loan fees and expenses, prepayment premiums, and make-whole provisions are included here.
- *Conditions precedent:* Here the lender specifies what final conditions are required before the loan is made. Generally, the items verify the borrower's current financial condition and might include payoff letters evidencing payment in full of any prior loans, payment of fees and expenses, delivery of current financial statements, results of lien searches, authorizations, insurance, absence of litigation, and passage of financial tests. In the case of secured loans, the agreement would specify the pledged assets and priority of lender claims. For revolving loans, these or similar conditions are set forth for each time there is a draw from the revolver facility.

- *Representations and warranties:* The borrower represents and warrants to the lender its business status with respect to several potential risk factors, including the existence of liens, subsidiaries, employee benefits and pensions, regulatory compliance, and places of business.
- *Affirmative covenants:* These are actions the borrower must do over the term of the agreement. Included in this section is a further assurance covenant that, among other things, will, in the case of a secured loan, generally require the borrower to cause any newly formed subsidiary to join the credit facility as a guarantor, thus preventing leakage of value from the collateral pool, which secures the loan.
- *Negative covenants:* These are actions the borrower must not do over the term of the agreement.
- *Events of default, remedies:* This section identifies what actions trigger default, what cures are available to the borrower to get out of default, and what rights the lender has if default is not remedied, for example, the lender's ability to demand repayment and accelerate its loan in advance of the stated maturity date.
- *Agent:* Some direct loans are shared among multiple lenders, each of which holds a pro-rata interest in the total loan package. The administrative agent is identified along with its duties and authorities. The administrative agent is generally the lead lender originating the loan. The agent is responsible for handling communications and cash movements between the borrower and the lenders and typically takes the lead in negotiating any amendments to the loan agreements, including covenant waivers.
- *Miscellaneous:* Loan agreements close with a list of assorted perfunctory items not material to the economic substance.

While the level and structure of interest payments found in the loan commitment section of the agreement represents the clear majority of the return on direct loans, we showed that covenant protection itself has value that can be theoretically measured by the Black-Cox model.

Covenants, and financial covenants in particular, are designed to protect the financial condition of the borrower for purposes of repaying the lender in full through controls on the borrower's income statement and balance sheet. These covenants are put forth in the loan indenture and monitored by the agent, who is usually the lead lender.

Covenants are generally divided into affirmative covenants and negative covenants.

A list of affirmative covenants would likely include the following:

- Corporate books and records as well as regular monthly or quarterly management reports and projections that assist the lender in understanding the ongoing operating condition of the borrower

- Evidence of compliance with payments on obligations, including rents, leases, insurance, pension payments, and taxes
- Evidence of maintenance of corporate existence, assets, and businesses
- Ongoing compliance with all applicable laws and regulations
- Observer rights at board of directors meetings

A longer list of negative covenants would likely include the following:

- Limitations on the ability of the borrower to take on additional debt, expressed either in dollars or as a percentage of total assets
- Limitations on the ability of the borrower to lend to a subsidiary or limitations on subsidiary debt
- Prohibition on speculation and permissions only for bona fide hedging
- Prohibitions on new liens, whether for business reasons or taxes
- Limitations on dividend payments or other distributions to equity investors
- Prohibitions or restrictions on asset sales, mergers, or consolidations
- Limitations on types of corporate investments
- Limitations on annual capital expenditures

More important, financial covenants that are less likely to be under the borrower's control may include the following:

- Minimum fixed charge coverage ratio, often expressed as EBITDA, as a multiple of required interest, lease, and similar payments
- Maximum (total and senior) debt to EBITDA ratio, often declining over the life of the loan and netting for cash on hand
- Minimum available balance sheet cash

The financial covenants generally fall into two camps: maintenance and incurrence. Maintenance covenants are stricter compared to incurrence covenants, requiring the borrower to continually satisfy a financial test. Incurrence covenants instead require application of a financial test only when a corporate action, such as new debt, is incurred. For example, a requirement that the borrower's debt not exceed a percentage of EBITDA is a common covenant. A maintenance covenant involving EBITDA might be very valuable to the lender and costly to the borrower given year-to-year potential volatility in EBITDA, particularly in cyclical industries. However, an incurrence covenant covering leverage would only be violated if the borrower were to exceed the covenant level via the incurrence of additional indebtedness. If the covenant level was exceeded solely because the borrower's EBITDA declined, the borrower would not be in breach of the covenant.

Consequently, differentiating the application of maintenance and incurrence tests becomes important in interpreting the strength of any covenant. Private direct loans typically make use of maintenance covenants, while publicly traded debt, such as high-yield bonds and some broadly syndicated loans, often only includes incurrence covenants. This difference makes theoretical sense given the relatively less liquid nature of direct loans.

Definitions are another important dimension in understanding covenants. For example, EBITDA plays a central role in many covenants, but the definition of EBITDA can itself become an important part of lender protection. Late in a credit cycle when lenders are competing more aggressively for deals, credit terms generally favor borrowers, and it is not uncommon for the definition of EBITDA in the loan agreement to expand and include add-backs such as expected reduction in operating costs and capital expenditures or expected improvements in sales that make the borrower look more creditworthy. Ideally, lenders should push for standard GAAP definitions grounded in current operating performance. Otherwise, covenants no longer have any meaning. In addition, financial covenants are typically set at a cushion to the borrower's actual financial condition. For example, if the borrower's actual senior leverage (senior debt as a multiple of trailing 12-month EBITDA) is 4.0 times at the initiation of the loan, the covenant level might be set at a modest cushion, such as 4.25 times. In the case of acquisition finance, a cushion is often set to a financial model. As the market for direct loans becomes more competitive, lenders will compete for deals by offering wider cushions. Similar to the use of add-backs, these covenant cushions make financial covenants less impactful.

Covenant lite is a term often used to describe loan agreements in which covenants are either watered down or eliminated and is a condition often seen later in a business cycle when credit is abundant, and borrowers have the upper hand in loan negotiations. The Black-Cox model helps measure the significant cost of covenant-lite loan agreements, particularly for unitranche and second lien loans. Lenders often note that covenants don't enhance the return on an otherwise bad deal. However, well-constructed covenants are important in that they give the lender a seat at the table in the event the borrower's financial condition declines and permit the lenders to restructure their loan packages to improve their position as creditor, including raising interest rates and fees, and accelerating their ability to force a company restructuring before the value of their collateral declines beyond recovery.

CHAPTER 13

Should Direct Loan Portfolios Be Leveraged?

Many investors in US middle market direct lending use leverage (borrow), typically at the fund level, to enhance return. Whether and how much to leverage is an important decision in constructing a direct lending portfolio. This chapter addresses how leverage affects direct lending return and risk and provides some guidance as to how the leverage question should be answered.

Exhibit 13.1 provides underlying fee and leverage assumptions that are representative of an institutional private fund vehicle. Those assumptions are then used in conjunction with the historical CDLI returns to project return and risk outcomes at varying leverage levels.

As an illustration, the net of fee return for this direct lending portfolio example is calculated in Exhibit 13.2, assuming leverage equal to 1.06 (106%) of net assets. This is the weighted average leverage used by BDCs on their loan portfolios over the last year ending March 31, 2022. The fees selected for our example are representative of an institutional account, but less than fees typically charged by the average publicly traded BDC.

The representations in Exhibit 13.2 are intended to reflect what an investor would have received since 2004 from a direct lending portfolio with the characteristics of the CDLI and a leverage level that asset managers (lenders) use to support those loan assets. Instead of using actual historical fee levels, fees more reflective of current institutional managers were selected, acknowledging that fees have come down over time as a by-product of greater scale in direct lending platforms and the desire to examine prospective performance rather than historical performance.

The calculation progression in Exhibit 13.2 begins with the 9.50% unlevered, gross of fee CDLI return since September 30, 2004, through March 31, 2022. Our example assumes that direct loan assets will return a level similar to the average over the last 17.5 years. Next, an additional

Direct lending asset returns	Cliffwater Direct Lending Index (CDLI)
Leverage (borrowing/net assets)	0.0 unlevered 0.6 average leverage for BDCs 1.0 leverage 1.5 leverage 2.0 leverage
Cost of debt (financing)	3.87%, equal to the average 2004–2022 historical financing cost of all BDCs in the CDLI, taken from 10-Qs/Ks. Financing spread equal to 2.28%, the difference between 3.87% total cost of financing and 1.59%, the average 3-mo. Libor rate for the same 2004–2022 time period
Management fee	1.00% of gross assets
Administrative expenses	0.20% of gross assets
Carried interest/preferred return	10%/6%

EXHIBIT 13.1 Indicative fee and leverage specifications for a direct lending portfolio.

9.50%	Asset return net of realized and unrealized losses
+ 10.07%	Gross additional return from leverage at 1.06 times NAV
– 4.10%	Cost of financing (@ 3.87% of borrowings)
= 15.47%	Gross of fee return
– 0.41%	Administrative expenses (@ 0.20% of gross assets)
– 2.06%	Management fees (@ 1.00% of gross assets)
13.00%	Return net of management and administrative fees
– 1.30%	Incentive fees (@ 10% of return net of management fee and expenses)
11.70%	Net return to investors
22%	Manager fees as a % of gross of fee return

EXHIBIT 13.2 Indicative direct lending portfolio after fees, expenses, and leverage.

10.07% is added to reflect the 106% leverage being used and equals 9.50% times 1.06.[1] The cost of leverage financing is assumed to equal 3.87%, the actual cost of debt financing loans in the CDLI over its history. The cost of leveraged financing in the example equals 4.10%, the 3.87% cost of financing multiplied by the 1.06× amount of financing. Together, the unlevered and 1.06× levered direct loan assets produce a 15.47% return net of borrowing costs but still gross of fees.

Fees are next deducted from the 15.47% return. Administrative fees equal to 0.20% of gross assets are subtracted. These fees, as a percentage of net assets, equal 0.41% (0.20% × 2.06). The term *gross assets* is generally used to refer to the combined value of both unlevered and levered direct loans. Since lenders and administrators must create and service all loans, administrative fees are often charged on all assets rather than net assets. In our example, both management and administrative fees are charged on gross assets. Consequently, the 1.00% management fee on gross assets is the equivalent to 2.06% (1.00% multiplied by 2.06) on net assets.

The last fee deduction in Exhibit 13.2 is the incentive fee, which is calculated after management fees and administrative expenses. The 1.30% incentive fee equals 10% multiplied by the 13.00% net return excluding the incentive fee. The example includes a 6% preferred return, but it does not affect the outcome since it is well below the 13.00% net return before application of the incentive fee. The net, after-fee return for the direct lending portfolio with average performance (CDLI) and 1.06 leverage ratio equals 11.70%. In this example, total management fees paid equal 3.36% of net assets and represent 22% of the direct lending portfolio's 15.47% gross return.

SIMULATED DIRECT LOAN PORTFOLIOS WITH LEVERAGE

The calculations for leverage and fees in Exhibit 13.2 are repeated, but instead of the 9.50% cumulative annualized CDLI return as a starting point, quarterly CDLI returns are used to create a simulated quarterly return series with leverage and after fees. Additionally, a quarterly return series is created for leverage levels 0.5×, 1.0×, 1.5×, and 2.0×. Exhibit 13.3 plots cumulative returns for the unlevered CDLI, which is gross of fees, the unlevered CDLI

---

[1] Average BDC leverage over the last year is used instead of the 0.66 (66%) 17.5-year historical average because BDC leverage was more restricted prior to 2019 and current leverage values are more representative of unconstrained financing support that is available to most institutional direct lending managed accounts.

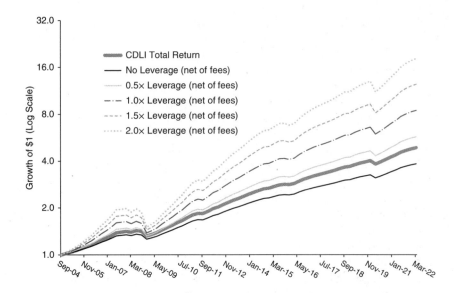

EXHIBIT 13.3   Performance simulation for direct lending portfolios with leverage, September 2004 to March 2022.

net of fees, and four levered CDLI return series, also net of fees. Annualized return and risk statistics are shown for the six simulated portfolio series in Exhibit 13.4.

As expected, return increases with leverage because direct lending returns, as measured by the CDLI, exceed the combined costs of financing, administrative fees, management fees, and incentive fees. Annualized returns range from 7.98% for an unlevered direct lending portfolio to 18.01% for a portfolio levered 2.0×. Very rarely are portfolios of direct loans leveraged more than 2.0× unless they are within a structured vehicle like a collateralized loan obligation, also known as a *CLO*. When leverage is used, the most common level is 1.0×.

Noteworthy is the reduction in return-to-risk ratio in Exhibit 13.4 as more leverage is used. Leverage increases risk as it increases return but return increases at a lower marginal rate compared to risk. For example, risk roughly doubles from the 3.25% unlevered portfolio to 6.50% for the 1.0× levered portfolio. Return does not double, but increases only by one-half, from 7.98% to 12.98%. Leverage does not bring double the pleasure because leveraged assets have lower returns due to the cost of financing, and administrative and management fees are typically charged at the same

	Return	Risk (Std. Dev)	Return /Risk	2008 Max Drawdown*	2020 Max Drawdown**
Cliffwater Direct Lending Index	9.50%	3.61%	2.62	–8%	–5%
CDLI, no leverage, after fees	7.98%	3.25%	2.46	–7%	–4%
0.5× Leverage, after fees	10.47%	4.87%	2.15	–13%	–7%
1.0× Leverage, after fees	12.98%	6.50%	2.00	–16%	–10%
1.5× Leverage, after fees	15.49%	8.12%	1.91	–21%	–12%
2.0× Leverage, after fees	18.01%	9.75%	1.85	–25%	–15%

*Max drawdown from June 30, 2008 to December 31, 2008.
**December 31, 2019 to March 31, 2020.

EXHIBIT 13.4 Simulated return and risk for levered direct lending portfolios, September 2004 to March 2022.

rate on levered assets as unlevered assets. Unlevered assets have a return-to-risk ratio equal to 2.46 but as leverage is applied the return-to-risk ratio declines to 1.85 for a 2.0× leveraged direct lending portfolio.

Investors might think about the optimal amount of leverage by comparing the 2008 and 2020 drawdown columns in Exhibit 13.4 with comparable data for private equity and real estate presented in Exhibit 3.1 in Chapter 3. Comparisons with publicly traded high-yield bonds and leveraged loans are interesting as well but risk statistics for those asset classes are based on market price and not determinations of SFAS 157 fair value.

Selection of leverage level likely depends on investor risk preference. Investors that are looking for a direct lending portfolio to have low risk and perhaps be a substitute for their traditional liquid fixed income portfolio are likely to select an unlevered or 0.5× levered direct lending portfolio. This might also be the choice of an investor that is new to direct lending and wants to build up some experience before adding the complexities of borrowing to the portfolio. For this investor, the 3.18% risk level for the unlevered, after-fee portfolio or the 4.87% risk level for the 0.5× levered portfolio is comparable to the 3.31% risk level for traditional fixed income risk as measured by the Bloomberg US Aggregate Bond Index.

Investors looking for a direct lending portfolio to be a component of a higher-returning portfolio, perhaps including private equity, are more likely to apply leverage to direct loans to get expected returns at a level comparable to private equity. To achieve the 12–15% level of return often targeted for private equity would require a leverage level between 1.0x and 2.0x. A 2.0x direct lending portfolio is perhaps optimal for a direct lending portfolio seeking private equity returns. Its 9.75% risk level shown in Exhibit 13.4 is roughly equal to the 10.05% private equity risk reported in Exhibit 3.1.

Investors looking to direct lending as an asset class that sits between stocks and bonds might find a leverage level equal to 1.0x the most attractive. The 6.50% risk level in Exhibit 13.4 is similar to the 5.09% risk level for equity real estate reported in Exhibit 3.1. Real estate is often viewed as an asset that offers cash flow, moderate risk, and good returns over time. A 1.0x levered direct lending portfolio might serve a similar and complementary role.

The analysis of leverage and risk is extended to drawdown in the last two columns of Exhibit 13.4. Both the GFC and COVID periods are included. Data analysts would generally consider the GFC as a 3-sigma economic and market event and COVID as a 1.5-sigma event. Drawdown has been a very useful alternative measure of risk since the GFC due to serial correlation of returns discussed in Chapter 3. Drawdown sharply magnifies the risk in leverage and is likely better understood by investors. By the drawdown measure, the unlevered direct lending portfolio looks clearly like a low-risk portfolio with a maximum drawdown equal to 7%, after fees, during a 3-sigma event. Most institutional portfolios fell 20% during the GFC and a 7% drawdown would likely be viewed as an attractive risk mitigator by most asset allocators. In the more recent COVID drawdown, the unlevered direct lending portfolio fell just 4%, again a good risk-off outcome from an absolute perspective and relative to other asset classes.

Even with one-half turn of leverage (0.5x) the 13% and 7% simulated drawdowns during the GFC and COVID, respectively, would look acceptable to most risk-averse investors, and both would have performed well above all asset classes except traditional fixed income.

A leverage level between 0.5x and 1.5x is what most institutional investors are engineering for their direct lending portfolios. This suggests direct lending is being viewed more as an asset class investors want to sit between stocks and bonds, providing high levels of cash flow (yield) at moderate risk.

PORTFOLIO CHARACTERISTICS, LEVERAGE, AND THE COST OF FINANCING

Chapters 11 and 13 together show there are two methods for increasing return (and risk) in direct lending. Chapter 11 showed return could be increased by lending to nonsponsored borrowers, smaller borrowers, and in a subordinated creditor position. This chapter showed that return could be increased by leveraging the direct lending portfolio through outside financing.

The leverage analysis presented in Exhibits 13.3 and 13.4 is based on a direct lending portfolio whose composition reflects the average characteristics of the direct lending market, captured by the CDLI, and a constant average cost of financing equal to 3.87% reflecting the historical average cost. A more refined analysis would tailor both the direct lending portfolio and the financing to specific circumstances. For example, Chapter 11 identified direct loan premiums that might influence portfolio yield and return. It would also seem reasonable to assume that the same or other risk factors might affect the cost of financing levered direct lending portfolios.

Exhibit 13.5 presents results from an analysis to identify which factors might explain differences in portfolio financing costs in the presence of leverage. A cross-sectional multiple regression was performed on 47 separate BDCs with data from the first quarter of 2022. The dependent variable was the cost of debt (Y) for the first quarter. Three independent variables were identified as potentially affecting financing costs: the amount of loan assets that are senior secured (X_1), the size of the direct loan portfolio (X_2), and the amount of leverage (X_3). Financing costs would be expected to be lower for senior debt and higher for subordinated debt. The size of the portfolio might

Regression Results		
Dependent Variable		
	Y = Cost of Debt (annualized)	
Independent Variable	**Coefficient**	**t-Stat**
X_0 = Intercept	6.11%	8.56
X_1 = % Senior	−2.63%	−3.42
X_2 = Asset Size ($ b)	−0.07%	−2.66
X_3 = % Levered	−0.16%	−0.52

EXHIBIT 13.5 Factors explaining the cost of financing leverage.

lower financing costs if scale could extract better financing terms. And, finally, financing costs would be expected to rise as more overall leverage is used.

The regression results in Exhibit 13.5 show that both loan seniority (X_1) and asset size (X_2) are statistically significant with t-statistics equal to -3.42 and -2.66, respectively. The -2.63% coefficient for loan seniority means that senior secured loans can be financed at a 2.63% lower rate when compared to subordinated loans. It is interesting that the incremental yield on second lien loans when compared to senior loans in Chapter 11 is not significantly greater than the incremental financing cost, likely explaining why subordinated loans are rarely financed. Asset size (X_2) also had a statistically negative impact on financing cost, reducing it by 7 basis points (-0.07%) for every additional $1 billion in loan assets. It is not surprising that very large lenders are able to secure cheaper financing from their bank and insurance company leverage providers.

Surprising is that leverage levels do not explain financing cost, with a statistically inconclusive t-statistic equal to -0.52 and directionally opposite of what would be expected. Deviations of actual financing costs from predicted costs suggests that, either other systemic factors are involved that were not captured or, more likely, the discrepancies are attributable to negotiating and structuring skills of CFOs at direct lending firms that put the financing in place. Traditional investor due diligence focuses mostly on the operational and risk management capabilities of the CFO, but with direct lending the position can also meaningfully enhance value (alpha) through negotiating lower financing costs with asset flexibility.

Fiduciaries approach leverage very cautiously, particularly when they have discretion over its use. This chapter showed that the low volatility found in direct loans makes leverage a likely acceptable addition to a portfolio. However, understanding the complexities of financing and its costs becomes ever more important as more leverage is used and should become an integral part of investor due diligence.

CHAPTER 14

The Democratization of Alternatives

Private assets have been represented in institutional portfolios for over three decades. Until recently these private assets have been focused almost exclusively on private equity and commercial real estate. But private debt has been slowly joining the other two, quietly forming a private assets trilogy. Currently, institutional investors maintain average private asset allocations equal to 23% of total assets, divided 13% to private equity, 7% to private commercial real estate, and 3% to private debt.[1] The 3% allocation to private debt is low, reflecting its recent creation as an asset class, but is now the most rapidly growing of the three within institutional portfolios.

The *democratization of alternatives* is a popular phrase used among asset management professionals and wealth managers to capture efforts to bring institutional-quality alternative offerings to high-net-worth and retail investors. Unlike institutional investors, individual investors have relied upon the 60–40 mix. In an effort to diversify investor portfolios further, asset managers have tried to introduce alternative investments into portfolio allocations. To date, these efforts have largely come in two waves.

The first began ten years ago, in the aftermath of the GFC, when asset managers launched many varieties of liquid alternatives in US-registered vehicles with a focus on safety and low correlation to stocks, which had just seen a 50% drawdown in 2008–2009. Much of this centered on alternative investment strategies that could be adapted to open-end mutual funds. Retail investors liked the liquidity and convenience associated with mutual funds, and SEC requirements limited fees, required liquidity, and restricted leverage levels. Popular at the time were hedge fund strategies (equity long/ short, macro, credit), real asset strategies (commodities, listed infrastructure, MLPs), liquid private equity, smart beta, and multi-asset strategies, including tactical asset allocation and risk parity.

---

[1]Cliffwater LLC, "Long-Term State Pension Performance Study, 2000 to 2021" (September 2022).

Much of this early democratization effort failed, at least commercially. This was due partly to an impressive rebound in publicly traded stocks that produced ten-year annualized return ending December 31, 2021, equal to 16.48% as measured by the S&P 500 Index. For the same ten-year period liquid hedge fund strategies struggled, producing a mediocre 2.57% annualized return.[2] Commodities, the liquid alternative for real assets, lost –5.41% per year.[3] By the end of the decade, no one wanted to talk about liquid alternatives.

The failure of liquid alternative funds could have been foreseen because they mostly relied upon the fragile success of manager skill (alpha) through hedge fund strategies. Instead, managers that experienced success through private hedge funds ended up being severely compromised by mutual fund requirements and diminished returns within the hedge fund industry generally, brought about by asset growth and market efficiency. Other liquid alternative strategies that relied upon asset class return (beta), such as commodities, produced lots of volatility but little return.[4]

The new second wave of alternatives democratization is now in full swing, having begun in earnest just a few years ago. This second wave has a much better chance of success because, from an investment perspective, it relies on the long-standing return liquidity premium from the private markets rather than trading securities in the public markets.

The key to the success of this second wave will be combining three important features: (1) earning an attractive return (7–15% net of fees at moderate risk), (2) finding the right investment vehicle that balances the underlying liquidity of private assets with investors' desire for liquidity, and (3) minimizing or eliminating investor inconveniences such as commitment paperwork, unexpected capital calls, late K-1s, and the layering of investment funds from recycling distributions. First wave funds solved (2) and (3) through open-end mutual fund structures but did not produce attractive returns. Early signs show that second-wave funds are having success producing desired investor returns using private assets and meeting investor demands for liquidity and convenience by deploying private assets into lesser known SEC registered vehicles meant to bridge the liquidity gap between daily open-end mutual funds and locked-up closed-end funds.

---

[2]HFRX Global Hedge Fund Index. One of the largest hedge fund of funds, the $4 billion Ironwood Institutional Multi-Strategy Fund LLC, a tender fund, produced a fairly unimpressive 5.86% ten-year return ending April 2022.

[3]Bloomberg Commodity Index.

[4]Remnants of commodity investing remain, but they have shifted back to the very old (gold) or the very new (bitcoin).

Chapters 15 and 16 cover the lesser-known investment vehicles that are leading the democratization of alternatives, particularly when it comes to investor access to private debt. These are BDCs, interval funds, and tender funds. But first the partnership model through which virtually all institutional investors allocate to private debt and other private assets is covered, a model that quickly challenges the patience of smaller investors.

THE PRIVATE PARTNERSHIP MODEL FOR INVESTING IN PRIVATE ASSETS

There are several ways investors can invest in middle market loans. The most common method, particularly among large institutional investors but also some ultra-high-net-worth investors, is private partnerships offered by direct lending asset managers. These private partnerships have a finite term, averaging seven years, as opposed to perpetual or evergreen investment vehicles with indefinite life. With the finite private partnership, the direct lending asset manager will take six months to a year to fundraise assets for the direct lending partnership. At the end of a successful fundraising effort the asset manager will have attained, say, $1 billion in binding investor commitments to the direct lending partnership. The $1 billion in commitments are not invested all at once but generally over a two- to three-year period as the asset manager originates loans to be placed in the partnership. Investor committed capital is called by the partnership intermittently as the asset manager needs cash to fund the loans that go into the partnership. Investors are generally given one to two weeks to wire cash to the partnership after it receives notice from the partnership that the funds are needed. New lending stops after the capital commitments have been invested in loans unless there is an additional reinvestment period that allows the asset manager to recycle cash from loan maturities or principal prepayments back into new loans. Reinvestment periods, if present, might extend another year or two. After the investment and reinvestment periods no additional loans are made and the completed partnership portfolio, consisting of 30 to 50 individual loans, moves into runoff with investors receiving cash proceeds from loan maturities and principal prepayments as they occur. In seven to ten years from when the commitment to the partnership is made, the investor can expect full recapture of committed capital and profits.

Investing in middle market direct loans through private partnerships is a cumbersome process, requiring a great deal of administrative and portfolio management attention. It also requires constantly committing to new direct lending partnerships every two to three years to maintain a consistent loan allocation because a single partnership alone offers loan exposure that ascends quickly over a couple years and then almost immediately descends over the next couple years. This pattern of cash flow requires the investor to commit to additional direct lending partnerships to fill the time gaps when legacy partnerships are unwinding.

All this detail can be a headache for investors who do not have the administrative and legal support, or investment expertise, to assemble and maintain a portfolio of private partnerships that will deliver the consistent outcomes reflected in the CDLI. Most large pension funds have those resources and prefer to invest in private partnerships, a legal format they know well from private equity investing. Others, including high net worth, family office, and smaller institutional investors, often do not have the required resources and have turned to other, more permanent vehicles to gain access to direct middle market loans.

CHAPTER 15

Business Development Companies (BDCs)

Business development companies have been the primary alternative to private partnerships for investors who seek a more simplified access to direct loans. Two other alternatives, known as interval funds and tender funds, are covered in Chapter 16. All three vehicles—BDCs, interval funds, and tender funds—are SEC registered, like mutual funds, which enable them to raise assets from a broad range of investors but also require them to adhere to certain investor type, investment, and transparency requirements. These SEC features give investors protections they may not find with private partnerships.

WHAT IS A BDC?

While differences exist, BDCs are in many ways like REITs (for real estate) and MLPs (for energy assets) in their cash-generating, tax-preference investment characteristics that appeal to investors. BDCs were created by Congress in 1980, under Section 54 of the Investment Company Act of 1940, to stimulate private investment in middle market US companies, which had suffered during the stagflation period following the steep 1973–1974 recession. Congress gave the BDC the advantage of electing to be private or exchange traded with a tax-free pass-through of investment income, but with some restrictions:

- SEC registration and oversight
- At least 70% of assets invested in nonpublic debt and equity in US corporations
- Maximum leverage equal to 2.0× net asset value (NAV)
- Annual distribution of at least 90% of income to shareholders
- Certain portfolio diversification constraints

Noteworthy is that the BDC is an SEC-registered investment company, subject to most of the same requirements as US mutual funds. These requirements include direct SEC oversight that should give BDC investors greater comfort when compared to private funds. At the same time SEC oversight can potentially bring higher costs, less investment flexibility, and unwanted transparency.

It is the requirement that 70% of assets be invested in nonpublic (private) debt and equity of US corporations that define the business of a BDC as making direct loans and providing equity financing. While equity is a permissible investment within the 70% requirement, virtually all BDCs concentrate their corporate financing activity on direct middle market corporate loans.

Prior to 2018, BDCs had been limited in their use of leverage to 1.0× their NAV. Expressed another way, BDCs had to maintain assets equal to at least 200% of their borrowings. In 2018, the passage of the Small Business Credit Availability Act allowed BDCs to increase leverage from 1.0× to 2.0× debt-to-equity, for example, maintain assets equal to at least 150% of their borrowings. Noteworthy is that BDC leverage levels increased from an average level of 0.71× net assets in 2017, before the increase in leverage allowance to 1.06× net assets for the four quarters ending March 2022. Leverage levels continue to increase slowly with most BDC managers targeting a 1.20× level. These arguably unconstrained leverage levels are slightly above the 1.00× leverage level suggested in Chapter 14.

Many BDCs can apply for, create, and invest in small business investment companies (SBICs) where loans are made to smaller companies. BDCs find the SBIC desirable because the SBIC provides low-cost, long-term financing at attractive leverage levels with subordination. Further, SBIC financing does not count against BDC debt limitations. However, SBIC financing is limited to $150 million for one fund and $225 million for more than one fund, which ultimately makes this type of financing a small part of the BDCs overall capital structure.

Many BDCs also invest in special purpose vehicles (SPVs). These take the form of joint ventures between the BDC and an outside institutional investor such as an insurance company or pension plan. Loans made by the SPV must be approved by both JV partners. The attractiveness of SPVs is that they can use financing that, like the SBIC, does not count against the borrowing limitations of the BDC. The limitation of SPVs is that they do not qualify for the 70% investment requirement in US corporations.

There are several operational requirements for running a BDC as an SEC-registered investment company:

- An independent board of directors
- A CEO, CFO, and chief compliance officer

- Independent legal counsel, administration, audit, and Sarbanes Oxley compliance
- Quarterly 10-K/Qs, board meetings, annual investment management agreement approvals, 8-Ks, and proxy statements
- Quarterly fair-value loan and portfolio marks determined by independent valuation firms and asset management and overseen by the BDC board.

BDCs elect to be treated as a regulated investment company (RIC) under Subchapter M of the 1986 Internal Revenue Code so that investment earnings pass through to investors without tax. However, to qualify as a RIC the BDC must also do the following:

- At least 90% of gross income must be from interest, dividends, and realized gains of securities.
- Pass a quarterly asset diversification test.
- Distribute greater than 90% of taxable income, equal to ordinary income plus short-term capital gains

The 90% requirement that BDC income come from interest, dividends, and realized gains of securities means BDCs do not generate unrelated business taxable income (UBTI). The absence of UBTI in BDCs is important and desirable to private institutional investors like endowments, foundations, and private pension plans that do not want to pay taxes on private investments and instead go to offshore vehicles that may limit the types of investments that can be held. The BDC cleanses UBTI for these investors.

BDCs also present tax advantages for non-US investors because they do not generate effectively connected income (ECI), which represents income generated in the US. The presence of ECI potentially creates a tax liability or tax withholding for the non-US investor operating in the United States. Nor is the non-US investor required to file a US tax return from a BDC investment. Consequently, an increased number of foreign institutional investors are looking at or have invested already in BDCs as a preferred structure to invest in direct lending.

The diversification test requires that at least 50% of the value of their assets consists of cash, cash items, US government securities, securities of other regulated investment companies, and other securities if such other securities of any one issuer do not represent more than 5% of their assets or more than 10% of the outstanding voting securities of the issuer. Also required is that no more than 25% of the value of their assets is invested in the securities (other than US government securities or securities of other regulated investment companies) of any one issuer or of two or more issuers that are controlled (as determined under applicable Internal Revenue

Code rules) by the BDC and are engaged in the same or similar or related trades or businesses (the diversification tests). These diversification tests are important, but generally BDC portfolios are well within the requirements.

BDCs can be internally or externally managed, though all but a few are externally managed by independent asset management firms. When externally managed, there is an investment management agreement between the BDC and the external asset manager that is approved by the BDC board annually. Annual contract approval is an SEC regulatory requirement that also applies to all registered mutual funds.

Most asset managers operating BDCs also offer private direct lending funds, in the form of private partnerships, to institutional investors. The SEC prohibits registered vehicles (like BDCs) and private funds from co-investing in the same securities, under Rule 17d. This means a loan originated by the asset manager cannot be divided into participations across the manager's client accounts, including the registered vehicle (BDC), without SEC permission. Consequently, almost all managers who operate BDCs request and are granted 17d exemptive relief from the SEC. The purpose of 17d is to prevent managers from cherry-picking securities, good or bad, to put in a registered vehicle.

The 17d exemptive relief also means BDC loan assets will look very much like the assets found in BDC managers' private fund offerings. Additionally, this means investors can look to the performance of the BDC as indicative of private fund performance. This is important because it suggests the CDLI, which is based on the performance of BDC direct loans, is also representative of the broader US direct lending marketplace represented by private partnerships.

Unlike REITs, registered vehicles such as mutual funds that invest in BDCs must disclose the fees and expenses of a BDC holding in their own disclosures. This flow-through is called acquired fund fees and expenses, or AFFE, and can materially affect the mutual fund's reported expense ratio. The sensitivity of mutual fund and ETF investors to expense ratios caused index providers to expunge BDCs from their indexes in 2014 not for investment purposes, but for the sole reason to reduce their reported expense ratios. Currently, the BDC industry is urging the SEC to reverse or modify its position on AFFE, arguing that BDCs are being unfairly singled out for AFFE disclosure when other asset classes like REITs and MLPs, which have management fees and expenses within their structures, are not disclosed. Unfortunately, AFFE disclosure limits institutional participation, though there are serious efforts to get this SEC administrative rule changed.

Another SEC mutual fund and ETF rule that also applies to BDCs is the 3% limit. Regulated investment companies cannot own more than 3% of the outstanding shares of a BDC without SEC permission (exemptive relief) or relinquishing voting rights. Unfortunately, the 3% limit, which is intended to limit fee pyramiding, also severely curtails corporate governance within the BDC industry. As discussed later, there are many poorly managed BDCs that might otherwise be corrected except that activist shareholders are limited from building a stock position in the target BDC beyond 3%. The limit severely curtails the influence an outside shareholder can exert on a poorly managed BDC and allows entrenched asset managers and directors to continue to disadvantage their shareholders. SEC changes to AFFE disclosures and the 3% limit would likely greatly expand and improve the BDC industry through parity in disclosure and a corporate governance solution to poor management. Beginning with the Ares Capital Corporation purchase of American Capital in 2017, many of the poorly managed BDCs have been acquired or replaced by better asset management teams, improving the overall quality of the BDC market.[1]

One positive note on corporate governance is that BDCs are not permitted to issue new stock if the price is trading below NAV without shareholder approval. Poor performing BDCs almost always trade below NAV, so they are at least restrained from diluting shareholder value by new share issuances. Unfortunately, this is small consolation to investors who have endured weak returns.

A couple of final BDC characteristics are worth noting. First, BDCs must also offer their corporate borrowers significant managerial assistance. Though potentially burdensome, borrowers seldom request such assistance from their direct lenders. Second, BDCs are permitted to charge management fees on gross assets, as opposed to net assets that deduct financed assets, and can charge incentive fees separately on (1) income and (2) net realized capital gains plus unrealized losses. These fee permissions are particularly generous to the BDC asset manager and not something generally found in institutional offerings of private funds. The separation of incentive fees for income and realized gains, net unrealized losses, does not meet institutional standards. Managers could stretch for yield in their loan originations to maximize the income incentive fee while recognizing this may increase realized losses over time. Best practice is to combine, not separate, the two incentive fees so the asset manager is incentivized to optimize total return rather than one component. A more complete discussion of fees is found in a later chapter.

Finally, BDCs offer investors greater convenience when compared to private partnerships. First, tax reporting is done through Form 1099 instead of K-1, which investors complain are often late and delay tax filing. Second, BDCs can offer shareholders immediate access and liquidity. Shareholders

---

[1]Large, well-managed asset managers, such as Crescent Capital, KKR, Oaktree, Blackstone, Barings, Carlyle, and Owl Rock, have replaced weaker BDC managers.

can buy or sell exchange traded BDCs daily and private BDCs are set up to be perpetual direct-lending vehicles allowing investors regular windows (generally monthly) to purchase or redeem shares, with some limitations.[2]

BDC INDUSTRY STATISTICS

Exhibit 15.1 provides summary statistics on the BDC market.

85	# of BDCs with assets >$50 million
41	# of BDCs with assets >$1 billion
9	# of BDCs with assets >$5 billion
$223 billion	assets held by all BDCs >$50 million
37	# of publicly traded BDCs
48	# of private BDCs
$52 billion	market capitalization of publicly traded BDCs
$121 billion	assets held by publicly traded BDCs
$102 billion	assets held by private BDCs
93%	% of gross BDC investments that are debt related
76%	% of gross BDC investments that are senior secured
9.77%	current gross yield on gross BDC assets
12.98%	current leveraged gross yield on net BDC assets (net of interest costs)
9.27%	dividend yield on Cliffwater BDC Index
1.21%	average management fee on gross BDC assets
0.82%	average incentive fee on gross BDC assets
0.38%	average expenses on gross BDC assets
4.97%	average fees and expenses on *net* BDC assets (NAV)

EXHIBIT 15.1 BDC industry statistics, March 31, 2022.

---

[2]Most private BDCs have monthly or quarterly shareholder redemption windows, but are limited to a 5% quarterly maximum, imposed at the fund level. This means redeeming shareholders can get all their money out as long as the total of all redeeming shares does not exceed 5% of shares outstanding. If total redemptions exceed 5%, each redeeming shareholder receives their pro rate share. For example, if requested redemptions total 10% of shares outstanding, each redeeming shareholder would be allowed to sell one-half of their requested amount. Investors would then have to wait until the next redemption window to sell remaining shares.

PRIVATE BDCs

BDCs can remain private or choose to be publicly traded on one of the major exchanges. Of the 85 BDCs with assets above $50 million, 37 are publicly traded and 48 are private BDCs. While there are more private than public BDCs, public BDCs represent the majority (54%) of assets managed within BDCs.

Private BDCs can be divided into two categories according to their long-term liquidity strategy for investors: (1) private-to-public BDCs and (2) stay-private or perpetual BDCs.

Until recently, asset managers preferred to raise assets as a private BDC and then become exchange traded through a public offering. Asset managers might prefer to sponsor a public BDC because it helps them build brand awareness, provides a source of permanent capital, and facilitates growth opportunity through new share offerings if the BDC stock trades above NAV. Investors also seem to prefer public BDCs because they provide ongoing liquidity and are generally larger, providing better direct loan diversification.

A popular strategy after the 2008 GFC has been for an asset manager to launch a private BDC, sell shares in a private offering, and then go public later. Sometimes the asset manager will offer lower fees to investors in the private BDC to encourage commitments by larger institutional investors. At IPO, those fees asset management charges increase but the institutional investor has the opportunity then to sell its shares, generally after some lock-up period. A private BDC would be necessary as a predecessor to the public BDC to acquire loans, funded by investor capital calls, so when the BDC goes public the funds raised in the public market would be immediately deployed into middle market loans rather than cash.

These institutional investors also have a reasonable expectation that they can sell their shares at a premium to NAV when the BDC goes public. For example, since the GFC, BDCs with strong asset management backing have had their shares trade at a 10–20% premium to NAV. Investors can potentially earn an 8–10% dividend through interest income while the BDC is in the private phase and earn an additional premium of 10–20% at IPO. It generally takes the private BDC about three to four years to be fully ramped to scale before being ready to IPO. Current yield plus the IPO premium together might provide a total return expectation between 10% and 15%.

Five examples of public BDCs that followed the path from private BDC to public BDC with a significant premium at IPO were Sixth Street (ticker: TSLX) in 2014, Goldman Sachs (ticker: GSBD) in 2015, Bain (ticker: BCSF) in 2018, Owl Rock (ticker: ORCC) in 2019, and Blackstone (ticker: BXSL) in 2021. Sixth Street Specialty Lending, Inc. was organized as a private BDC in December 2010. It concurrently raised capital through a private offering of its shares to institutional investors and called committed capital as it made direct loans. Large institutional backing came from pension funds of the States of New Jersey, Oregon, Ohio, and Arizona, as well as the high-net-worth arm of Morgan Stanley. Private BDCs that intend to go public generally want to build a retail investor base, like that brought by Morgan Stanley, that will provide greater liquidity on IPO and will be a more representative shareholder base post-IPO.

In its private offering, Sixth Street Specialty Lending agreed to go public within four years or gradually liquidate the BDC loan holdings as they matured. The BDC went public in an IPO after four years in March 2014, traded at an early 20–30% premium to NAV, and has since averaged an approximate 20% premium. During its private phase the BDC earned an 11.66% net annualized return for its shareholders. The IPO would have increased the annualized return to private shareholders from 11.66% to a range of 16–19% depending on when the shareholder sold shares in 2014.

Goldman Sachs BDC, Inc. followed a similar path as Sixth Street Specialty Lending but two years later. Their private BDC was launched in 2013 and the BDC conducted an IPO in May 2015. It initially traded at a 10–20% premium to NAV and has since averaged an approximate 15% premium. Except for Bain Capital, whose IPO timing may have been unfortunate, the other private-to-public BDCs have had successful IPOs.

Another related private-to-public route, which will likely gain popularity, is a private BDC being acquired at a premium by its sister public BDC. Golub Capital uses this technique to grow its public BDC (ticker: GBDC). In 2015, Golub launched a private BDC (GCIC), offering advantageous terms to institutional investors. That private BDC grew to over $1 billion in net assets before it was acquired by GBDC in 2019 at a 7% premium to net assets.

The most popular type of BDC today is the stay-private, perpetual BDC. Perpetual BDCs allow investors to purchase shares, generally monthly, not on an exchange at market prices, but in a private transaction at NAV. The BDC repurchases shares at NAV but limited to monthly or quarterly with a limit, generally 5% of outstanding shares per quarter. These perpetual BDCs enjoy current favor because their share volatility is much less than publicly traded BDCs and it is easier to raise capital by selling shares without restriction. Most notably, Blackstone broke all records recently, raising $18 billion in investor capital for a private perpetual BDC known as BCRED. Success brings imitators and several other perpetual BDCs have been formed to access this market.

Exhibit 15.2 provides a listing of all private BDCs.

It is not uncommon for asset managers to have multiple private BDCs. Owl Rock, Goldman Sachs, Golub, and Barings are examples. These multiple offerings generally have different investment objectives or different

Name	SEC Code	Net Assets in $ Thousands
Blackstone Private Credit Fund	1803498	$17,902,407
Owl Rock Technology Finance Corp	1747777	$3,457,234
Owl Rock Core Income Corp.	1812554	$2,763,379
Franklin Square Energy	1501729	$1,783,915
Owl Rock Capital Corp III	1807427	$1,663,566
Franklin BSP Lending Corp	1490927	$1,498,382
Apollo Debt Solutions BDC	1837532	$1,356,706
Owl Rock Capital Corp II	1655887	$1,341,968
Morgan Stanley Direct Lending Fund	1782524	$1,190,918
TCG BDC II	1702510	$1,149,202
New Mountain Guardian III	1781870	$1,142,290
Golub Capital BDC 3	1715268	$1,115,718
Goldman Sachs Private Middle Market Credit II	1772704	$1,007,775
CION (Apollo)	1534254	$922,453
TCW Direct Lending VII	1715933	$918,854
HPS Corporate Lending Fund	1838126	$913,586
Barings Private Credit	1859919	$853,407
NMF SLF I	1766037	$750,228
Stone Point Credit Corp	1825384	$639,292
HMS Income Fund (Main Street Capital)	1535778	$616,627
Barings Capital Investment Corp	1811972	$609,599
Runway Growth Credit Fund	1653384	$597,466
Monroe Capital Income Plus	1742313	$497,611
Goldman Sachs Private Middle Market Credit	1674760	$497,435
SL Investment Corp	1825590	$427,902
Trinity Capital	1786108	$424,041
Audax	1633858	$406,993
Nuveen Churchill BDC	1737924	$402,677
Kayne Anderson BDC	1747172	$387,182
TCW Direct Lending	1603480	$382,568

EXHIBIT 15.2 Private, non-listed business development companies, March 31, 2022.

(continued)

Name	SEC Code	Net Assets in $ Thousands
AB Private Credit Investors Corp	1634452	$373,791
Oaktree Strategic Income II	1744179	$338,163
TriplePoint Global Venture Credit	1792509	$295,094
Venture Lending & Leasing IX	1717310	$240,069
Franklin BSP Capital	1825248	$237,668
AG Twin Brook BDC	1666384	$186,445
SCP Private Credit Income BDC	1743415	$180,928
Commonwealth Credit Partners BDC I	1841514	$142,570
Carey Credit Income Fund (Guggenheim)	1618697	$139,809
NC SLF	1844684	$134,436
BlackRock Direct Lending Corp.	1834543	$87,730
Venture Lending & Leasing 8	1642862	$68,661
WTI Fund X	1850938	$67,364
NexPoint Capital	1588272	$62,947
Golub Capital Direct Lending Corp	1868878	$58,952
BC Partners Lending Corporation	1726548	$46,327
Carlyle Secured Lending III	1851277	<u>$15,422</u>
Total Net Private BDC Assets		$50,279

EXHIBIT 15.2 (*continued*)

shareholder objectives; for example, one may stay private and another private to public.

PUBLICLY TRADED BDCs

There are 39 publicly traded BDCs with a combined market capitalization equal to $52 billion at June 30, 2022. A listing of those public BDCs is shown in Exhibit 15.3.

Some of the largest and highest-quality asset managers operate publicly traded BDCs, including BlackRock, Blackstone, Goldman, Carlyle, KKR

Publicly Traded BDC	Ticker	Percentage of Market Cap
Ares Capital	ARCC	19.49
FS Investment	FSK	12.47
Owl Rock	ORCC	10.30
Blackstone Secured Lending Fund	BXSL	7.90
Prospect Capital	PSEC	6.12
Golub Capital	GBDC	4.86
Hercules Technology	HTGC	4.10
Goldman Sachs BDC	GSBD	3.63
Sixth Street Specialty Lending	TSLX	2.97
New Mountain Finance	NMFC	2.64
Oaktree Specialty Lending Co	OCSL	2.61
Barings BDC	BBDC	2.21
Bain Capital Specialty Finance	BCSF	1.89
SLR Investment	SLRC	1.59
TCP Capital	TCPC	1.51
Apollo Investment	AINV	1.48
Carlyle Secured Lending	CGBD	1.44
Trinity Capital Inc.	TRIN	1.14
Pennant Park Floating Rate	PFLT	1.08
Crescent Capital	CCAP	1.04
Capital Southwest	CSWC	1.04
Fidus Investment	FDUS	0.94
Triplepoint Venture	TPVG	0.88
Pennant Park	PNNT	0.87
Gladstone Capital	GLAD	0.75
Whitehorse Finance	WHF	0.66
Horizon Tech. Finance	HRZN	0.63
Saratoga Capital	SAR	0.57
BlackRock Kelso	BKCC	0.57
Stellus Capital Inv.	SCM	0.53
Portman Ridge Finance Corporation	PTMN	0.47

EXHIBIT 15.3 Publicly traded business development companies, June 30, 2022.

(*continued*)

Publicly Traded BDC	Ticker	Percentage of Market Cap
Monroe Capital	MRCC	0.40
Oxford Square	OXSQ	0.38
OFS Capital	OFS	0.30
First Eagle Alternative Capital	FCRD	0.21
Great Elm Capital	GECC	0.19
Investcorp Credit	ICMB	0.13
		100

EXHIBIT 15.3   *(continued)*

and Oaktree. The largest publicly traded BDC is managed by Ares Capital (ARCC), a firm well known not only for its direct lending but also distressed private funds. It is the largest BDC because (1) it was a very early entrant, starting its BDC in 2004, (2) it has been one of the best performing BDCs since its beginning, and (3) the Ares BDC has made major acquisitions of troubled BDCs in the past and has had success turning them around. For example, Ares acquired American Capital BDC in 2016 and acquired Allied Capital BDC in 2010.

BDC MARKET INDEXES

There are three popular indexes tracking the public BDC market: S&P BDC Index (SPBDCUP), the Cliffwater BDC Index (CWBDC), and the MVIS US Business Development Index (MVBIZD), which is the successor index to the Wells Fargo BDC Index (WFBDCPX). All three indexes are capitalization-weighted, but unlike the Cliffwater BDC Index, the S&P and MVIS indexes are float adjusted and cap any single BDC to no more than 10% and 20%, respectively.

The capped index weightings on any single BDC causes a major reweight-ing from traditional capitalization weighting because ARCC, arguably one of the longest tenured and best-performing BDCs, has a 19.49% weighting by market capitalization but only a 10% weight in the S&P BDC Index.[3] Such a limitation causes extra portfolio turnover and transaction costs as the Ares excess weighting must be rebalanced every quarter to the remaining

---

[3]The MVIS BDC Index appears to have changed its capped weighting to 20% from 10% when it replaced the Wells Fargo BDC Index.

BDCs. The limitation is also contrary to the efficient market hypothesis that market capitalization weighting provides the highest risk-adjusted return for the average investor. While index providers sometimes argue that limiting an outsized market weighting improves diversification, most (95%) of the benefit of diversification occurs with the first 13 BDC positions and the 19% Ares market weighting does not interfere with achieving a very diversified portfolio. For these reasons, the Cliffwater BDC Index is used to provide analysis of the public BDC market. Information on the Cliffwater BDC Index, including a return history back to 2004, can be found at www.BDCs.com.

BDCs: A TALE OF TWO MARKETS

The public BDC market is often described as two-tiered, with a group of strong performing BDCs backed by shareholder friendly management teams with large platforms, and another group of weak performing BDCs backed by smallish boutique firms whose BDCs are poor performing and who take advantage of their captive shareholders through unnecessarily high fees. While the entire BDC market trades near NAV, the first group consistently trades at a premium to NAV while the second group consistently trades at a discount, sometimes a severe one. As pointed out previously, the second group exists only because the 3% limit restricts the corporate governance tools available to shareholders and activists broadly to force changes to management.

BDC DIVIDEND YIELD

Most investors are attracted to public BDCs because of their dividend yields, which represent most of their quarterly earnings from interest income, net of losses and management fees. Exhibit 15.4 provides a history of dividend yield for the Cliffwater BDC Index dating back to its start date in September 2004.

Post-GFC dividend yields on the Cliffwater BDC Index have remained within an 8–11% yield range, with a significant spike occurring during COVID. Most of the fluctuations in dividend yield have not been the result of changing underlying loan yields but, instead, price fluctuations in BDC shares. Unlike the CDLI, which maintains loan values at NAV, the Cliffwater BDC Index is market price based and shares can trade above or below NAV.

Exhibit 15.5 provides the history of price premiums or discounts for the Cliffwater BDC Index price compared to the Cliffwater BDC Index NAV.

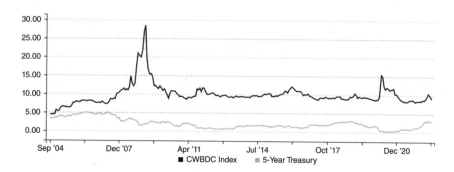

EXHIBIT 15.4 Comparison of Cliffwater BDC Index and five-year Treasury yields.

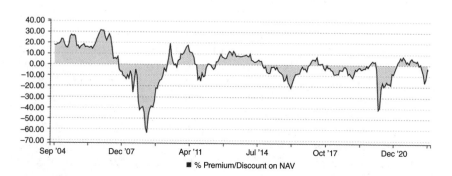

EXHIBIT 15.5 Cliffwater BDC Index price premium or discount to NAV.

Investors often look at BDC premiums and discounts as an indicator of relative value, choosing to buy at discounts and sell at premiums. Sometimes BDCs can sell at significant discounts to NAV as they did most recently during COVID. Some astute investors with knowledge of the BDC market purchased individual BDCs at discounts up 60% of NAV. When the market rebounded, some of these investors doubled their investment in less than one year. The three-year effective maturity of BDC underlying loan portfolios makes buying BDCs at discount a particularly successful trading strategy because, if the loan fundamentals are good, the discount will have to converge to NAV as principal matures or prepays over a three-year window.

BDC TOTAL RETURN

Exhibit 15.6 reports the cumulative return for the public BDC market using the Cliffwater BDC Index from its inception on September 30, 2004. The volatile lighter line shows the growth of $1,000 invested through August 17, 2022. The $1,000 would have grown to $3,726 and an annualized return equal to 7.62%, including dividend income.

The smoother, darker line shows the return on NAV, equivalent to the BDCs' return on equity capital. Over the same time, the net operating return for the Cliffwater BDC Index equaled 7.91%, annualized. The difference in operating and market return is because BDCs were trading at a 15% premium to NAV in 2004 and a 5% discount in 2022. The lesson is that shareholder returns do follow BDC fundamentals over time, but market premiums and discounts can negatively or positively affect performance, particularly over shorter time periods.

Exhibit 15.7 examines just the price component of total return and compares it to NAV. In both cases, interest or dividend income is stripped from the return calculation.

The dividend yield for the CWBDC Index has averaged about 10% over the entire Index history. However, as Exhibit 15.7 depicts, NAV have declined, losing value at an annualized rate equal to –2.19%. This rate of loss, when de-levered by the 0.69× historical average leverage ratio for BDCs, gives an equivalent unlevered realized loss equal to –1.29%, roughly equal to the –1.08% historical realized loss ratio for the CDLI (see Exhibit 2.1).

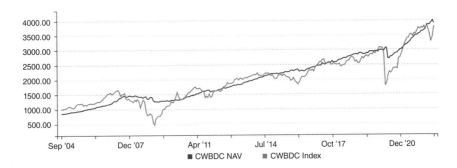

EXHIBIT 15.6 Comparison of market return and net operating return for Cliffwater BDC Index.

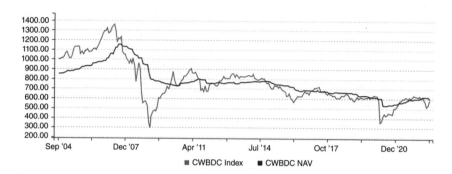

EXHIBIT 15.7   Comparison of price return and NAV return for Cliffwater BDC Index.

Visual inspection of Exhibit 15.7 suggests BDC premiums and discounts do a pretty good job forecasting net realized and unrealized gains and losses, though they tend to overshoot their target. This might be interpreted as efficient market pricing, as future realized or unrealized losses are anticipated by market pricing well before they occur in the financial statements. This also suggests an existing BDC discount may not be a value opportunity but rather an expectation that NAV may decline to meet the discounted price rather than the other way around.

CHAPTER 16

Interval and Tender Funds

Together with BDCs, interval funds and tender funds are pooled investor vehicles intended to give investors access to investments that are not liquid enough to offer in daily open-end mutual funds or exchange traded funds. Interval funds are covered first because, next to BDCs, they have become the preferred vehicle for investors trying to access the benefits of private debt in a semiliquid and convenient way.

INTERVAL FUNDS

Interval funds are SEC-registered pooled investor vehicles operated under the Investment Company Act of 1940. They are intended to have an indefinite life, unlike private partnerships. What is unique to interval funds is their requirement to allow investors/shareholders to redeem their shares for cash at defined periodic time intervals, typically quarterly. On setup, the asset manager sponsoring the interval fund can set redemption frequency and limits. For example, most interval funds set their redemption frequency to be quarterly, though monthly or semiannually is sometimes seen.

Redemption limits are applied at the fund level, not the individual shareholder level and can range between 5% and 25% of net assets at each redemption date. Like the redemption frequency, the redemption limit is set in advance, contained in the fund prospectus, and must be adhered to by the fund. Most interval funds set their quarterly redemption limit at 5% of net assets. This means shareholders who want to get all or some of their money out of the fund can do so quarterly unless the redeeming shareholders in aggregate are requesting to redeem more than the redemption limit, which equals 5% in this example. Should a quarter's total redeeming assets equal 7% of net assets, for example, each redeeming shareholder would receive 5/7ths of their requested redemption amount and 2/7ths would remain in the interval fund. There is no automatic rollover of unfilled redemption requests to the next quarter and no queuing system. Each quarterly redemption cycle is independent of the last. Shareholders are notified in advance of redemption dates, generally 30 days, and shareholders can submit their redemption requests up to the date of redemption. Redemption proceeds are received one or two days after the redemption date.

Investors contribute to an interval fund by being issued new shares valued at NAV at the time of issuance. Most interval funds issue shares either daily, monthly, or quarterly. Shares are typically nontraded; all share transactions are with the fund itself. The ability to invest immediately, without a strung-out series of capital calls, is an important convenience valued by non-institutional investors. This feature also allows investors to skip the cumbersome subscription agreements that private partnerships require.

Virtually all interval funds elect regulated investment company status, which allows them to pass through in dividends substantially all income and net realized gains (minus short-term losses) to investors. This pass-through status avoids any tax levy at the fund level. Instead, investors receive a familiar 1099 at year-end, replacing the often-delayed K-1 sent to limited partners often months after year-end.

Most interval funds pay quarterly dividends equal to their cash income but allow for a dividend reinvestment election for investors that want to grow their fund allocation.

Interval funds and BDCs are both SEC-registered funds with many similarities, but one very important difference is the regulatory limit on the amount of leverage (borrowing) that can be used. Fund borrowing is limited to 2× net asset value for BDCs but a much lower 0.5× NAV for interval funds.[1] The higher permissible leverage granted to BDCs is the result of Congressional legislation that exempts BDCs from SEC mutual fund leverage limits they otherwise would have to adhere to, as interval funds must.

The tighter leverage restrictions have apparently not hampered interval fund growth over the last several years, though they still remain a fraction of the size of the BDC market. On June 30, 2022, publicly traded and private BDCs collectively held $110 billion in investor assets, almost doubling over the previous three years. Interval funds focused on private debt held $27 billion in investor assets, a fivefold increase since 2019.

Exhibit 16.1 provides a listing of credit-oriented interval funds.

---

[1]For every $1 of investor capital, a BDC can borrow an additional maximum of $2, giving the BDC a total of $3 to invest in direct loans. An interval fund can borrow only 50 cents for every $1 of investor capital. Leverage limits for BDCs and interval funds can often be expressed as asset coverage ratios, that is, the minimum dollar amount of assets as a percentage of fund borrowing. The minimum asset coverage ratios for BDCs and interval funds equal 300% ($3.00/$1.00) and 150% ($1.50/$1.00), respectively.

Name	Ticker	Net Assets in $ Millions
Cliffwater Corporate Lending Fund	CCLFX	$8,200
PIMCO Flexible Credit Income Fund	PFLEX	$3,024
Stone Ridge Alternative Lending Risk Premium Fund	LENDX	$2,372
CION Ares Diversified Credit Fund	CADUX	$2,342
Variant Alternative Income Fund	NICHX	$1,935
Carlyle Tactical Private Credit Fund	TAKNX	$1,303
PIMCO Flexible Municipal Income Fund	PMFLX	$1,189
Lord Abbett Credit Opportunities Fund	LCRDX	$945
Cliffwater Enhanced Lending Fund	CELFX	$686
Apollo Diversified Credit Fund	CRDIX	$537
KKR Credit Opportunities Portfolio	KCOUX	$515
BlackRock Credit Strategies Fund	CREDX	$435
First Eagle Credit Opportunities Fund	FECRX	$405
FS Credit Income Fund	FCRIX	$290
Blackstone Floating Rate Enhanced Income Fund	BGFLX	$297
Alternative Credit Income Fund	RCIIX	$260
Flat Rock Opportunity Fund	FROPX	$177
Oaktree Diversified Income Fund Inc	ODIDX	$147
Bluerock High Income Institutional Credit Fund	IIMFX	$82
AFA Multi-Manager Credit Fund	AMCLX	$40

EXHIBIT 16.1 Private, non-listed credit interval funds, June 30, 2022.

Interval funds are also a popular vehicle for equity real estate, holding $20 billion in investor capital.

TENDER FUNDS

Tender funds are very similar to interval funds. The major difference is that share repurchases are not fixed by timing, size, or price. Basically, tender funds can repurchase shares when they want, in any amount they want, and at a price that may differ from NAV. This flexibility is very unlike interval funds whose share repurchases come at fixed intervals, up to fixed amounts, and at NAV. Tender funds have gained traction among asset managers who provide investors access to private equity where the liquidity of underlying investments is long term and uncertain, which practically makes any promise of short-term liquidity a serious challenge. In the second wave of democratization of alternatives, private equity managers are choosing tender funds. These managers are few but include firms such as Partners Group, Stepstone, and Hamilton Lane.

CHAPTER 17

Selecting Direct Lending Managers

There is no passive option in direct lending; it is only accessible through active management. It is a dynamic market as lenders continuously originate and refinance middle market corporate loans every three to five years, mirroring the private equity market but with greater velocity. The CDLI captures the collective (asset-weighted) work product of the direct loan managers represented in the Index, but it is not investable. Manager/lender selection, therefore, is part of investing in direct loans.

Not surprisingly, some managers have produced better outcomes than others, and by wide margins. The purpose of this chapter is to explore the factors that differentiate direct loan managers and offer suggestions on what characteristics best typify managers who will be successful. But before proceeding, a brief case study is presented to illustrate the importance over time in selecting the right manager.

SELECTION MATTERS

Exhibits 17.1a and 17.1b provide actual direct loan performance from two of the earliest and largest direct lending managers for the September 31, 2004, to March 31, 2022, time period. Both manager track records are audited and included in the CDLI. A comparison of the exhibits shows clearly that not all managers are alike when executing a direct lending investment program.

A dollar invested with Manager A at September 30, 2004, would have grown to $8.66 as shown in the top, heavy line in Exhibit 17.1a, representing a 13.13% annualized return, gross of fees, and unlevered. Manager A's 13.13% asset performance is also 3.67% above the 9.46% return for the CDLI (see Exhibit 2.1), indicative of significant skill at direct lending. Also impressive is that the 3.67% excess return above the CDLI did not all come from yield. Manager A's income return grew to $7.19, a 11.93% annualized income return compared to 10.79% for the CDLI, a yield difference of 1.14%.

EXHIBIT 17.1a   Performance of successful Manager A.

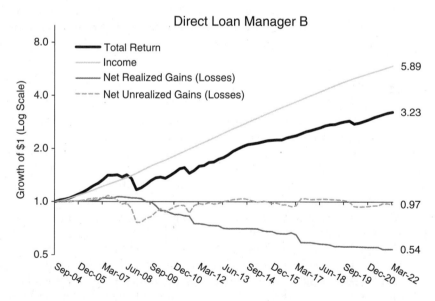

EXHIBIT 17.1b   Performance of unsuccessful Manager B.

Manager A is unusual in their ability to generate realized gains over this period when direct loans almost always incur realized losses from defaults. Manager A produced these realized gains primarily through acquisition of secondary pools of direct loans at discount during periods of distress, like the 2008 GFC, and a strong record of low credit losses on directly originated loans. While the CDLI incurred realized losses equal to –1.08% over this period, Manager A produced realized gains equal to 1.33%, or an excess return from realized gains equal to 2.41% (1.33% + 1.08%). The 2.41% is the realized gross-of-fee alpha produced by Manager A.

Annualized unrealized losses for Manager A and the CDLI over the measurement period were similar, equal to –0.23% and –0.19%, respectively. Therefore the 3.67% annualized difference in total return between Manager A and the CDLI can be divided into 1.14% from excess yield, 2.41% from excess realized gains, –0.04% from excess unrealized losses, and a residual 0.16% that is attributable to reinvestment of excess returns from excess yield and gains. (The 0.16% is sometimes referred to as a cross-product term.)

Manager B's track record, shown in Exhibit 17.1b is a completely different story, underperforming the CDLI in both income generation and realized losses.

A dollar invested with Manager B at September 30, 2004, would have grown to $3.23 as shown in the heavy line, less than one-half of Manager A, and representing a 6.93% annualized return, gross of fees, and unlevered. Manager B's 6.93% asset performance is 2.53% below the 9.46% return for the CDLI, reflecting poor past performance coming from large realized losses that were not offset by higher income. In fact, Manager B's income return of 10.66% was about the same as the CDLI income return of 10.79%, but their realized losses equaled an annualized –3.46%, and well above the CDLI –1.08% realized loss return. A reasonable expectation is that yield and realized losses are inversely related, with investors getting rewarded in higher yields for higher credit risk. That was certainly not true for Manager B. Manager B's performance record does show a small annualized unrealized loss at period's end equal to –0.17%, about the same as the CDLI. Therefore, the 2.53% total return shortfall for Manager B relative to the CDLI is virtually all attributable to poor underwriting that translated into large, realized credit losses.

This case study demonstrates that manager selection matters, and sometimes a lot. Accepting that, what should an investor look at when selecting a direct lender? For example, should investors just select direct lenders that offer the highest yields? After all, a higher yield would give the investor at least a better starting point, absent any other information.

MANAGER DIRECT LOAN YIELD

Direct lending returns are driven by three primary factors: yield, credit losses, and fees. Yields attract the most attention when evaluating direct lenders because they are an overwhelming source of return, easily calculated, and always available.

Exhibit 11.1 showed that investors hunting for yield can fall into a kind of yield trap because absolute direct loan yields vary by the types of risks taken. At any point in time investors shopping for yield will find a range of yields being generated by direct loan managers. Exhibit 17.2 reports yield variations across BDC managers for their underlying assets for years 2005 through 2021. Yield is calculated by dividing interest income by average gross assets. Each dot represents a different direct lending manager.

Casual inspection of Exhibit 17.2 suggests that both the level and dispersion of manager loan yields remains relatively stable over time. The asset-weighted average is shown as the heavy line and represents CDLI interest income. CDLI interest income plots below the median of manager yields due to asset weighting. The slight downward slope in interest income is largely attributable to declining Libor over the period shown, a trend that is reversing.

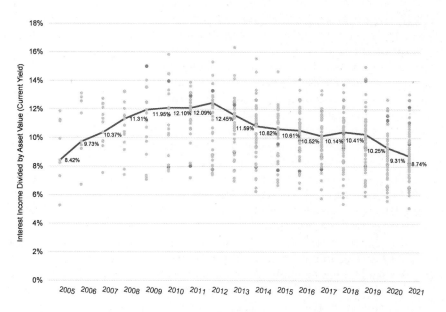

EXHIBIT 17.2   Yield (interest income) by direct loan manager, 2005 to 2021.

The dispersion of yields is measured by standard deviation each year. It averages 1.80% over the entire time period, meaning approximately two-thirds of managers build loan portfolios with yields within a 3.60% range.

The dispersion in manager yields is best understood by combining the risk premium architecture presented in Exhibit 11.1 with actual direct loan manager exposures to risk factors, as shown in Exhibit 17.3. The diagram illustrates the variation among managers in exposures to risk factors at a single point in time. These manager risk factor exposures remain roughly constant over time, reflecting each manager's preferred style of loan origination. Each bubble represents a single manager, and the number is only for identification purposes. The size of each bubble is not a risk factor and measures direct loan assets under management.

The horizontal axis measures the average size of the borrower in the manager's portfolio. This is the fourth risk factor identified in Exhibit 11.1. Size is measured by EBITDA and ranges up to $100 million, which is broadly considered the upper end of the US middle market. Beyond $100 million in EBITDA, borrowers generally have accessed the broadly syndicated bank loan markets for financing. Recently this has been changing, with borrowers using private debt managers for financing that went to the syndicated market in the past.

Note the wide dispersion in borrower size averages across direct loan managers, with equal numbers of managers operating at different size strata. Also, there does not appear to be a relationship between the size of manager and average size of borrower. Often, investors are concerned that as managers grow in assets they are forced to do bigger deals. While this tendency is found in other asset classes, it has yet to materialize in direct lending.

The vertical axis in Exhibit 17.3 measures manager average exposure to sponsored or nonsponsored borrowers, the third risk factor identified in Exhibit 11.1. Unlike the symmetric distribution of borrower size, the distribution of sponsored and nonsponsored exposure favors sponsored borrowers with an average overall exposure to sponsored borrowers equal to roughly 77%. There also appear to be more direct lenders lending to sponsored borrowers and for those lenders to be larger. Lenders to nonsponsored borrowers frequently point out the increased time and effort required to underwrite their loans. If true, then it would be logical to expect fewer assets and managers doing nonsponsored loans.

Perhaps most noticeable is the smaller number and size of direct lenders operating in the nonsponsored lower middle market. This would mean that many managers are purposefully foregoing the full yield premiums found in smaller nonsponsored loans. This likely is attributable to the ability of asset managers to scale their businesses more easily by lending to sponsor-backed borrowers.

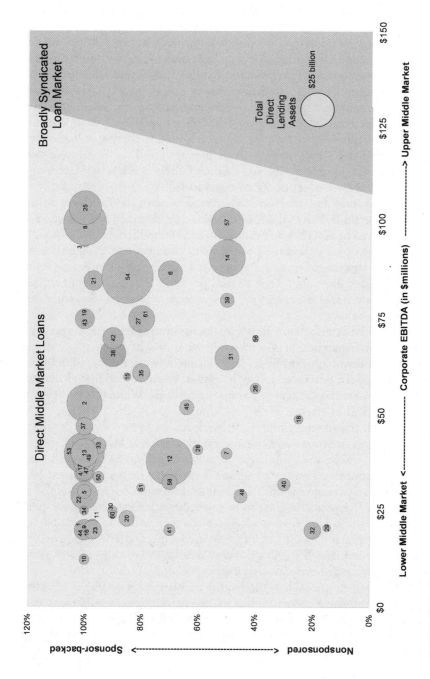

EXHIBIT 17.3 Manager exposure to direct loan risk factors, March 31, 2022.

The last risk factor from Exhibit 11.1 is credit risk and is measured in Exhibit 17.3 by the darkest bubble. Lenders focused on senior loans are displayed in darkest shading. Lenders making primarily subordinated loans are shown in lightest shading. Lenders with a broad mix of senior and subordinated loans are in medium shading. By number, managers making mostly senior loans and those that invest in both senior and subordinated debt are roughly equal, though senior-only managers are larger in size. Only one manager in the sample focuses exclusively on subordinated debt, probably because the availability of subordinated debt is less predictable, scalable, and lenders will also find themselves competing with hedge funds and other special situation managers for these borrowers.

The middle market yield potential measured by the risk premiums in Exhibit 11.1 measured 6.6% (1.7% nonsponsored premium, plus 1.6% lower middle market premium, plus 3.3% subordinated premium) on March 31, 2022. The actual range in middle market yields, from high to low, offered by direct lending managers equaled 6.2% for the same date shown in Exhibit 17.2. Excluding the highest and lowest yielding managers, the dispersion in return equaled 5.4%. This variation in yield among direct lenders is significant but largely explained by risk factor exposures for those managers. The regression of manager risk factors and yields produced an R-square equal to 0.52, meaning that 52% of the variability in manager yield is explained by the risk factors. Combining the 52% R-square between yields and risk factors with the 1.80% cross-sectional standard deviation in yields implies that the standard deviation of yields across direct lenders that *is not* explained by risk factors equals a smallish 1.25%.

It appears that direct lenders have some ability to affect yield in a way other than by taking on factor exposures rewarded by high-yield premiums. And it is likely the 1.25% dispersion not explained by risk factors are created by differences in the extent to which managers self-originate loans, earning full deal fees (OID) versus participating in smaller or larger club deals and receiving partial or no fees. Another explanation is that some direct lenders engage in an industry focus, such as venture or health care lending, which have higher asset volatility and therefore higher yields, as explained in Chapter 10. And, of course, the presence of covenants is another important factor, also explained in Chapter 10.

In the broader credit markets, and for the direct lending market as well, the level of interest income (yield) likely represents beta. In most cases differences in yield can be explained by the major risk premiums identified in Chapter 11 or other factors unrelated to manager skill. In the market for financing, even in the middle market, there are sufficient competitive pressures among lenders that yield anomalies would seem hard to come by.

CREDIT LOSSES ACROSS DIRECT LENDERS

Risk premiums provide a very useful explanation for the different yields found in US middle market direct lending but there is not sufficient evidence that they are useful in explaining credit losses, the second component in the calculation of direct lending returns. Instead, the variability in realized credit losses appears thus far to fall at the footsteps of the lender itself and their underwriting capability.

Exhibit 17.4 parallels Exhibit 17.2. In Exhibit 17.4, realized credit gains (losses), rather than interest income, are shown by calendar year for individual direct lending managers together with the CDLI, which represents an asset-weighted average.

Dispersion among manager realized gains (losses) in Exhibit 17.4 is significant and exceeds differences found for interest income. The average annual cross-sectional standard deviation of realized gains (losses) equals 3.36% for the entire period and rises to 4.94% during the 2008–2010 subperiod when losses from the GFC were realized. By contrast, the cross-sectional standard deviation in interest income was 2.34% for the entire period and 2.48% during the 2008–2010 GFC subperiod. Statistically speaking, an investor focus on a lender's ability to manage credit losses is significantly

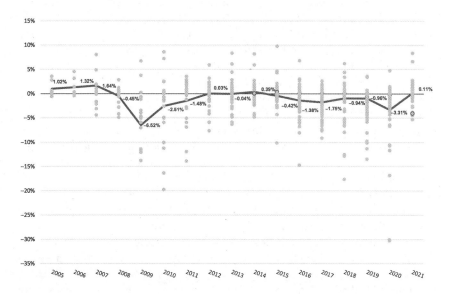

EXHIBIT 17.4   Net *realized* gains (losses) for direct lending managers and the Cliffwater Direct Lending Index, by year.

more important than their ability to generate interest income. Expressed differently, managing credit losses is 2.1× more important than income generation, calculated by the ratio of variances (the square of standard deviation).

The 3.36% cross-sectional standard deviation in realized gains (losses) across direct lending managers is very meaningful considering that the standard deviation of CDLI returns over time is 3.63% (Exhibit 3.1). This is not like traditional stocks and bonds where active manager risk (alpha risk) is a very small percentage of overall market risk (beta risk). In direct lending, individual manager risk can exceed the risk of the direct lending asset class itself.

Exhibit 17.5 presents realized gains (losses) in another way by showing cumulative net realized gains (losses) by direct loan manager. The length of track record varies across managers with many starting after the GFC. As a result, Exhibit 17.5 contains track records of net realized gains (losses) of differing lengths. The dark line represents aggregate CDLI net realized losses. However, the graphic is useful in showing the long-term dispersion of realized gains (losses) across managers and not just yearly dispersion.

A key question is whether the risk factors that explain so much of the differences in direct lending interest income among managers also explain differences in manager realized credit gains (losses). Finding an answer that

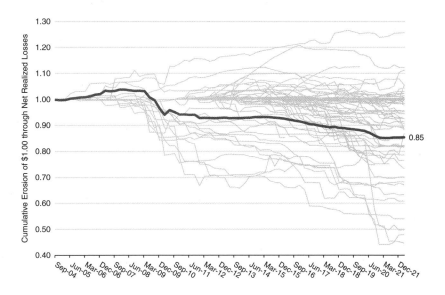

EXHIBIT 17.5 Cumulative net *realized* gains (losses) for direct lending asset managers and the Cliffwater Direct Lending Index (heavy dark line), September 2004 to March 2022.

is statistically meaningful is difficult because realized credit losses are concentrated over just a few years, 2008–2010, covering a small sample set of direct lenders. Most of the remaining years are largely credit benign with modest credit losses. In those years differences in portfolio yield may reflect perceived risk of default, but without actual defaults a statistical relationship won't be found.

The correlation between calendar year interest income and realized credit gains (losses) equals –0.39, suggesting that higher yield direct lending portfolios tend to experience lower realized credit gains (larger realized credit losses). Assuming higher yields reflect greater credit risk, the negative correlation is directionally correct. However, the R-squared equals just 16%, meaning that yield explains a low percentage of the variation of credit losses across direct lenders.

These results likely mean that credit losses across individual direct lenders are better explained by differences among lenders in their skills at sourcing, underwriting, and work-out capabilities. This would be lender alpha.

TOTAL RETURN

Historical data on yield and credit gains (losses) suggest that direct lender performance can vary widely across managers. Yields vary widely across direct lenders given their exposure to risk factors and realized credit losses vary widely due to differences in underwriting skill. And the lack of correlation between yield and credit loss increases the dispersion of manager returns, rather than reducing it. A wide dispersion among direct lenders in calendar year total return (incorporating yield, realized gains [losses], and unrealized gains [losses]) is indeed found in Exhibit 17.6.

The average cross-sectional standard deviation equals 6.56%, which is high for asset classes, but low compared to private equity, and has implications for portfolio construction discussed in Chapter 20. A major takeaway from this dispersion analysis is that the selection of direct lending managers is very important and that the risk found in manager selection likely exceeds the risk found in the asset class itself. This means that the common approach of hiring a single manager to gain exposure to direct lending and then adding managers as allocations increase probably presents unnecessary risks. Better to hire several direct lenders at the outset to get a better chance of asset class characteristics.

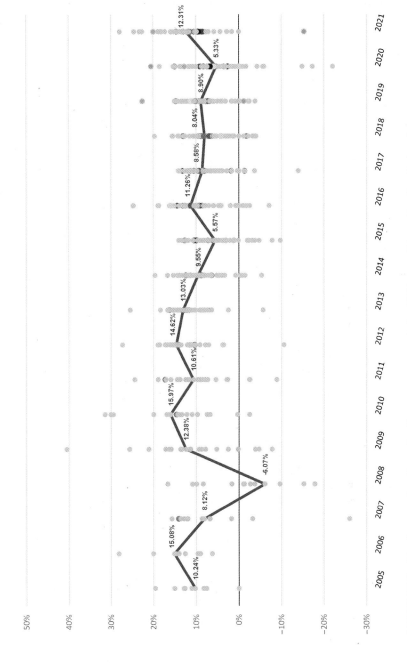

EXHIBIT 17.6 Total return for direct lending managers and the Cliffwater Direct Lending Index, by year.

DIRECT LENDING MANAGERS

Direct loans are bespoke agreements between lenders and borrowers. As such, successful investment outcomes are dependent on the quality of the direct lending manager(s) selected by the investor.

Unlike ten years ago, investors today have a variety of asset management firms to select from. The population of direct lending managers has grown rapidly since the GFC and continues to expand in line with the growth in direct lending assets. Unlike many other traditional and alternative asset classes, there has yet to appear any significant concentration in assets among a few firms. As of December 31, 2022, there were roughly 300 global direct lending firms, 200 located in the United States. These firms combined managed $856 billion in direct lending assets globally, with $650 billion in the United States and $200 billion in Europe. Direct lending in Asia is in its infancy with perhaps a dozen managers investing $6 billion in direct loan assets.

An institutional approach to selecting a direct lender likely involves a multifaceted analysis, such as the one described in Exhibit 17.7. Like most other asset classes, a small minority, perhaps 20% of available managers, meet the highest qualifications and fiduciary standards. There is generally another group of 20–30% that are of institutional quality but lack a few

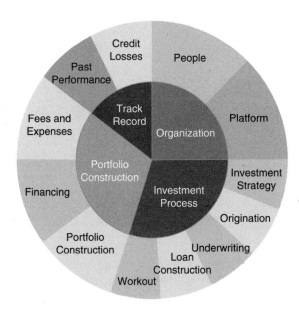

EXHIBIT 17.7 Due diligence checklist for middle market direct lender.

characteristics that put them in the highest grouping. Finally, roughly 50% or more available managers are unlikely to produce good outcomes due to multiple deficiencies.

ORGANIZATION

Successful money management firms have experienced investment and operational personnel with good resources at their disposal. Ideally, the investment people have been working together under one roof for a long period of time. But for a few managers, many direct lending organizations have been newly formed over the past ten years and thus don't have long histories. In those cases, the professional team may have worked together at a bank or nonbank financial lender prior to the GFC and were recruited to an asset management firm or started a new firm during the GFC. This is in fact a common scenario in direct lending, at least in the United States. Many successful direct lending professionals today have pedigrees going back to pre-GFC nonbank commercial lenders such as GE Capital and CIT. Others came from commercial banks such as Continental, First Chicago, Fleet, and the New York investment bank proprietary trading desks. These professionals were well trained and experienced in middle market corporate lending well before direct lending became popular.

Operations has a critical role to play at any direct lending organization. Unlike stock and bond managers, for whom every security has a digital identifier with terminal access to all sorts of data and a great number of operational functions are outsourced, most direct lenders deal with loan documentation and terms that require identification, measurement, and compliance that is not available off the shelf. While some functions can be outsourced to capable vendors, this does not change the need for the direct lender to input data, feed it to the vendor, and verify accuracy. Several of the early direct lending firms built their own administrative systems for lack of good off-the-shelf products. That is one reason administrative expenses for operating a direct lending portfolio can be high, averaging around 0.40%.

INVESTMENT STRATEGY

Most direct lending managers have a similar investment strategy: maximize interest and other income and avoid losses from defaults. They can differ greatly in how they execute and that is where lenders are differentiated. Borrower type and size are the most significant differentiators, as described in Chapter 11. Most direct lenders deal only with borrowers backed by private equity sponsors. Here, the number and depth of these relationships with private equity firms is very important and can be verified through reference checks. It is also useful to know the reputation of the private equity firms, particularly in dealing with their portfolio companies during downturns.

Only a few asset managers lend exclusively to nonsponsored borrowers. More often a direct lender will source both sponsored and nonsponsored borrowers. With nonsponsored lenders it is likely more challenging to do just about everything. Yields are higher but investors in lenders to nonsponsors need to also assess the rate at which loans can be made and exited. In both cases they are likely much slower. For example, nonsponsored companies are likely to have fewer corporate actions (liquidity events).

Direct lenders typically differentiate themselves into lower middle market, middle market, and upper middle market. The lower middle market would be borrowers with EBITDA less than $25 million while the upper middle market are borrowers above $75 million in EBITDA. Lender focus is usually based on existing sponsor relationships or other sourcing avenues. Lenders in the upper middle market need to guard against excesses, like covenant-lite, that slip down from the broadly syndicated bank market to the upper middle market for direct loans. Lenders in the lower middle market see more stable borrower metrics and terms but need to pay more attention or allocate more resources to problem loans and exit strategies.

Lenders will also differentiate by the level of credit risk taken. Some are senior secured only while others look at the totality of the business they are lending to and may lend at several levels, including subordinated. Unitranche lending, which combines senior and junior loans so that the lender becomes a single turnkey source of financing for the borrower is rapidly growing in popularity. To be successful, unitranche loans need to be priced lower than the typical senior/junior debt structure. The positive is that investors may get more money to work with unitranche lenders, but the negative is that the investor gives up yield for risk taken.

A smaller group of direct lenders focuses on certain industries. Health care and technology (venture) lending are two examples. These lenders take advantage of the higher yields (beta) offered by these higher risk industries and seek to mitigate risk of default (alpha) through specialized industry expertise.

ORIGINATION

Direct lenders originate loans, but not entirely. The classic direct lender sources loan deals, structures the loan documentation, holds the entire loan to maturity and likely after refinancing, monitors the borrower for covenant compliance, and works out the loan in the case of borrower distress.

For sourcing and structuring, together called *origination*, the direct lender receives compensation in the form of deal fees that are paid up front or original issue discount that, while accounting treatment can vary, is usually amortized as income over the life of the loan.

Roughly 20% of the direct lenders today are of this classic variety. Another 70% may self-originate but could also participate in small club deals where a few direct lenders agree to participate jointly in a loan pari passu. In these cases, the club may be formed because the loan is too large for the direct lender who found the deal, or that lender might invite other lenders to diversify into more loans as other club members reciprocate. With smaller clubs, deal fees are shared but not always equally. Finally, fewer than 10% of direct lenders do not originate deals but lend only through participations from large lead arrangers like an Antares or Golub. These direct lenders effectively outsource the origination process. Their loan portfolios forgo the extra income, but they are typically much more diversified by number of loans and industry. While origination sounds great and produces extra income and perhaps an informational advantage relative to borrowers, it also can present a bottleneck to the investment opportunity set that can frustrate portfolio construction and risk management.

Most direct lenders organize origination and underwriting functions together on industry verticals. There are exceptions where the origination team operates independent of the underwriting team, a model traditionally found in commercial bank lending. The move to combining these functions is likely due to the need for speed of execution and the ability to bring industry expertise to the borrower early in the underwriting engagement.

UNDERWRITING

In theory, underwriting is the process of structuring financing to fit the needs of the borrower while at the same time assessing risk. Risk assessment includes the concepts of expected default frequency and recovery given default. Expected default frequency addresses the size of the loans relative to firm assets and cash flow to minimize the future probability of a default happening. Recovery given default refers to having sufficient security so that if default occurs there is an opportunity for full recovery of loan proceeds.

In practice, borrower financials and proposed loan amounts are used by the loan manager to determine implied credit ratings, or shadow ratings, based on comparisons provided by major rating agencies. For example, loan leverage levels (loan to EBITDA) for the proposed loan at issuance is compared to equivalent measures determined by rating agencies for different quality grades, from single A to CCC. The proposed loan is given a shadow rating that best matches its leverage level at issuance. In turn, the shadow rating is used to set pricing (yield) based on what the loan market is currently offering for that risk.

Underwriting is generally performed by the industry specialist, which is then reviewed more broadly by an investment committee.

Of course, loan managers consider many financial variables, not just leverage levels, in their mapping of a specific loan to a rating agency's letter rating. Hence, the loan manager is basically rating the loan, not the rating agency. But loan managers generally rely on rating agency letter grades to accurately reflect risk. Market yields for each rating then sets the price for accepting that level of risk.

LOAN CONSTRUCTION AND MONITORING

A general discussion on loan agreements and covenants was covered in Chapter 12. Direct lenders use the underwriting process to settle on loan terms and covenants that will be required to finance the borrower. In most cases direct lenders use the services of outside law firms that specialize in structured finance to assist in constructing and negotiating loan terms. Compliance with the loan agreement requires ongoing monitoring of borrower financials. Most loans have maintenance covenants that require periodic (quarterly) collection of data from the borrower and covenant testing.

WORKOUT

The final step of the investment process is workout of the loan in case a default occurs. Oftentimes the default is technical and that requires the borrower to pay a fee or greater interest rate as a remedy. In situations where there is an actual default stemming from a fundamental problem with the borrower, the lender will need specialized expertise and resources to maximize recovery value. Not all direct lenders have these skills. Some direct lenders operate as part of larger alternative asset management firms that include private equity and distressed capabilities. These direct lenders are better positioned to handle the recovery process versus the alternative of a distressed sale.

PORTFOLIO CONSTRUCTION

The most common vehicle for investing in corporate direct loans is private partnerships with limited life. Asset managers who construct portfolios of direct loans for private partnerships seek to optimize return and risk, subject to the level of committed assets, the period of time designated for investment, and deal flow opportunity during the investment period. Like private equity, most investors in direct lending will have concurrent commitments to more than one direct lending manager because no single manager can optimize the entire direct lending opportunity set. Understanding this, the direct lender should optimize their own opportunity subset and let the investor optimize the full direct lending opportunity through multiple managers. This design has worked well for institutions investing in private equity and private real estate.

Understanding they will not be responsible for investors' overall market diversification (beta), direct lenders instead maximize the yields they can manufacture while minimizing credit losses (alpha). Investors will commit to several direct lending funds of complementary strategies to optimize their overall allocation to direct lending. But direct lenders don't always agree on this view of portfolio construction. Some design their portfolios to be more turnkey, believing their investors want to one-stop their direct lending exposure. These managers generally have been in business longer and have investors that may have relied principally on one manager. Other managers have very focused direct lending strategies with a greater emphasis on return maximization and who should represent one component of an overall direct lending allocation.

Exhibit 17.8 provides some general statistics on 50 of the largest direct lenders and their private partnerships, a group that collectively manages $649 billion in direct lending assets. These statistics should provide some guidance on how actual portfolios are managed.

2008	Average Year Firm Launched
$12 billion	Average direct lending assets managed
62%	Percent of firms managing BDCs
50	Average # of direct lending professionals
$455 million	Median fund gross assets
78%	Average % first lien (senior secured)
13%	Average % of first lien that is unitranche
0.98×	Average leverage used
1.97×	Maximum leverage used
$50 billion	Average borrower EBITDA
80%	Average % sponsor-backed loans
75	Average # portfolio credits
9.3%	Average net IRR (internal rate of return)
8.1%	Average cash yield
0.25%	Average annualized loss ratio

EXHIBIT 17.8 Portfolio characteristics for direct lending private partnerships.

The portfolio statistics for the sample of private partnerships are not dissimilar from BDCs. This should not be too surprising because many asset managers offer both private partnerships and BDCs. Noteworthy is the 0.98× average leverage for private partnerships, which is very similar to the value found in BDCs, whose leverage averages 1.09× and is constrained by regulation to less than 2.0×. Looking back at the portfolio characteristics for BDCs in Chapter 15, it appears that asset managers operate their BDCs and private partnerships in very similar ways across portfolio composition and financing.

The average number of loans at 75 is adequately diversified for a single fund but probably not for an investor, particularly when leverage averages 0.98×. That means the average position size, as a percentage of NAV, equals 1.3%. One default, with an offsetting 50% recovery rate, would lower the IRR of the private fund by roughly 13 basis points over its five-year life. Given that loans have limited return upside, most investors would want to have broader representation of credits through multiple funds.

The 0.25% realized credit loss ratio for the average manager in Exhibit 16.8 stands out compared to the 1.08% realized credit losses reported for the CDLI. The low loss ratio for the 50-firm sample set in Exhibit 16.8 is due to two reasons. First, the sample is biased toward larger managers who became large because they have achieved better performance, presumably from lower loss rates. If investors can select better managers, ex ante, then the 0.25% loss rate may be a better predictor of future loss rates compared to the 1.08% loss rate for an unbiased universe of direct lenders. Second, the lower 0.25% loss rate is not surprising because the sample set is also biased toward direct lenders that started businesses after the GFC. Their average loss rates will be lower than the 1.08% CDLI loss rate whose calculation gives equal weight to pre- and post-GFC loss outcomes.

It is important to understand the portfolio construction strategy for any individual loan manager and how it fits into an investor's overall portfolio.

LEVERAGE FINANCING

Most middle market direct lenders enhance yields by using a modest amount of leverage, ranging from none to 2.0× net asset value. The higher levels of leverage are used for senior secured middle market credits while portfolios of subordinated and mezzanine loans use little or no leverage. As reported, the average BDC and direct lending private partnership generally operate with leverage levels between 0.9× and 1.2×. Unlevered direct lending portfolios are available from some managers. Also, collateralized loan obligations (CLOs) holding middle market loans are growing in popularity with leverage levels between 4.0× and 5.0×. The higher leverage levels for middle market CLOs are made possible by strict rules for the allocation of loan cash flows that protect those providing senior financing. This presents income uncertainty and price volatility to those investors providing capital (NAV) that generally does not appeal to institutional investors wanting consistent cash flow and low volatility.

There are several methods for financing assets purchases, each with pros and cons. The first is the subscription line. These credit facilities have recently become very popular and are banks, insurance companies, or specialty finance firms that will lend BDCs or private partnerships against their undrawn committed capital. Consequently, subscription lines are a temporary source of financing, existing only until committed capital is fully drawn by the general partner. The amount of financing under the subscription line depends on several factors, including the size of the fund and the creditworthiness of investors. Subscription lines are relatively cheap, priced at 1.50–1.75% over Libor, but like revolving loans, the lender pays an unused commitment fee, typically 0.25%. Subscription lines are very useful early in a fund's life when the portfolio is being ramped up and does not have the diversification necessary to satisfy asset-based lenders. Subscription lines have also become a popular way to boost the internal rate of return (IRR) calculation of performance since income is generated on little to no net asset value. However, some investors have gotten frustrated with a manager's borrowing on uncommitted capital rather than just calling capital because the undrawn commitments may be held by the investor in reserves that are earning less than the financing costs of the subscription line.

The second and most common financing method is for the direct lender to enter into an agreement creating a revolving credit facility. The facility provides the direct lender financing as needed (revolving) subject to limits. The financing is provided by multiple parties, including banks and insurance companies, arranged by a syndication agent, and guaranteed by the underlying portfolio of loan assets. The revolving credit facility is generally costlier with a 2.25–2.50% spread over Libor and a 0.375% charge on unused amounts. But unlike a subscription line, the revolver is a more permanent source of financing with a four- or five-year maturity.

A third financing method is the creation of a special purpose vehicle (SPV). SPVs are lending vehicles, also with four- or five-year maturities, secured by loans placed in the SPV. Costs tend to be somewhat higher than revolvers at a 2.50–3.00% spread over Libor. They also tend to be more manually intensive. There are many types of SPV facilities, including the availability of term financing, flexibility in asset-level approvals, and the ability to use them as warehouse financing for CLO takeouts, or for rated structures.

A fourth financing source, and one more commonly found in permanent capital structures like BDCs or interval funds, is longer maturity (five-plus years) unsecured and subordinated notes issued in private placements or through public offerings. These generally have fixed rates at higher costs. Managers issuing private placements have the option to enter into an interest rate swap matching floating rate to fixed rate payments. On a swap-adjusted basis the financing might cost a little more but it is very flexible and easy to support compared to SPV facilities, which can require significant resources.

A fifth source of financing is issuing public fixed rate debt with intermediate term maturities. This financing option is generally available only to asset managers running large BDCs or interval funds that can rationalize the rating and syndication costs. These publicly traded bonds are sold primarily to retail investors.

A sixth source of financing can come from the small business administration (SBA). The SBA was established in 1958 by Congress to stimulate small business growth and, today, is responsible for roughly $25 billion in loans to small businesses. Direct lenders can access SBA financing by getting licensed by the SBA to set up a small business investment corporation (SBIC). The SBIC is akin to a private partnership where the direct lending asset manager is the general partner and institutional investors are limited partners. SBICs are attractive to its investors—general and limited partners—because they can issue SBA-guaranteed debentures at ten-year maturities, with no principal amortization, at favorable interest rates compared to other traditional sources of financing, and at levels up to 2.0× investor capital. However, SBA financing is limited to $150 million per SBIC and $350 million for multiple SBICs under a common manager. SBICs must also direct their loans or other investments to qualifying companies, which are generally smaller middle market companies with EBITDA less than $10 million or companies in industries or sectors designated by the SBA for favorable treatment.

Understanding how direct lending managers arrange their sources of financing, how cash flows from loan assets match the interest and principal repayment requirements of credit facilities, and how financing costs are optimized across the potential sources, is a critical component of investor due diligence.

FEES AND EXPENSES

Chapter 19 discusses manager fees in some detail. Fees have generally been coming down as they have in most other asset classes. Part of the reason in direct lending is asset growth has allowed managers to reduce costs as increased scale has widened operating margins. Also, the entry of institutional investors has brought greater attention to both the level and structure of manager fees. But not all direct lenders have the same strategy, and more labor-intensive strategies will continue to charge higher fees.

TRACK RECORD

The lack of a track record history through the GFC has been a hindrance to evaluating many of the direct lending firms formed after 2008. A few direct lenders do have track records that extend well before the GFC and are generally able to provide sufficient granularity to decompose returns into income, realized losses, and unrealized losses. Direct lenders that operate BDCs are required to provide this detail to shareholders so the information is readily available and verifiable. Detailed performance data from direct lenders that do not operate BDCs is often not available from the manager. This is because direct managers generally follow the performance practices of their private equity brethren and report only total net performance by fund by vintage year. Unfortunately, it is impossible to glean information on a lender's credit loss experience from a performance presentation of this type. Without changing their reliance on IRR, more direct lenders are now supplementing performance disclosures with default and recovery histories.

In the case of direct lenders formed after 2008, an understanding of their abilities during downturns requires parsing performance histories at prior firms, which is more difficult, but generally the investor can come to some conclusion as to whether the current team or its individual members successful navigated the GFC. That said, there is nothing better than actual audited returns during a downturn to verify underwriting and workout capabilities.

CHAPTER 18

Loan Valuation

How accurate are valuations in the absence of a tradable market for middle market loans? This is an important question for most investors in direct corporate loans for several reasons. First, many investors in public BDCs focus on the price-to-NAV ratio (the BDC market price divided by net asset value) as a potential measure of under- (over)-valuation, signaling a buy or sell opportunity. If NAV is incorrect, so is the valuation signal. Second, manager fees are based on NAV so mistakes in valuation can potentially cause fee overpayments. Third, a growing group of direct lending pooled vehicles allow investors to purchase or sell units at NAV. Private BDCs, interval funds, and tender funds, as well as other registered and nonregistered, open-end pooled vehicles are examples. For instance, if NAV is *overstated*, excess value is passed from the new shareholders making investments to existing shareholders, and at the same time excess value is passed from existing shareholders to withdrawing shareholders. Excess value flows in the opposite direction when NAV is understated. This chapter addresses how direct loan values are determined and whether investors can rely on them.

As background, the Financial Accounting Standards Board (FASB) defines asset value as fair value,[1] prescribed by ASC 820 most recently in 2011. ASC 820 defines fair value as "the price that would be received to sell an asset or paid to transfer a liability in an orderly transaction between market participants at the measurement date." In outlining a discovery process that will find fair value, ASC 820 segregated assets into three categories (Level 1, Level 2, and Level 3), each with a different process for determining fair value.

Level 1 assets are liquid assets with valuations based on quoted prices readily available in active markets. Level 1 assets typically include listed equities, listed derivatives, mutual funds, and any other assets that have a regular mark-to-market pricing mechanism, generally via a central exchange. Investors should have a high confidence in Level 1 valuations except perhaps

---

[1] Private, nontraded assets were historically valued at historical cost, adjusted for write-ups or write-downs, prior to ASC 820 and fair value accounting.

during extreme events. Level 2 assets generally trade in inactive markets and rely on values (quotes) provided by market participants rather than real-time transactions on a central exchange. These assets are often priced through indicative quotations from multiple broker dealers and then averaged. Examples of Level 2 assets include credit default swaps and corporate debt. Most derivative securities are considered Level 2 assets even though the valuation for the underlying security may be readily available on a central exchange. Level 3 assets are generally those that are not traded or traded infrequently and, therefore, fair value cannot be determined by market-related activity or inputs. The fair value of Level 3 assets can only be estimated by using significant assumptions as inputs to a valuation model.

Direct corporate loans are Level 3 assets.[2] There may be some exceptions when the direct loans are lightly traded, in which case they might be treated as Level 2. While ASC 820 gives broad discretion in setting fair value for Level 3 assets, there are several straightforward models available to price corporate loans. The key inputs are the most recent borrower financials, recent changes, and most likely a valuation model that maps the circumstances of the loan being valued to a pool of other loans with similar circumstances that have a credit rating. Pricing can then be discovered once a rating equivalent is agreed on. Importantly, asset managers develop written valuation policies that guide how it is valuing Level 3 assets and a compliance function confirms that these policies are being consistently followed.

Common practice is for direct loans to be valued quarterly. Another, not dissimilar, valuation process is used for determining the value of liabilities if financing is used. NAV equals the fair value of assets minus the fair value of liabilities. It is also common for the asset manager to use an independent external valuation firm to value its Level 3 loans at least once a year with the loan manager setting values during the off quarters. Best practice is quarterly independent valuations, though these can be costly, and so managers generally weigh the net benefits of this practice to shareholders.

The quality of ASC 820 fair value protocols as they apply to Level 3 assets and direct US middle market corporate loans in particular can be tested by comparing, in the aggregate, quarterly pricing for high-yield bonds and broadly syndicated bank loans, both of which are Level 2 assets, with the fair value determination of direct loans captured by the CDLI. More granular comparisons of individual loans or groups of loans with equivalent Level 2 loans might reach different conclusions, but the comparison in Exhibit 18.1 between direct loan values and traded high-yield bonds and bank loans should provide guidance about the pricing behavior and accuracy of diversified loan portfolios over time.

---

[2]Level 3 assets comprised 91% of total BDC assets on March 31, 2022.

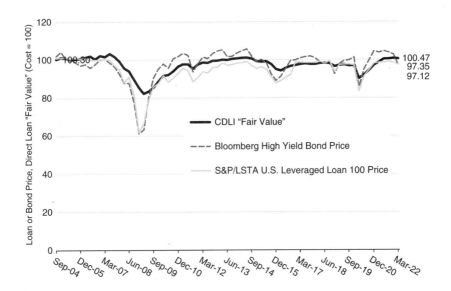

EXHIBIT 18.1 Price comparison for direct loans, high-yield bonds, and bank loans, March 2004 to March 2022.

Quarter valuations for the three indexes are plotted in Exhibit 18.1. Casual inspection suggests that pricing for direct loans, as measured by the CDLI, tracks the short-term directions of high-yield bonds and bank loans, and for the most part direct loan values lie between their Level 2 counterparts. The exceptions are the 2008 financial crisis and, to a lesser extent, the 2015–2016 oil crisis and 2020 COVID crisis. The valuation divergence for direct loans during the oil crisis was likely due to the difference in energy sector weights between the CDLI, where energy represented less than 5% of the Index, and high-yield bonds and bank loans, where energy represented well over 10% of those indexes. The valuation divergence for the GFC and COVID crisis has to do with the fact that high-yield bonds and leveraged loans are publicly traded, and providers of liquidity to sellers demand a premium yield (lower price) for supplying that liquidity. This public market feature, not present in the private markets, causes greater price volatility for high-yield bonds and leveraged loans.

The markedly greater divergence between direct loans and publicly traded high-yield bonds and loans during the GFC had another element not present during COVID. At December 31, 2018, there was a 25-point difference in valuation, which surely did not originate from changing fundamentals of the underlying companies across the three indexes. At the time, liquid high-yield bonds and loans were popular collateral in structured vehicles carrying high leverage. The unwinding of these vehicles caused selling pressure and lower prices on Level 2 risky assets that did not affect direct loans, which were held in banks, insurance companies, and BDCs. Effectively, direct loan values were set to reflect ASC 820 orderly transaction pricing rather than the market dislocation pricing occurring at the time. It is interesting that in a post-GFC update the FASB included in its Level 3 pricing guidance the concept of risk adjustment in pricing when there is significant measurement uncertainty. However, this guidance has apparently not come into play in subsequent downturns.

Direct loan valuations in Exhibit 18.1 also appear less volatile, apart from the 2008 financial crisis. This lower volatility is also reflected in the calculation of return volatility reported in Exhibit 3.1 where direct loans had a 3.63% standard deviation compared to 9.54% for the S&P/LSTA Leveraged Loan Index and 10.56% for the Bloomberg High Yield Bond Index. Direct middle market loans in fact may be less volatile than these publicly traded bank loans and bonds. But an alternative explanation could be that the Level 3 valuation process must somehow be flawed and that those setting fair value are not doing so conditioned only on information as of the valuation date but also implicitly take account of past prices and future expectations. If true, this creates a smoothing of prices over time, lowering the measured standard deviation of return.

A test for the presence of smoothing would be a positive finding of serial correlation in direct lending returns. Serial correlation measures the correlation of returns with returns' prior periods. If there is no smoothing, serial correlation equals zero. This is the ideal random walk world, where past prices do not influence current or future prices. If serial correlation is positive and equal to 0.50, for example, it means that past prices do explain current pricing to a degree equal to 25% (equal to 0.50^2).

Returns can also be found to have correlation not only with the immediate prior quarterly return but also quarterly returns extending back in time. A common manifestation of this effect used to occur in private real estate and private equity returns where serial correlation persisted up to a four-quarter lag. This produced significant smoothing in returns, causing risk calculations based on these returns to be understated. The cause of the serial correlation in these smoothed returns was intermittent independent valuations, mostly annually, without the rigorous guidelines of ASC 820. Since the GFC the integrity of valuations has become a greater priority for all private asset classes.

The integrity of direct loan valuations can be tested by measuring serial correlations of various time lags for direct lending quarterly returns.

Quarterly CDLI price returns, not total returns, are used because valuation impacts change in price but not income. The CDLI quarterly price return equals realized plus unrealized capital gains (losses) divided by NAV.

Serial correlations in CDLI price returns equal to 0.40, 0.21, 0.00, and −0.02 are found for one-quarter lag, two-quarter lag, three-quarter lag, and four-quarter lag, respectively. In a regression where the CDLI quarterly price return is the dependent variable and each of the four prior quarter price returns are independent variables, only the immediate prior quarter shows statistical significance with a *t*-statistic equal to 3.06. Keeping only the immediate prior quarter price return as the only independent variable increases the *t*-statistic to 3.55 with a beta coefficient equal to 0.40 and an R-squared equal to 0.16. It is interesting to compare the serial correlation for CDLI price returns with the Morningstar LSTA US Leveraged Loan 100 Index price returns. For the same time period, positive serial correlation also exists for the Morningstar LSTA US Leveraged Loan 100 Index price returns with a beta coefficient equal to 0.15, but the correlation equals only 0.15 and the *t*-statistic equals 1.26, which is not statistically significant. Therefore, while some short-term price smoothing exists within private direct lending, it is short-lived (one quarter), represents a minor percentage of the return (16%), and is mitigated by the existence of positive serial correlation in traded leveraged loans as well.

These measurements suggest modest and short-lived smoothing in direct lending valuations. Modest is understood as a correlation equal to 0.40, meaning that the prior quarter explains only 16% (equal to 0.40^2) of the current quarter valuation. Short-lived is understood as a *t*-statistic that is only statistically significant for the immediate prior quarter. This observation applies to the CDLI, a proxy for direct lending overall. Individual direct lender returns may display higher, lower, or no serial correlation, depending on their specific valuation process.

The 3.63% measured risk for the CDLI in Exhibit 3.1 can be revised knowing the NAVs on which the returns are calculated display some smoothing. Using the 0.40 serial correlation as input, the CDLI risk level can be mathematically unsmoothed to a value equal to 4.62%, or 1.38× the measured standard deviation. This unsmoothing adjustment is relatively small but can become important in applications involving leverage or where investors trade on NAV. It can be shown mathematically as well that if loan returns have the appearance of smoothing in the manner described, then the valuation error, measured by standard deviation, in any one quarter, equals plus or minus 0.52% (52 basis points).

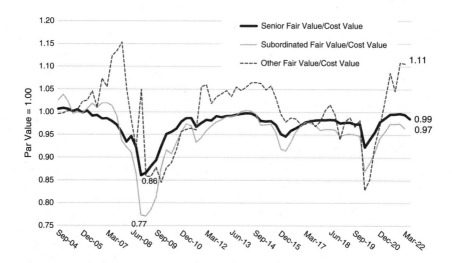

EXHIBIT 18.2 Comparison of fair value versus cost (principal) value for senior and subordinated loans within the CDLI, September 2004 to March 2022.

SENIOR VERSUS SUBORDINATED LOAN PRICING

CDLI pricing in Exhibit 18.1 is decomposed in Exhibit 18.2 into three components by seniority: senior secured, subordinated, and other.

Exhibit 18.2 takes a closer look at middle market loan values by grouping loans into senior and subordinated subsets to better understand pricing and volatility associated with credit seniority. Loan values for each subset are plotted from the 2004 CDLI inception. The heavy line represents the asset-weighted average price for senior loans (including unitranche) and the lighter line represents the same for second lien and subordinated loans. The dashed line represents the asset-weighted price for an "Other" category, which includes equity-related holdings (equity, warrant, CLO equity, other) within CDLI that are sometimes attached to middle market loans.

Clear valuation differences exist between senior and subordinated middle market loans within the CDLI. Senior loans are less volatile and hold their value better in down markets compared to subordinated loans. These fair value changes also inform risk calculations. The standard deviation of return (excluding interest income) measures 2.94% for senior loans and 5.20% for subordinated loans. The standard deviation of the equity-related "Other" category measures 9.51%, much closer to the 16.58% standard deviation of the Russell 3000 Index.

VALUING DIRECT MIDDLE MARKET LOANS USING STATISTICAL METHODS

Independent valuation firms and asset managers value direct loans quarterly by either comparing prices of loans with similar characteristics (loan-to-value, industry, EBITDA growth, etc.) or modeling future cash flows adjusted for the probability of default and likely recovery. The uniqueness of each loan can make this an arduous and expensive task.

It can be shown that valuing middle market loans in the aggregate, or some large subgroup of loans, can be achieved through statistical techniques with reasonably high accuracy, using a broad index of liquid loans as the source of price discovery for illiquid middle market loans. Exhibit 18.3 shows the statistical relationship between prices for senior-only and subordinated middle market loans with prices for the Morningstar LSTA US Leveraged Loan 100 Index using quarterly data for the 2005 to March 2022 time period.

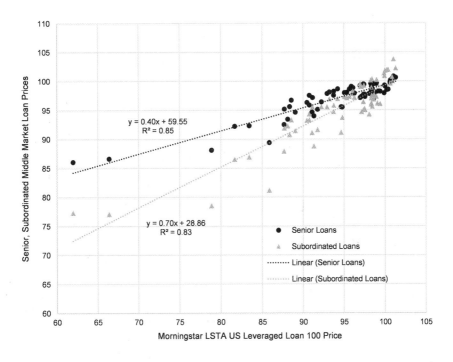

EXHIBIT 18.3 Price relationship between middle market loans and liquid leveraged loans.

The quarterly price for the Morningstar LSTA US Leveraged Loan 100 Index is used as the independent variable in Exhibit 18.3 while the quarterly asset-weighted prices for senior loans and subordinated loans from the CDLI are used as separate dependent variables. Quarterly markers identify pairings of senior or subordinated middle market loan prices with the quarterly price for the Morningstar LSTA US Leveraged Loan 100 Index. The regression lines and regression results in Exhibit 18.3 define the historical price relationship between private and public loans. For both regression lines, the R-squared figures of 0.85 and 0.83 are very high for direct senior loans and subordinated loans, respectively.

Second, the slope coefficients, or betas, between senior and subordinated loan prices and the Morningstar LSTA US Leveraged Loan 100 prices are different and in the expected direction. Senior middle market loans have 0.40 beta to leveraged loans while subordinated loans have a 0.70 beta to leveraged loans. Again, the betas are well less than 1.00 because middle market loans do not provide the liquidity to investors that leveraged loans do. The higher 0.70 beta for subordinated loans reflects their greater sensitivity to general economic risks, both equity and credit.

The statistical analysis presented in this chapter can be refined, of course, but the point is that valuations of diversified direct loan portfolios possess links to the broadly syndicated leveraged loan market that can be very useful when intra-quarter price discovery is needed. Diversification matters for valuation because individual loan price estimation errors will cancel out in an unbiased way the greater the number of individual loans in the portfolio. In fact, any error in the valuation of a portfolio of loans will fall by the reciprocal of square root of the number of loans in a portfolio, if valuations of individual loans are truly independent of each other. For example, say the average valuation error on an individual loan is a consequential plus or minus 3% of its true value. For a portfolio of 30 loans, the valuation error for the overall portfolio drops to 0.5%. For a portfolio of 1,000 loans the valuation error drops to 0.1%, an error rate that is at the threshold for immaterial in fund accounting.

CHAPTER 19

Investment Fees

Investors continue to inquire about fees and the value proposition offered by active management, particularly for the higher fees found in alternative investments. This chapter updates fee data on investment services for middle market corporate direct lending, identifies unique features found in direct lending fees, presents an apples-to-apples fee measurement protocol to better compare managers who have different fee structures, and, finally, gives statistical results that attempt to explain why some managers might reasonably have higher or lower fees compared to the average.

Fee, expense, and portfolio information was collected from 49 direct lending managers who collectively manage $541 billion in direct lending assets as of September 31, 2021, and offer limited partnership interests in private partnerships on which our fee analysis is based. Portfolio information includes use of portfolio leverage, loan seniority, borrower size, and allocations to nonsponsored borrowers, all characteristics found to explain differences in loan yields, and which may also explain fee differences as well. While the 49 funds examined are not identical, they are substantially similar in their focus on middle market lending as an investment strategy with the majority of capital provided by institutional investors.

Exhibit 19.1 provides results from our updated direct lending fee survey covering data collected during the fourth quarter of 2021. Fees are broken down into management (column 1) and incentive (columns 4 and 5). Management and incentive fees are combined to report total fees (columns 6 and 8).

A single set of loan assumptions underlie the results. Unlevered middle market loan yields, including original issue discount (OID) and other prepayment fees,[1] are assumed to equal 7.75% with a 0.50% annual credit loss ratio. Our research suggests these gross yield and loss rates are consistent with the study group whose portfolio of middle market loans are 89% senior, 78% sponsor-backed, with a $50 million EBITDA

---

[1]OID and fees paid to lenders from early prepayment of principal.

	(1)	(2)	(3)	(4)	(5)	(6)	(7)	(8)
	Mgmt. Fee Rate (%)	Leverage	Effective Mgmt. Fee on NAV (%)	Carried Interest (%)	Preferred Return (%)	Total Fees on NAV (%)	Gross Yield (%)	Total Fees as % of Gross Yield
Average	1.10	1.07×	1.89	13.1	6.1	3.14	12.01	26
Asset-Weighted	1.07	1.25×	1.99	12.9	6.3	3.34	12.83	26
GAV Average	1.03	1.18×	2.15	12.1	5.8	3.35	12.51	27
NAV Average	1.25	0.79×	1.25	15.3	6.6	2.63	10.76	25
10th Percentile	1.50	1.50×	2.53	17.5	7.0	4.15	13.93	32
25th Percentile	1.25	1.25×	2.25	15.0	7.0	3.47	12.81	30
50th Percentile	1.00	1.00×	1.91	15.0	7.0	2.97	11.70	26
75th Percentile	1.00	1.00×	1.50	12.0	6.0	2.54	11.70	24
90th Percentile	0.79	0.46×	1.12	10.0	5.0	2.20	9.30	20
10th–90th Range	0.71	1.04×	1.41	7.50	2.0	1.95	4.63	12

NAV = net asset value (investor capital only).
GAV = gross asset value (investor capital + assets financed through borrowings).

EXHIBIT 19.1 Direct lender fees.

borrower size. Additionally, borrowing costs are assumed to equal 2.80% and administrative and other costs equal 0.42%, both consistent with the characteristics for the study group of direct lenders.

MANAGEMENT FEES

Column 1 in Exhibit 18.1 reports survey results for management fees. Direct lending management fees are most often charged on invested, not committed, assets, and all 49 direct lending managers in our survey charge on invested assets. Private equity managers almost universally charge fees on committed assets during a fund's investment period. This difference is likely explained by legacy practices, more robust deal flow, shorter investment periods, and a shorter deal life compared to private equity. Fees on invested assets reduces both overall fees and mitigates or eliminates the J-curve phenomena.

Of the direct lending managers, 35 of the 49 (71%) charge fees on gross assets (GAV)[2] while the remaining 14 managers base their management fees on net assets (NAV). Outside direct lending, other forms of structured finance (such as CLOs), and some real estate structures, we seldom find management fees charged on gross assets. The argument for charging fees on gross assets is that the resources required of a manager to deploy assets is the same regardless of whether those assets are invested or levered, and, in fact, additional resources may be required to maintain the leverage. Weighted by assets, 75% charge management fees on GAV and 25% on NAV.

Column 1 shows considerable variability in management fees, only a fraction of which is explained by whether fees are charged on net or gross assets. The 10th–90th percentile fee range equals 0.71%, which is a very meaningful difference for any asset class.

LEVERAGE

Column 2 reports leverage statistics for the survey group. Most managers use leverage in their private funds (only four do not) with an average equal to 1.07x.[3] Not surprisingly, managers who charge management fees on gross assets use more leverage than those that do not. However, those same managers have a lower average management fee (column 1, rows 3 and 4).

EFFECTIVE MANAGEMENT FEE

Column 3 adjusts the headline fee in column 1 and expresses fees as a percentage of net assets (NAV). Average management fees increase from 1.10% to 1.89% of net assets due to some managers charging fees on levered assets (GAV). Of course, for them, the stated average 1.03% management fee on GAV becomes 2.15% as a percentage of net assets.

---

[2]Gross assets (GAV) include both investor capital (NAV) plus assets from leverage (borrowings).

[3]Leverage is expressed as a multiple of net assets (NAV). A value equal to 1.07x means that the private fund uses borrowings equal to 1.07 multiplied by its net assets, for a gross asset value equal to 2.07 multiplied by net assets.

CARRIED INTEREST

Column 4 reports carried interest statistics for private debt funds. The vast majority of managers in the survey charge an incentive fee. The average incentive fee equals 13.1%, which is well below the ubiquitous 20% incentive fee found in private equity, with 10% and 15% incentive fees being the two most commonly found. As might be expected, managers who charge management fees on gross assets tend to have lower incentive fees than those charging management fees on net assets, at 12.1% versus 15.3%, respectively.

PREFERRED RETURN

The average preferred return equals 6.1%. This is lower than the typical preferred return of 8% for private equity, likely reflecting lower return expectations for direct lending. In almost all cases direct lending funds require a 100% catch-up after the preferred return is achieved. Private equity funds generally apply a 50% catch-up, which is more investor friendly.

TOTAL FEES ON NAV

Direct comparisons of fees can be difficult with the variety in structures and use of leverage. Therefore, we create a single fee measure in column 6 that represents the sum of asset fees and incentive fees, as a percentage of net asset value. We calculate total fees on NAV by averaging combined management and incentive fees as a percentage of NAV across managers. The average direct lending manager imposes a combined fee equal to 3.14% of net assets. The average gross of fee expected return equals 12.01%.

TOTAL FEES AS PERCENTAGE OF GROSS INCOME

Column 7 looks at the proportion of gross return that is paid to managers either through management or incentive fees. The 26% average is not materially different from what is found in private equity.

FACTORS EXPLAINING FEE VARIATION

A significant proportion of manager fee variation can be explained statistically by four factors. Leverage is the dominant factor explaining higher fees; explaining lower fees are size of borrower, allocation to senior loans, and allocation to sponsor-backed borrowers.

In addition to these management fees, the survey showed direct lending private partnerships charged an additional 0.42% of NAV in nonmanagement expenses, including administrative costs, custody, professional fees, and other costs. Together with management fees, total fees and expenses for direct lending private partnerships are found to equal 3.56% of net asset value.

COMPARISONS TO BDC FEES

Fees are higher for BDCs when compared to private partnerships. The all-in fee of 3.56% of NAV found for private partnerships compares to 4.79% for BDCs, a significant 1.23% difference.[4] The higher fee for BDCs is not explained by greater leverage. The asset-weighted average leverage for private partnerships equals 1.25×, as reported in Exhibit 18.1, which is greater than the 1.09× asset-weighted average leverage for BDCs. Corrected for the difference in leverage, the 1.23% fee difference would be higher.

Several reasons explain the higher fees for BDCs. BDC management fee rates are slightly higher compared to private partnerships, but importantly, those rates are applied to gross assets for virtually all BDCs but only 70% of private partnerships charge management fees on gross assets. The 1.99% effective management fee on net private partnership assets compares to 2.35% for BDCs. Second, BDC incentive fees average 16.9% compared to 12.9% for private partnerships. This difference in incentive fee rate causes BDCs to charge roughly 59 basis points more on net assets compared to private partnerships. Finally, BDC administrative costs are higher, averaging 70 basis points on net assets compared to 42 basis points for private partnerships. Summing the higher BDC management fees (0.36%), the higher incentive fees (0.59%), and the higher administrative costs (0.28%) equals 1.23%, the all-in difference between BDC and private partnership fees.

The recent success of stay-private BDCs is based in part on bringing down fees. Several BDC launches have significantly cut fees in hopes of rapid fundraising.

DIRECT LENDING FEES AND ALIGNMENT OF INTEREST

Investors in direct lending should be aware of three issues with the fee structures common to private partnerships and BDCs that may cause the financial interests of managers and investors to part.

---

[4]Asset-weighted annualized fees paid over the previous three years ending March 31, 2022, to all 87 publicly traded and private nontraded BDCs whose loan assets comprise the CDLI.

- The first is charging incentive fees on interest income, the primary source of private debt return that reflects payment to the lender for taking credit risk. There is no reason for incentive fees to be earned on earnings that reflect the return to beta, in this case credit risk. Further, such a structure is only going to incentivize the lender to take more credit risk so as to get greater yield and, hence, incentive fees. Better that the lender receives incentive compensation for avoiding or minimizing losses, though unfortunately such fee structures are rare. What is worse is BDCs typically have separate incentive fees for income and gains (losses). This means BDC lenders potentially can incur damaging credit losses and still collect an incentive fee on income.
- Second is the majority of lenders charge fees on gross assets rather than net assets. This gives the lender an incentive to prioritize leverage to maximize management fees, doubling the amount for the average manager. Similar to (1), the incentive is to take risk.
- Third is lender incentive fees generally have a low hurdle rate, less than unlevered loan yields, with a 100% catch-up after meeting the hurdle. In private equity the catch-up generally equals 50%. This again encourages the lender to maximize yield sufficient to earn the entire catch-up and nothing more. Such a severe fee step up and step down can lead lenders to make decisions that are not in the investor's interest.

Fortunately, direct lending fee levels and structure are moving in the right direction and some individual lenders are offering attractive terms to their investors.

CHAPTER 20

Portfolio Construction

Today, virtually all institutional investors follow the same four-step process when constructing a multi-asset portfolio. Step one is to identify asset classes that might be considered as part of a multi-asset portfolio. Generally, these asset classes have positive long-term real returns. Other asset class factors considered are short-term return volatility, correlation to other asset classes, liquidity, and market size. Step two is adopting a benchmark index for each asset class that will represent it both in the asset allocation and portfolio monitoring processes. The third step is selecting a target mix of asset classes that will comprise a portfolio that best meets client objectives. And the final step is structuring/selecting securities or funds that will constitute each asset class with the objective of mirroring or exceeding the benchmark index in some beneficial way. Sounds straightforward, but investors often encounter frustrations in implementing this process. This chapter focuses on how private debt has worked its way into the institutional multi-asset mainstream and what the challenges have been.

DIRECT LENDING BENCHMARKS

Investors, as fiduciaries, require a means to measure the performance of managers to whom investment discretion is being given and fees paid. With private assets portfolios there are three general approaches to benchmark selection, none of which is ideal.

The first option is to find the publicly traded index that is most representative of the private asset portfolio in question. For private real estate this is a REIT index. For private equity it's the Russell 3000 Index or similar index. The closest public equivalent index for corporate direct lending is either the Morningstar LSTA US Leveraged Loan 100 Index or Credit Suisse Leveraged Loan Index. Private assets can generally outperform these public equivalent indexes over longer periods of time but over the short term there can be wide discrepancies between the private asset class and the public index. It becomes difficult to tell whether wide differences are attributable to the manager(s) selected or the failure of the public benchmark to adequately capture private asset characteristics that causes performance to diverge from the public benchmark.

The second option is to use performance data from vendors that produce return universes of similar funds and composites from data collected on individual funds. Useful and comprehensive fund universe data is available for most private equity and real estate portfolios, but not yet for private debt until very recently. Cambridge Associates, Burgiss, and Prequin are three commercial vendors that now provide private debt return universes. But the problem with universes of comparable funds is that the data collection process can be subject to selection biases that may overstate actual achievable returns. As well, composite returns based on the databases may not reflect the specific investment strategy being followed by the investor. Therefore, these universe databases often lack information on underlying company holdings that would help define an appropriate benchmark for portfolio construction purposes.

The third option is an index constructed of actual private securities. A good example is the NCREIF Property Index[1] (NPI), which consists of thousands of commercial real estate properties across the United States and whose data are collected quarterly and consolidated into industry-wide information and index returns. Unfortunately, there is no equivalent database and index available for private equity. The CDLI is constructed in the same way as the NPI except the source of its data is public filings while NPI data are submitted to NCREIF by fund managers. The NPI and CDLI are good performance comparisons with actual portfolios, except both the NPI and CDLI are before all fees and expenses and private asset managers almost always report performance net of fees and expenses, making performance comparisons accurate only if adjustments for fees are made.

THE IMPORTANCE OF A BENCHMARK

Exhibit 20.1 examines institutional asset class performance as compared to commonly used benchmarks. The distribution of asset class returns covering the ten-year period ending June 30, 2021, is shown across seven major asset classes used by 65 state pension systems. Pension assets for these

---

[1]National Counsel of Real Estate Investment Fiduciaries.

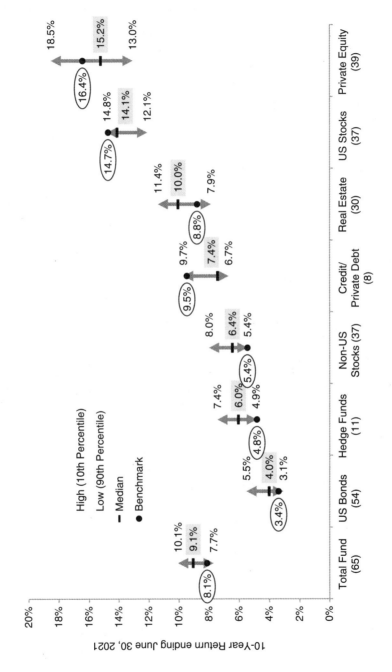

EXHIBIT 20.1 Ten-year state pension fund returns ending June 30, 2021, total fund and by asset class.

65 systems total over $3.5 trillion and are a good representation of how institutional capital is managed.[2] Not all 65 state pensions that reported ten-year total fund returns ended June 30, 2021, also reported all asset class returns. The number of state funds represented in each asset class distribution is located below the asset class labels along the horizontal axis.

The arrows in Exhibit 20.1 display the range of individual state pension returns from low (the 90th percentile return) to high (the 10th percentile return) along with their values. Median returns are shown on the right with a dash mark depicting where within the arrow the value falls. Finally, a black dot is shown for each asset class identifying the benchmark commonly used for each asset class. The benchmark return is identified by the circled value to the left of the arrow.

Exhibit 20.2 shows additional information, including the benchmarks used for each asset class and the 10th–90th mid-range return spread within each asset class. This spread is useful in understanding the extent to which investment professionals constructing asset class portfolios track benchmark returns.

Several observations that should be comforting to investors come from Exhibits 20.1 and 20.2. The first is that higher risk asset classes show higher return. Bonds have the lowest return and the lowest risk. Stocks have the highest return and highest risk among liquid asset classes. The performance of non-US stocks is probably a disappointment over the ten-year period, but when combined with US stocks, which many argue is more appropriate, the global performance of stocks (~10%) is about where it is expected to be.

The second observation is that private asset classes have performed better than public asset classes. Private equity achieved the highest return, with a 15.18% median return among state pensions, which was greater than the 14.10% and 6.45% median returns for public US and non-US stocks, respectively. Private equity is generally distributed about 70% to US partnerships and 30% to non-US partnerships, so an equivalent weighted public stock equivalent would be 11.81%.[3] Consequently, state pensions earned a return that was 3.36% (15.18% minus 11.81%) higher on their private equity than they would otherwise have earned on their public equity. It is not surprising these numbers are driving state pensions to allocate more assets to private equity.

Private real estate returned 10.04% for the ten-year period and was the next highest returning private asset class, as most might expect. Most

---

[2]Data is sourced from state pension Annual Comprehensive Financial Reports (ACFRs).

[3]Equals $0.7 \times 14.10\% + 0.3 \times 6.45\%$.

	Total Fund	US Bonds	Hedge Funds	Non-US Stocks	Credit/Pri-vate Debt	Real Estate	US Stocks	Private Equity
10th Percentile	10.07%	5.52%	7.45%	7.99%	9.70%	11.37%	14.77%	18.47%
Median Return	9.07%	4.01%	6.05%	6.45%	7.42%	10.04%	14.10%	15.18%
90th Percentile	7.70%	3.09%	4.89%	5.44%	6.69%	7.85%	12.08%	13.04%
Benchmark Return	8.13%	3.40%	4.82%	5.45%	9.46%	8.78%	14.70%	16.39%
Benchmark Percentile	80%	77%	100%	90%	37%	80%	13%	35%
10th–90th Mid-Range	2.37%	2.43%	2.56%	2.55%	3.01%	3.52%	2.68%	5.43%
Count	65	54	11	37	8	30	37	39

Benchmarks:

Total Fund	70% Global Stocks (MSCI ACWI Index), 30% Fixed Income
US Bonds	Bloomberg Aggregate Bond Index
Hedge Funds	HFRI Fund of Funds Index
Non-US Stocks	MSCI ACWI ex US Index
Credit/Private Debt	CDLI
Real Estate	NCREIF Index (NPI)
US Stocks	Russell 3000 Index
Private Equity	Cambridge Associates Private Equity Index

EXHIBIT 20.2 Distribution of state pension asset class returns, total fund and by asset class.

state pensions do not allocate much, if any, to public REITs because of their smaller size and very high volatility. For the same ten-year period, REITs, as measured by the FTSE NAREIT Equity REIT Index, returned 9.34%, which was less than what state pensions earned on the private real estate portfolios.

Our third observation relates to private debt, only now are there a sufficient number of public funds allocating directly to private debt with ten-year track records that some conclusions can be drawn. Institutional investors use terms such as *credit*, *private credit*, or *private debt* to describe a newly forming asset class. The composition of most of these allocations is a mix of direct lending and opportunistic credit, though some investors also include smaller allocations to public high-yield bonds, broadly syndicated loans, and distressed debt. There are now eight state pension systems with dedicated policy allocations to this asset class with ten-year track records.

Selecting a benchmark for a dedicated credit asset class has been a challenge for institutional investors. Thus far, the majority have chosen to use publicly traded benchmarks such as the Morningstar LSTA US Leveraged Loan 100 Index or the Bloomberg High Yield Corporate Bond Index plus a 1–2% return premium. This approach will generally produce low benchmark returns as compared to the likely performance of private debt. For example, the Morningstar LSTA US Leveraged Loan 100 Index returned just 4.06% annualized over the ten-year period shown in Exhibit 20.1. This proposed benchmark would have fallen below all actual state pension private debt returns even with a 2% return premium tacked on. Although an easy benchmark to beat if invested in private debt, a public credit index fails to represent the types of credit in virtually all private debt allocations.

The CDLI is shown as a benchmark in Exhibit 20.1. Its 9.5% annualized return, while ranking high among actual private debt returns, is a better benchmark because of its representation. Should investors want to include some allocation to public credit with their credit allocations, a better benchmark scheme would be percentage allocations to CDLI and the Morningstar LSTA US Leveraged Loan 100 Index.

The third observation is perhaps more unsettling to investors in alternative investments. Exhibit 20.2 reports the dispersion of individual state pension asset class outcomes, measured by the 10th–90th mid-range statistic, is more pronounced in private asset classes than public asset classes. This may suggest institutional investors are having a much harder time deciding how to construct the private portfolios that they want to allocate to from a top-down asset allocation perspective. Private debt allocations are equally vulnerable to this phenomenon, with a 3.01% mid-range value.

The distribution of returns for public asset classes, measured by the 10th–90th mid-range, is about the same: 2.68% for US stocks, 2.55% for non-US stocks, and 2.43% for US bonds. Portfolio construction for all three of these asset classes involve the wide use of indexing or active risk diversification brought by using multiple managers that individually are well diversified and focused on benchmark risk, the result of returns varying significantly from benchmark returns. The comparatively tight dispersion in returns across these three asset classes reflects a portfolio construction process among institutional investors that is, for the most part, very tightly controlled and driven by the portfolio construction of the targeted benchmark index.

The ten-year returns for hedge funds are also tightly dispersed with a 2.56% mid-range similar to public asset classes. The low dispersion for hedge funds may be attributable to a well-established and accepted benchmark, the HFRI Fund-of-Funds Index.

Exhibits 20.1 and 20.2 suggest that institutional investors need to recognize that portfolio construction *within* private asset classes can be as important as the amounts allocated to these asset classes. In short, portfolio construction may be more important than asset allocation when it comes to private assets.

And regarding the emerging private debt asset class, institutional investors will likely migrate benchmarks like the CDLI that capture returns of private debt investments rather than an often disconnected public index alternative.

THE CDLI AS A PRIVATE DEBT BENCHMARK

The challenges to finding a single benchmark that serve both objectives of performance measurement comparison and portfolio construction may be too great for private debt generally and corporate direct lending specifically. The CDLI has the best chance, given its similarity in construction to the NPI and the general, though not unanimous, acceptance of that index as a benchmark for equity real estate allocations.

There are six characteristics of good benchmarks:[4]

■ Unambiguous
■ Investable
■ Measurable

---

[4]Jeffrey V. Bailey, Thomas M. Richards, and David E. Tierney, "Benchmark Portfolios and the Manager/Plan Sponsor Relationship," *Current Topics in Investment Management* (Harper & Row, 1990).

▪ Appropriate
▪ Reflective of current investment opinions
▪ Specified in advance

Unambiguous means the securities and asset values in the index are known. The loan securities in the CDLI and their fair values are published quarterly in ten-Q/K SEC filings, thereby meeting this criterion. Other useful information included in the quarterly 10-Q/Ks includes specific borrower, industry classification, yields, and seniority.

Investable means the securities are available to be held as a passive investment if the investor wants to forgo active management. This criterion is not suited for private assets since it is the active manager who creates the security or loan in this case. However, the CDLI is composed of direct loans within BDCs, most of which are publicly traded and index funds of BDCs that exist for investors who choose that option. Conceptually, the CDLI is available as a passive investment option through a BDC index fund but the BDC index fund is much more volatile.

Measurable means a return on the benchmark can be calculated on a regular basis and within a reasonable time. The CDLI is published within three months after quarter-end. While not as timely as public indexes, which are updated at end of day, the timing of the CDLI is similar to the NPI and a full quarter ahead of the publication of most private fund universe data.

Appropriate means the index reflects the activity or investment style of the manager. The CDLI fits this criterion by the simple fact that it is composed of the loans managers underwrite.

Reflective means the manager is knowledgeable of the securities in the index. Unlike public securities, where the assumption of perfect information creates market efficiency, the private markets are characterized by information asymmetry where managers possess proprietary information on the securities they underwrite. However, the disclosure of the names of borrowers in the CDLI provides all managers the opportunity to acquire information about the borrower and participate in refinancings. Therefore, the CDLI meets the *reflective* requirement of a good benchmark to the closest extent available to a private benchmark.

Specified in advance means the benchmark is known to the manager in advance of the evaluation period. The CDLI meets this criterion with the only qualification being the three-month lag in reporting quarterly returns, but with the understanding that private asset reporting can't be as continuous as with publicly traded securities.

With the understanding that private asset benchmarks by their very nature can't perfectly fit the criteria laid out for the ideal benchmark, the

CDLI meets five of the six criteria and falls short to a degree on *investability* because of its gross-of-fee calculation. The CDLI could be adjusted for fees, however, by deducting an appropriate fee rate. By contrast, an equivalent public benchmark, such as the Morningstar LSTA US Leveraged Loan 100 Index, falls short on the *appropriate* criterion, meaning the broadly syndicated loans within the Morningstar LSTA US Leveraged Loan 100 Index are not middle market loans that are appropriate securities for the direct loan manager's portfolio. Fund universes and composite returns based on them fall short on the *investability* and *reflective* criteria. Some private funds in the universe are not available to investors and, therefore, not investable. Also, private fund holdings are considered intellectual property by the managers and not disclosed. Therefore, managers have no information about the underlying holdings against which they are being evaluated.

In summary, there is no ideal benchmark for direct lending, but this is also a problem that applies to all private asset classes. While the most common benchmark used currently is an equivalent public index, like the Morningstar LSTA US Leveraged Loan 100 Index or the Bloomberg High Yield Bond Index, more investors are shifting to the CDLI because it better represents what loan managers invest in.

DIVERSIFICATION

Some of the early investors in direct lending selected just one or a couple of direct lenders, perhaps to gain understanding of the asset class or as an opportunistic investment within private equity. Now that institutional investors are beginning to make larger and targeted allocations to private debt as an asset class, a more structured approach to portfolio construction is needed.

Leaving the benchmark choice aside, the presence of direct loan risk factors (Exhibit 11.1) and loan manager exposures to those risk factors (Exhibit 17.3) provide useful guidance for portfolio construction.

First is the recognition that no one loan manager can represent the US corporate middle market for direct loans. In fact, it is not even close. Not only does the average manager have too few loans but also each manager has different exposures to risk factors and premiums. Unless the fiduciary wants to provide long-term direction on what parts of the direct loan market are most favorable—and they don't—then a multiple-manager structure is an absolute requirement.

Regarding risk factor exposures, fiduciaries should target the aggregate exposures of the direct loan market, as represented by the CDLI, when they are selecting direct lenders as a group. Markets tend toward efficiency, even private ones, and aggregate characteristics are more likely to produce the best risk-adjusted returns. Given the more focused tendencies of individual loan managers as reported in Exhibit 17.3, it will likely take five or more direct lenders to achieve a portfolio that sufficiently captures the variety in middle market loans.

Second is the recognition that the lack of diversification among managers will likely expose the overall portfolio to other factor risks that are diversifiable with likely no sacrifice in long-term return. These include sponsor risk and industry risk. Approximately 75% or more of borrowers are sponsored-backed. In a typical direct lender profile, sponsor-backed loans are not broadly diversified across private equity firms but instead one or a few firms represent an outsized percentage of loans originated by the direct lender. By itself, this is not necessarily a bad thing as the lender may have a very good relationship with one or two private equity firms that result in regular deal flow with benefits that can be passed along to investors. However, a portfolio consisting of only one or two direct lenders has a good chance of having excessive exposure to a few private equity firms. In effect, the investor ends up with not only direct lender manager risk but also private equity manager risk. A portfolio with multiple direct lenders will diversify the private equity firm risk underlying the sponsor-backed loans made by the direct lenders.

The US corporate middle market is well diversified across industries. Investors will likely take on unnecessary and non-compensated risk by concentrating loans in one industry or subset of industries. That industry risk increases the probability of defaults. From a practical perspective, this was recently illustrated during the oil crisis in 2015 and 2016. A lender skilled at picking energy borrowers would still produce outsized realized and unrealized losses because of the industry downturn, even though the lender's borrower performed better when compared to the average energy borrower.

Exhibit 20.3 reports Global Industry Classification Standard (GICS) sector weights for direct corporate loans in the CDLI at March 31, 2022. One modification has been made to the sectors. An "Other" sector replaces the GICS Real Estate sector because the direct lending represents corporate, not real estate loans. The "Other" category captures mostly structured financial assets collateralized by corporate loans.

The pie chart in Exhibit 20.3 shows that the direct lending market is well diversified across GICS sectors. The largest sector is information technology

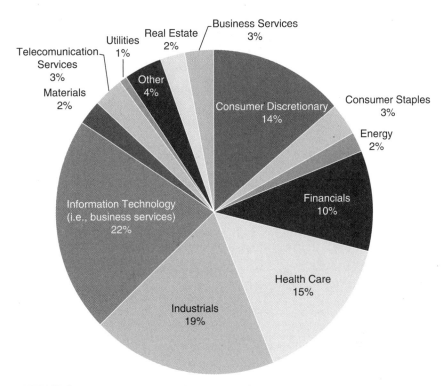

EXHIBIT 20.3 CDLI industry weightings, March 31, 2022.

at 22% of total loan assets, with the next two largest sectors, industrials and health care, comprising 19% and 15%, respectively, of total loan assets.

Exhibit 20.4 provides GICS sector weights for the Russell 2000 Index of middle market and smaller company stocks, which should have industry weightings similar to direct middle market loans.

Russell 2000 Index sector weightings for stocks are very similar to the CDLI sector weightings for direct loans. Differences lie in two sectors. Financials represent 16% of the Russell 2000 Index and is one of its largest sectors, while representing just 10% of the CDLI. This difference is likely explained by middle market banks not needing access to direct loans through the private markets when they have customer deposits to finance their investment activities. The second difference is the 8% weighting to real estate in the Russell 2000 Index and 2% weighting in CDLI. In the other direction, information technology represents 22% of the CDLI but a much lower 15% of the Russell 2000 Index.

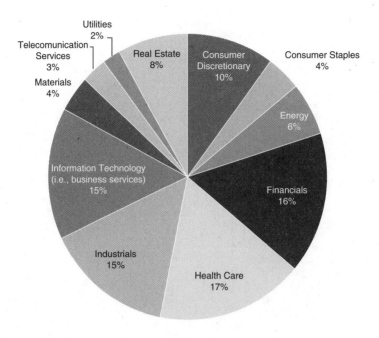

EXHIBIT 20.4   Russell 2000 industry weightings, March 31, 2022.

A well-constructed portfolio of direct loans should produce a diversified sector profile like that found in Exhibit 20.3. This is much more likely to be achieved when multiple managers are used because individual direct loan managers seldom have a portfolio of loans that is sector balanced. Unlike traditional stock and bond managers who can easily optimize portfolios to ensure sector diversification, direct lending managers have much greater difficulty creating sector weighting neutrality, even if they had a desire to do so. Consequently, investors need to consider the sector imbalances in the managers they select and actively pursue combinations of managers that achieve sector diversification.

Diversification is perhaps best measured non-statistically by the number of individual loans (credits) in the overall portfolio. The larger the number of credits, the more credit losses will approach and eventually equal market averages, in this case the realized credit losses for the CDLI and over 10,000 loan holdings. The investor reaches that extreme by hiring all 80+ direct lenders represented in the CDLI. Obviously, executing on that strategy is administratively costly unless the investor builds a portfolio of publicly traded BDCs. A combined portfolio that held 250 to 500 individual credits would seem appropriate for an objective to achieve risk-adjusted returns at or above the CDLI. With leverage, the number of credits might be even greater.

The final factor is the level of confidence in the abilities of the direct lender, primarily to underwrite risk well and produce below-market credit losses. Qualitative factors and quantitative factors, such as those covered in Chapter 17, are important. Most institutional investors err on the side of more managers when constructing a portfolio and narrow the list over time as experience reveals a clearer picture of manager skill.

Top-performing institutional investors implement disciplined and diversified portfolio construction techniques to asset classes. As allocations to direct lending and private debt increase, investors need to follow the same best practices for portfolio construction followed in other private asset classes. There is no single best answer, but having a good benchmark and guidelines to maintain diversification are necessary for favorable long-term outcomes.

CHAPTER 21

Expected Returns and Risks from Direct Lending

Previous chapters discussed the different dimensions of corporate direct lending. This chapter and Chapter 22 provide an institutional framework for assessing direct lending relative to other asset classes and determining the appropriate allocation to direct lending within an overall portfolio.

Somewhat surprisingly, the institutional approach to asset allocation has not changed much since the 1980s. Prior to 1980, a centralized top-down approach to asset allocation did not exist. Instead, institutional investors allocated assets to a few good balanced managers, who in turn made decisions as to how to allocate assets across different asset classes, which at that time were only a handful. Pensions, endowments, and foundations (collectively, fund sponsors) moved to a single allocator model in the 1980s because the balanced manager approach showed poor returns, charged high fees, and was not integrated with benefit obligations and spending rates. Consultants, who previously focused almost exclusively on manager selection, emerged to assist their institutional clients with asset allocation and asset-liability management.

With control of asset allocation, fund sponsors and their advisors forecast long-term return and risk for individual asset classes, define an "efficient frontier" of asset mixes that maximize return at different levels of risk, and select the asset mix from the efficient frontier that best fits the risk-taking desired by the fund sponsor. The efficient frontier portfolio that best matches the level of risk desired by the fund sponsor is called the optimal portfolio, or more frequently, the policy asset mix, and becomes part of the fund sponsor's investment policy statement. This process, known as an asset allocation study, is repeated every three to five years. Most asset allocation studies do not closely integrate liabilities into the selection of the policy asset mix except for corporate pension plans that have less tolerance for variability of required pension contributions. These plans have sought to eliminate changes in their unfunded liabilities by matching the interest rate risk (duration) of their assets with that of their liabilities, which typically is in the 9- to 12-year range.

The growth of corporate direct lending, or more broadly private debt, among institutional investors will partly depend on its defined role within the context of asset allocation studies. A critical step will be for investment consultants, who have great influence over asset allocation decisions, to judge private debt as an investment that is sufficiently permanent, scalable, and unique in terms of possessing investment characteristics that are not otherwise incorporated in other mainstream asset classes already widely used in asset allocation studies. If this happens, private debt will become more widely used as a distinct asset class for asset allocation studies, and potentially a permanent fixture in policy asset mixes. That is now happening in earnest, as more and more of the largest US public pension systems are including private debt as a separate asset class within their policy asset mixes, at levels up to 20% of total assets and an average allocation equal to 6.39% for those pension funds that have a designated allocation to private debt.[1]

In cases where private debt is *not* modeled by institutions as a separate asset class, another factor that will affect the growth of its adoption is the choice of the broader asset class within which private debt is considered a subcategory. In some cases, private debt is included within a private equity or private assets program. Since most institutions view private equity as a return-enhancing strategy, private debt, even though it may have superior risk-adjusted returns than private equity, might be viewed as having a drag on performance. This can have a particularly dampening effect on the demand for private debt in cases where investment staff receive performance-based compensation. This can work in the opposite way when private debt is included within a broader fixed income allocation. In these cases, private debt can significantly enhance the yield and return profile of a public fixed income portfolio, even alongside high-yield bonds and other non-investment grade debt exposure.

Chapter 8 presented the case for treating credit as a separate asset class. The purpose of this chapter is to provide the inputs necessary to integrate private debt into an asset allocation study.

---

[1]Cliffwater 2021 annual state pension study.

EXPECTED RETURN

The following equation gives a simple and concise expression for determining expected return.

$$Expected\ Return = [Cash\ Yield + Cash\ Flow\ Growth] + Change\ in\ Valuation$$
$$+ Manager\ Alpha$$

The two variables in brackets represent the strategic component of return because they incorporate long-term asset class fundamentals, which returns will eventually mirror. The sum of current cash yield plus cash flow growth is generally referred to as the Gordon model. Change in valuation measures asset price changes that would come about, for example, if price-earnings ratios changed, if the yield curve shifted up or down, or if overall credit spreads shifted. Valuation changes are viewed as sources of short-term volatility, with limited impact on long-term returns. Therefore, this component is generally not included in the expected return estimate used in asset allocation studies. Finally, manager alpha is the concept of managers creating idiosyncratic returns not attributable to the general market. Since manager alpha is highly variable and ephemeral, it generally has been industry practice not to include manager alpha in expected returns. The exception is for those asset classes that would otherwise not be considered for inclusion except for a significant, positive contribution from manager alpha.

There are two asset classes for which manager alpha is a significant contributor to expected returns, helping to drive allocations in a policy investment mix. The first is private equity. Allocators typically assume a return premium over public equity when developing their private equity expected returns, usually in the range of 3–5%. This premium might partly be attributable to a liquidity premium, in which case it is not alpha and would be reflected in an otherwise higher current cash yield compared to public stocks. The other source of the return premium is manager alpha, which could come from opportunistically buying companies below their intrinsic value or making improvements to the company's revenue growth and/or profitability in ways unique to the manager. For most asset classes, the uncertainty in forecasting manager alpha is high because these markets are generally efficient, and manager alpha has not been found to be significant and persistent over an extended period. Private equity has been an exception to this, where excess returns have been significant and persistent.

For example, data from state pension systems covering the period from 2000 to 2021 show private equity portfolio returns in aggregate earned net returns equal to 11.0%, annualized, which exceeded public equity returns by 4.1%, justifying an expected return premium in the 3–5% range.[2]

The second asset class where manager alpha is integral to its expected return is hedge funds. A 2–5% manager alpha is a typical range for modeling hedge fund expected returns. Also, investors don't generally think about cash yield and cash flow growth in the context of hedge funds. Instead, a forecast of equity beta gives a percentage level of participation in overall stock market cash yield and cash flow growth. For example, if hedge funds are expected to have an equity beta equal to 0.20, and if expected stock cash yield plus cash flow growth equals 7%, then hedge funds will be expected to derive a 1.4% return (0.20 × 7%) from its exposure to stocks. The sum of 1.4% and the level of manager alpha the allocator selects equals the expected return for hedge funds.

This backdrop should be useful for developing an expected return for corporate direct lending that is consistent with how expected returns are developed for other asset classes in an asset allocation study.

Fortunately, developing expected returns for corporate direct lending is straightforward with a likely lower estimation error than most other asset classes. Despite this, there are several nuances to consider.

Using this expected return equation, a first try at forecasting cash yield might be either the current yield or yield-to-three-year takeout for the CDLI. The current yield on the CDLI is probably a better measure for calculating expected return because if NAV is at a premium or discount to principal value, it assumes no amortization, while yield-to-three-year takeout assumes a three-year amortization window and, if used, would overstate long-term expected returns. The current yield on the CDLI was 7.77% on March 31, 2022.

An adjustment to cash yield might be for expected changes in short-term rates over the ten-year forecasting period. Historically, short-term rates have tracked expected inflation, but on March 31, 2022, the three-month Treasury bill was yielding just 0.48%, which was well below the 2.47% expected inflation over subsequent ten years.[3] Depending on when T-bill yields rise,[4] an upward adjustment from the 7.77% March CDLI current yield to an expected 9.76% ten-year CDLI current yield[5] is warranted because direct loan benchmark rates are effectively tied to T-bill yields.

---

[2] "Long-Term Private Equity Performance: 2000 to 2021," Stephen Nesbitt, Cliffwater LLC, June 13, 2022.

[3] The ten-year break-even inflation rate on March 31 equaled 2.83%.

[4] As of this writing (September 1, 2022), T-bill rates had already risen to 2.87%.

[5] 9.76% = 7.77% + (2.47% − 0.48%).

Using the 9.76% adjusted CDLI current yield also assumes the risk premiums within the corporate direct lending market will remain consistent with the premiums measured on March 31, 2022. While the current premiums undoubtedly will move around over time, their current value will likely be an unbiased estimate of future premiums. Another approach could be to look at historical risk premiums or historical current yields for corporate direct lending and use those. The problem with this approach is that it ignores the starting point, to which expected returns can be very sensitive, even over ten-year periods.

The second component of expected return—cash flow growth—is likely a negative number for direct lending and should be set to equal expected realized credit losses over the ten-year forecasting period. The 1.08% annual rate in realized credit losses should be a good first approximation of future expected credit losses. Lower credit losses might be used if the forecast was based on the presumed selection of more-skilled managers.

Finally, change in valuation is generally ignored for asset allocation studies. It is also less important for middle market direct lending where fundamentals and valuations are more stable and, unlike stock price-earnings ratios, valuations are not subject to wide swings. Manager alpha can also be ignored for expected return. CDLI returns and fundamentals reflect the weighted average efforts of the underlying managers, and if manager alpha exists, it is already embedded into cash yield and cash flow growth.

Exhibit 21.1 provides a calculation for ten-year return forecasts for corporate direct lending that would be suitable inputs into present-day institutional asset allocation studies. Two prospective portfolios are modeled. The first column represents an unlevered direct lending portfolio, and the second column represents a typical 1.00× levered portfolio.

The assumptions in lines 1 to 8 are intended to mirror the typical investment characteristics and terms for a diversified direct lending portfolio. However, actual direct lending portfolio specifications and portfolio size can alter terms. Consequently, the calculations in Exhibit 21.1 should be viewed as representative for corporate direct lending on March 31, 2022. That said, direct lending returns have been remarkably stable over time, evidenced by CDLI performance, which underlies the performance of private partnerships, BDCs, and other pooled private debt vehicles.

Expected gross yield equals 9.76% (line 1) and is above the 8.76% interest income reported in Exhibit 2.3 for the CDLI during the trailing four quarters ending March 31, 2022. The higher expected yield compared to actual yield comes from anticipated increases in short-term interest rates that will affect the base reference rate for direct loans. The 9.76% gross yield is assumed to be the same for both unlevered and levered strategies. Credit losses (line 2) equal the historical average realized losses for the

		Unlevered Portfolio	Levered Portfolio
Assumptions			
1	Gross Yield on Direct Loans	9.76%	9.76%
2	Credit Loss Rate	−1.08%	−1.08%
3	Leverage	NA	1.00×
4	Management Fee (on net assets)	1.25%	1.25%
5	Incentive Fee	NA	10%
6	Preferred Return	NA	7%
7	Admin Expenses (on net assets)	0.42%	0.42%
8	Cost of Financing	NA	4.47%
Expected Return Calculation			
9	Unlevered Portfolio Cash Yield	9.76%	9.76%
10	+ Gross Yield from Leverage	NA	9.76%
11	− Interest Cost of Leverage	NA	−4.47%
12	= Gross Levered Portfolio Cash Yield	9.76%	15.05%
13	− Expected Credit Loss	−1.08%	−2.16%
14	= Net Yield before Fees	8.68%	12.89%
15	− Management Fees	−1.25%	−1.25%
16	− Administrative Expenses	−0.42%	−0.42%
17	= Net Yield after Mgmt Fees and Admin Expenses	7.01%	11.22%
18	− Incentive Fees	NA	−1.12%
19	= Expected Return on Direct Lending	7.01%	10.01%
Notes			
20	Total Mgmt and Incentive Fees	1.25%	2.37%
21	Fees as % of Net Yield Before Fees	14%	18%

EXHIBIT 21.1 Calculation of expected return for corporate direct lending.

CDLI. Leverage at 1.00× (line 3) is roughly equal to the 1.07× average used by levered private direct lending funds (Exhibit 19.1). Management fees at 1.25% of net assets (line 4) is the most likely rate found for levered and unlevered funds charging on net assets rather than gross assets. The 10% incentive fee (line 5) is subject to a 7% preferred return (line 6). The 7% preferred return does not affect the incentive fee calculation because the full 1.12% incentive fee still results in 10.01% return, well above the 7% preferred return. Administrative expenses (line 7) are assumed to equal 0.41% but they can vary in practice. Administrative expenses are generally lower for private funds and higher for registered vehicles like BDCs. Like management fees, administrative fees can sometimes be charged on gross assets. The 4.47% cost of financing the 1.00× leverage (line 8) approximately equals the annualized weighted average interest cost for obtaining leverage among BDCs during the year ending March 31, 2022, adjusted upward for anticipated short-term T-bill interest rate hikes.

The expected return calculation starts in line 9 with a 9.76% current yield for both unlevered and levered portfolios. The expected return on the unlevered portfolio is straightforward. Deductions for credit losses (line 13), management fees (line 15), and administrative expenses (line 16) leave a net yield and expected return equal to 7.01%. Manager fees (line 20) as a percentage of net yield before fees (line 14) equals 14% (line 21).

The levered portfolio adds 9.76% (9.76% × 1.00) in leveraged yield (line 10) but deducts 4.47% (4.47% × 1.00) in financing costs, resulting in a 15.05% gross levered cash yield (line 12). Subtracting expected credit losses of 2.16% (1.08% × 2.00) gives a net yield before fees equal to 12.89%. Further subtracting management fees and administrative expenses produces a 11.22% return (line 17) on which incentive fees are based. The full incentive fee equal to 1.12% (10% × 11.22%) is deducted to arrive at an expected return equal to 10.01% for the levered direct lending portfolio (line 19). Total fees (line 20) as a percentage of net yield before fees (line 14) equals 18% (line 21).

Looked at in isolation, most institutional investors should find corporate direct lending with a 7% unlevered or 10% levered expected return compelling when compared with recent total fund returns. A 21-year performance study by Cliffwater LLC covering all state pension plans with fiscal years ended June 30, 2021, representing over $3.5 trillion in assets, found that pension assets produced a 6.69% compound annual return, less than the 7–8% actuarial assumed returns. Since the 2001 to 2021 period covers two bear markets and two bull markets, the 6.69% return would seem very representative of what pensions might achieve looking ahead. In fact, none of the 65 state pensions in the study achieved returns above their actuarial return over the 21-year period.

In the same Cliffwater study, the average annual risk for individual state pension portfolios, measured by standard deviation, equaled 10.93% for the 21 years ending June 30, 2021. By comparison, the return standard deviation for the CDLI equaled 3.69% over its 17.5-year history. In Chapter 13, risk calculations for direct lending portfolios with various amounts of leverage were derived based on historical CDLI data and fee assumptions. Risk calculations ranged from a 3.25% standard deviation for an unlevered direct lending portfolio to 9.75% standard deviation for a direct lending portfolio at 2.0× leverage. Even at the high 2.0× leverage the direct lending portfolio risk is below the average total portfolio risk for state pensions.

While the comparative time periods do not precisely overlap, it seems reasonable to conclude the addition of corporate direct lending to large state pensions would be accretive, increasing pension returns and reducing risk. This outcome would be similar if applied to other institutional asset pools.

Asset allocation studies begin with a review of return assumptions for all available asset classes. Exhibit 21.2 provides a detailed matrix with expected returns, risks, and correlations for 19 traditional and alternative asset classes, most of which are considered in asset allocation studies. Expected returns are represented by the compound return in the first column and were created using the previous equation and applying it to each asset class. Long-term expected returns for major asset classes are generally similar across consultants and other allocators.

EXPECTED RISKS

Expected risk is shown in the third column of Exhibit 21.2. The public asset classes rely on historical measures alone. The private asset classes use historical data in combination with unsmoothing techniques and links to public asset classes to arrive at risk forecasts that are more economically based, rather than accounting based. For example, the risk forecast shown for unlevered private debt, which is based on direct lending, equals 4.00%, which is slightly higher than the 3.63% historical standard deviation found in Exhibit 3.1. Unlike expected returns, risk estimates for private asset classes can vary widely across consultants, who often use different techniques for forecasting risk.

Correlations are shown in the remaining columns in Exhibit 21.2. As with expected risk, correlation forecasts rely on historical measures for the liquid asset classes and unsmoothed mechanisms for the private asset classes.

Values for the Consumer Price Index are added to the asset classes near the bottom of Exhibit 21.2, as many allocators want to gauge the sensitivity of their asset mix policies to changing inflation. This has received special interest recently with the concern over what will happen to asset values if inflation and interest rates rise. The correlations of asset classes with CPI inform investors whether asset classes will react positively to rising inflation (positive correlation) or negatively to rising inflation (negative correlation). The last row shows the inflation beta, a measure of asset class return sensitivity to changes in CPI inflation. Note that unlevered direct lending has a forecast inflation beta equal to 0.55, meaning that if inflation unexpectedly increases 5.00% over some time period, the return on direct lending will increase an additional 2.75% over the same time period. This relationship

	Compound Return (%)	Average Return (%)	Annual Risk (%)	US Stocks	Non-US Stocks	Emerging Markets	Global Equity	Core U.S. Bonds	10-yr Treasury	3M LIBOR (Cash)	10-yr TIPS	High Yield Bonds	Bank Loans	Private Real Estate (UL)	Public REITs	Private RE Partnerships	Private Equity	Hedge Funds	MLPs	Private Debt (UL)	Private Debt (L:1.0)	Public BDCs
US Stocks	7.00	8.45	17.00	1.00																		
Non-US Stocks	7.00	8.62	18.00	0.85	1.00																	
Emerging Markets	7.50	10.88	26.00	0.85	0.80	1.00																
Global Equity	7.30	8.87	17.70	0.90	0.90	0.85	1.00															
Core U.S. Bonds	3.70	3.78	4.00	0.00	0.00	0.05	0.00	1.00														
10-yr Treasury	3.00	3.32	8.00	-0.20	0.00	0.00	-0.05	0.85	1.00													
3M LIBOR (Cash)	2.55	2.57	2.00	0.00	0.00	0.05	0.00	0.05	0.00	1.00												
10-yr TIPS	3.00	3.25	7.00	0.00	0.15	0.15	0.10	0.80	0.65	-0.05	1.00											
High Yield Bonds	5.85	6.46	11.00	0.65	0.60	0.60	0.60	0.19	-0.15	-0.15	0.30	1.00										
Bank Loans	5.90	6.15	7.00	0.55	0.10	0.40	0.40	0.05	-0.20	0.20	0.30	0.80	1.00									
Private Real Estate (UL)	7.35	8.48	15.00	0.50	0.45	0.40	0.45	0.00	-0.10	0.00	0.30	0.65	0.40	1.00								
Public REITs	6.35	8.77	22.00	0.70	0.65	0.65	0.65	0.15	0.00	-0.15	0.20	0.65	0.50	0.75	1.00							
Private RE Partnerships	8.35	12.85	30.00	0.50	0.45	0.40	0.45	0.00	0.05	0.00	0.00	0.70	0.50	0.75	0.65	1.00						
Private Equity	10.00	12.00	20.00	0.80	0.70	0.60	0.70	0.00	-0.20	0.00	0.00	0.65	0.50	0.70	0.60	0.60	1.00					
Hedge Funds	5.20	5.30	4.40	0.70	0.70	0.65	0.70	0.00	-0.25	-0.10	0.15	0.70	0.80	0.20	0.55	0.20	0.30	1.00				
MLPs	7.30	10.18	24.00	0.50	0.50	0.54	0.51	-0.05	-0.20	0.00	0.15	0.65	0.65	0.35	0.35	0.35	0.50	0.60	1.00			
Private Debt (UL)	8.00	8.08	4.00	0.65	0.60	0.60	0.60	0.19	-0.15	-0.15	0.30	0.80	0.80	0.65	0.65	0.70	0.80	0.70	0.65	1.00		
Private Debt (L:1.0)	9.65	9.97	8.00	0.65	0.60	0.60	0.60	0.19	-0.15	-0.15	0.30	0.80	0.80	0.65	0.65	0.70	0.80	0.70	0.65	0.97	1.00	
Public BDCs	7.35	9.35	20.00	0.80	0.75	0.70	0.80	0.00	-0.10	0.00	0.10	0.75	0.50	0.70	0.70	0.70	0.80	0.75	0.60	0.90	0.90	1.00
CPI	2.85	2.87	2.20	-0.10	-0.05	0.40	0.00	-0.20	-0.25	0.70	0.80	-0.05	0.30	0.35	0.35	0.35	-0.10	0.50	0.20	0.30	0.30	0.10
Equity beta				0.86	0.92	1.25	1.00	0.00	-0.02	0.00	0.04	0.37	0.16	0.38	0.81	0.76	0.79	0.17	0.69	0.14	0.27	0.10
Inflation beta				-0.77	-0.40	4.73	0.00	-0.36	-0.41	0.64	2.55	0.25	0.95	2.39	3.50	4.77	-0.91	1.00	2.18	0.55	1.09	0.91

EXHIBIT 21.2 Expected return, risk, and correlations across asset classes.

189

is entirely consistent with the floating rate characteristic of direct loans. By contrast, conventional fixed income with fixed rates has a negative inflation beta. Core US bonds have an expected inflation beta equal to −0.36. This has also been consistent with rising rates over the past year when core bond portfolios with fixed interest rates have reported negative returns.

Also shown are equity betas for the asset classes in the second to last row. Direct lending is assumed to have a positive correlation with stocks and, unlevered, a 0.14 equity beta. This level of equity beta is also consistent with events during the 2008 GFC. The CDLI fell 6.5% during calendar 2008, only 15% of the 42.2% drop in global stocks, measured by the MSCI All Country World Index.

Not so favorable is the high 0.80 correlation between direct lending and private equity. This level of correlation means that 64% (R-square) of the variability in direct lending returns is explained by volatility in the underlying equity of the companies lent to. This also sounds reasonable given the Chapter 10 discussion of loans as a short-put option on corporate assets. Volatility in the valuation of corporate assets is directly absorbed by corporate debt and equity with the split determined by the amount of leverage. In comparison to other asset classes, direct lending is attractive for being high cash yielding, low risk, and with positive interest rate and inflation sensitivity. Its negatives are lack of liquidity and diversification potential. The lack of diversification also extends to publicly traded high-yield bonds and bank loans, whose correlations with direct lending are also expected to be high because the underlying borrowers in all three asset classes are companies inextricably linked to the business cycle.

CHAPTER 22

Asset Allocation

Asset allocation studies are intended to formulate diversified portfolios of asset classes that will maximize long-term return within acceptable levels of risk. With the expected returns, risks, and correlations in Exhibit 21.2 as inputs, portfolios of maximum return can be calculated for varying levels of risk using optimization software. Collectively these optimized portfolios form what is called an efficient frontier.

Ideally, investors who are fiduciaries select a portfolio risk level that is prudent, which means a risk level peers might select facing similar circumstances. This prescription for decision-making has turned circular in recent years and potentially concerning as returns for otherwise prudent portfolios are insufficient to meet enterprise required returns, such as actuarial interest rates, moving fiduciaries to select higher risk, higher return asset mixes, which are now deemed prudent because others are doing the same. The concern is that return, not risk, is now driving asset allocation studies.

Along the way fiduciaries have looked to alternative investments as a potential solution for improving return without excessive risk. Commercial equity real estate was the earliest alternative to stocks and bonds in the 1980s but lost its bloom during real estate busts of the early 1990s and again in 2008–2009. Allocators have systematically increased risk forecasts for real estate over time without commensurate increases in return. As a result, asset allocation studies have kept real estate at modest allocation levels.

Private equity, borne from the "conglomerate discount" phenomena of the 1970s, first made its way into institutional portfolios in the early 1980s and successfully produced returns well above public equities over time. Despite its success, it is unusual for private equity allocations to exceed 10% in asset allocation studies because the perceived risk is higher than public equity, and it incurs higher implementation costs. Despite these concerns, fiduciaries have been increasing their allocations to private equity in recent years.

Hedge funds emerged as an alternative investment after the 2008 GFC to achieve equity-like returns with lower bond-like risk. The thinking was that private equity and hedge funds together could produce a return that was 3–5% more than a stock and bond combination at a similar risk level. So far only one-half of that formula has worked. Private equity has exceeded public equity by significant amounts but hedge funds have struggled to produce returns commensurate with their risk, complexity, and fees.

Nonbank finance, and corporate direct lending specifically, was reinvigorated by GFC-related bank failures and subsequent regulation that drastically restricted bank risk-taking. Unlike hedge funds, which had a legacy of earlier success for endowment and family office investors, nonbank finance had less institutional history and was not viewed as a mainstream asset class. The purpose of this book has been to educate fiduciaries and investors about direct lending and other areas of private credit so they can assess whether to include these assets into the asset allocation process.

Exhibit 22.1 uses the inputs provided in Exhibit 21.2 and standard optimization software to illustrate what recommended allocations to direct lending might look like from future asset allocation studies. For these purposes, the list of asset classes has been narrowed down to eight, where direct lending is included twice, one unlevered and the other levered at 1.00×. Also, instead of showing the entire efficient frontier, only portfolios with risk levels of 10%, 12%, and 14% are displayed, with the values selected because they span risk levels taken by most institutional investors.

Section (a) in Exhibit 22.1 considers only unlevered direct lending alongside stocks, bonds, real estate, and private equity. The allocations reported in section (a) are subject to a maximum of 40% to the illiquid assets and no more than 20% in any individual private asset class. The optimal portfolio allocation to unlevered direct lending is significant, averaging 11%, and inversely related to the desired amount of risk. Also noteworthy is the distribution of allocations across private assets. For all three risk levels allocations to private assets are at their maximum limit of 40% and the redistribution from direct lending to private equity is predictable. Noteworthy is that real estate receives a smaller allocation compared to private equity and direct lending.

Section (b) expands the optimization to allow for leveraged direct lending, which alters the optimization outcomes. Levered direct lending is preferred to unlevered and receives a maximum 20% allocation because of its higher return. This is true across the three risk levels. The higher allocation to levered direct lending comes from private equity, which previously had been increased as the sole source of higher return. Real estate remains basically unchanged.

Optimized Asset Mixes

	Global Stocks	Core Bonds	Real Estate	Private Equity	UL Direct Lending	1.00x Direct Lending	Bank Loans	High-Yield Bonds	Return	Risk
(a) max 40% to private assets; max 20% to single private asset class										
Lower Risk	28%	32%	6%	20%	14%				7.37%	10%
Medium Risk	37%	23%	9%	20%	11%				7.81%	12%
Higher Risk	47%	13%	12%	20%	8%				8.18%	14%
(b) same as (a), but levered direct lending permitted										
Lower Risk	30%	30%	5%	15%	0%	20%			7.80%	10%
Medium Risk	42%	18%	6%	14%	0%	20%			8.22%	12%
Higher Risk	54%	6%	8%	13%	0%	20%			8.58%	14%
(c) same as (b), but bank loans, high-yield bonds permitted and max 25% on credit asset classes										
Lower Risk	29%	26%	5%	15%	0%	20%	5%	0%	7.86%	10%
Medium Risk	41%	14%	6%	14%	0%	20%	5%	0%	8.28%	12%
Higher Risk	53%	2%	7%	13%	0%	20%	5%	0%	8.64%	14%

EXHIBIT 22.1 Optimized portfolios with direct lending, unlevered and levered.

Section (c) adds high-yield bank loans and high-yield bonds as liquid credit-oriented asset classes to the optimization. The thought is to separate out the allocations to direct lending in sections (a) and (b) caused by liquid credit exposure from other return and risk characteristics unique to direct lending. In so doing, credit exposure (bank loans, high-yield bonds, unlevered direct lending, and levered direct lending) is limited to no more than 25% of the total portfolio. The optimized portfolios again leave an optimized allocation to levered direct lending at 20% of total assets.

As a generalization, asset allocation studies that include corporate direct lending with return and risk assumptions like those identified in Exhibit 22.2 should produce allocations to direct lending at 10–20% of total assets with a preference for modestly levered direct loans. In some ways, direct lending might be viewed as a lower risk complement to private equity. Both are desirable and their relative allocations dependent on the level of risk desired by fiduciaries making asset allocation decisions. Real estate is an important contributor to overall portfolio return and risk, but allocations are smaller compared to other private asset classes.

Hedge funds are one of the asset classes notably absent in the Exhibit 22.1 analysis. Optimal portfolios at lower risk levels (standard deviation <10%) include allocations to hedge funds, allocations to lower risk alternatives such as infrastructure, and reallocations from levered to unlevered direct lending.

CHAPTER 23

Direct Lending Performance Under a Volcker-like Fed Policy Regime

As of this writing inflation is unacceptably high and potentially systemic. The Federal Reserve, whose job is to control inflation, is reaching back 40 years, opening the inflation-fighting playbook written by Paul Volcker, Fed chairman under Ronald Reagan. Volcker's weapon of choice (or necessity) was interest rates, raising them to 18–19% in 1980–1981, up from 6–8% for most of the prior decade.[1] The Volcker playbook was successful, bringing inflation down from a high of 15.8% to 4.5% over the 1980–1984 time period. But it was costly, causing a recession that produced a 2.6% decline in real GNP and a 6% jump in the unemployment rate to 10.8%.[2]

The capital markets were not spared. Stocks fell 17% and investment grade bonds fell 11%.[3] These declines might seem modest compared to contemporary drawdowns, but they followed a decade with no real return for stocks or bonds. The non-investment grade bond market, still in its infancy, saw a 20% cumulative default rate (12% in cumulative losses) for the 1982–1985 time period.[4] Corporate earnings suffered as well, falling 18%.[5]

---

[1]Federal Funds Effective Rate (source: FRED).

[2]Normalized unemployment at the time was 5% or more, unlike today's 3% levels.

[3]S&P 500 Index and Long-Term Government Bonds (Ibbotson), respectively. Drawdowns for both stocks and bonds were dampened by the high dividend and coupon yields at the time.

[4]Standard and Poor's Ratings Direct, January 2004. The broadly syndicated loan market was nonexistent at the time and bank commercial and industrial loan data are unavailable.

[5]S&P 500 earnings per share. US corporate profits in the aggregate fell 16% (Source: FRED).

The Fed's task today might appear less challenging. The starting point for inflation is lower, 8% versus 16%, as is the starting point for interest rates, 3% versus 7%. However, there is more leverage (debt) in the financial system today after decades of innovation and post-GFC Fed accommodation. In other words, the same change in interest rates will likely have a greater impact on consumer spending and business profits than 40 years ago.

This chapter underwrites direct lending in a Volcker-like policy regime, understanding that the direct lending did not exist 40 years ago and therefore has no historical comparison. The same is nearly true for traded non-investment grade debt. In 1980 the high-yield bond market was in its infancy, awaiting Milken's reign later in the decade, and the leveraged loan market did not exist. Fortunately, the economics of direct lending are fairly straightforward, and a few reasonable inputs can give investors some confidence on the return and risk ahead for direct lending as the Fed pursues its Volcker-like policies.

DIRECT LENDING RETURN FORECAST UNDER A VOLCKER-LIKE POLICY REGIME

As described throughout these chapters, direct lending returns can be parceled into four variables, as follows:

$$Direct\ Lending\ Return = Income \pm Realized\ Gains(Losses)$$
$$\pm Unrealized\ Gains(Losses) - Fees$$

A five-year forecast shows total direct lending losses doubling compared to the previous five years, but higher credit spreads and increased base rates offset those losses completely. The five-year time frame matches in length the time period beginning December 1980 during which Volcker successfully completed his deflationary plan.

Exhibit 23.1 contains current run rates as well as return forecasts over one and five years, annualized, for a typical institutional senior secured direct lending private fund that is levered 1:1 under a Volcker-like regime that succeeds over a five-year period but suffers a significant recession in the interim.

Income

Interest income will almost certainly increase under a Volcker playbook, at least initially and for two reasons. First, direct loans are floating rate, receiving a short-term reference rate of interest generally tied to three-month

	Current Run Rate (%)	Annualized Five-Year Return Forecast (%)
3-mo. Libor	3.60	4.50
+ Credit spread w/OID	7.00	7.50
+ Levered (1:1) spread	5.00	5.00
= Interest income	15.60	17.00
+/– Realized losses	–2.00	–3.80
+/– Unrealized losses	0.00	–1.00
– Fees and expenses*	–3.14	–2.97
= Direct lending return	10.46	9.23

*Assumes 1.25% management fee on net assets, 12.5% carry, and 0.40% expenses on net assets.

EXHIBIT 23.1 Direct lending return forecast.

Libor or SOFR plus a credit spread.[6] The Fed Funds interest rate is expected to climb from 4.5% to 5.5% based on the forward rates curve and Fed pronouncements. Presumably, at this higher interest rate level the Fed expects to get inflation under control. Three-month Libor averages about 35 basis points above the Fed Funds rate.

For senior secured loans, the credit spread has averaged 6.90% over the previous five years ending June 30, 2022.[7] The higher credit spread expected over the next one and five years is a result of greater market uncertainty (higher VIX) that would most likely be associated with a Volcker scenario, as it was in 1981–1985.

However, the extra return associated with one turn of leverage remains constant, assuming that spread expansion on income also occurs with financing.

Realized Losses

Realized losses are generally delayed from the occurrence of a recession. The GFC is used to benchmark realized losses for a Volcker scenario, totaling 19% (9.5% unlevered) over five years with most of the defaults occurring

---

[6]Libor will be the reference rate for illustrative purposes, understanding that SOFR is its replacement. SOFR averages about 15–20 basis points below Libor.

[7]Credit spread equals the average yield on CDLI-S over the last five years minus the average three-month Libor yield over the last five years.

in years three through five. The unlevered 9.5% is the cumulative realized credit loss rate on the CDLI[8] for the 2008–2010 period.

Unrealized Losses

Over the five-year period, annualized unrealized losses are expected to total 1.0%. Initial unrealized losses will be higher (forecasting future realized losses) but assuming Fed policy is successful in taming inflation, any unrealized markdowns are expected to ultimately reverse.

Fees and Expenses

Management fees and expenses are 1.25% and 0.40%, respectively, on net assets, with a 12.5% incentive, representative of a top-tier direct lending manager.

ASSET CLASS COMPARISONS UNDER A VOLKER-LIKE POLICY REGIME

In Exhibit 23.2 the direct lending return forecasts for direct lending are compared to forecasts for other major liquid asset classes. The forecasts are as of September 23, 2022, and therefore *are in addition to* year-to-date gains/losses for direct lending (+1%), stocks (–20%), and investment grade bonds (–14%).

The 1.3% return forecast for stocks is characterized by an additional 22% drawdown from September 22, 2022, levels, followed by a slow recovery. The percentage decline in earnings per share is similar to that experienced during 1981–1982 and the decline in price-earnings ratio reflects the impact of projected higher interest rates. The historical 60-year relationship between interest rates and price-earnings ratio is described in Exhibit 23.3.

The equation in Exhibit 23.3 quantifies the inverse relationship between the ten-year Treasury bond yield and S&P 500 price-earnings ratio. A 1% increase in the ten-year Treasury bond is associated with a 1.23 point reduction in price-earnings ratio. At current price-earnings levels, a 1% increase in rates is associated with a 7% drop in stock prices.

---

[8]Please see disclosures at the end of this report for further information on the CDLI and CDLI-S.

	Current Cliffwater Ten-Year Expected Return (%)	Annualized Five-Year Forecast (%)	Notes
Direct Lending	**10.46**	**9.23**	**Levered 1:1, see Exhibit 1**
US Stocks	7.00	1.30	*One-year*: 18% short-term EPS decline and 1.6× drop in P/E ratio *Five-year*: EPS recovers to 2022 levels, P/E slightly below current levels to reflect higher 4.0% terminal ten-year Treasury yield
Inv. Grade Bonds	4.55	4.10	*One-year*: rise in ten-year Treasury to 5.0% *Five-year*: ten-year Treasury falls to 4.0%, 1% above 3% inflation rate
Cash	2.35	4.50	Three-month Libor

EXHIBIT 23.2 Direct Lending compared to other asset classes.

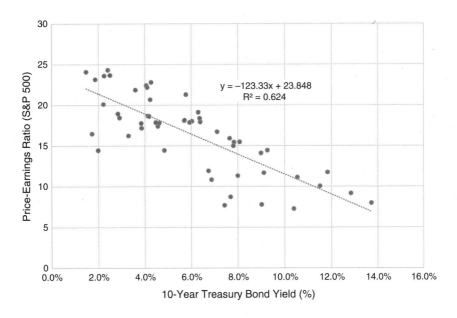

$$y = -123.33x + 23.848$$
$$R^2 = 0.624$$

EXHIBIT 23.3 60-year history of interest rates and price-earnings ratios.

The forecast negative return on investment grade bonds (Bloomberg Aggregate Bond Index) combines the expected increase in interest rates over the forecast period with the 6.4-year duration for investment grade bonds. Cash returns are expected to exceed the expected inflation rate consistent with the switch from quantitative easing to Volcker-like quantitative tightening.

Direct lending's relatively short maturity (five years), absence of interest rate risk, credit seniority, and covenant protection should help the asset class weather a Volcker-like scenario, both absolutely and relative to other asset classes.

CHAPTER 24

Enter SOFR

irect middle market loans are floating rate, meaning the lender gets paid a current short-term interest rate plus a yield spread, the size of which reflects the credit risk of the underlying borrower. The short-term interest rate or reference rate had historically been Libor or, less often, a T-bill rate. The typical Libor or T-bill maturity is three months, though a one-month maturity is sometimes used. Libor rates historically averaged 25 basis points over T-bills, but more during times of distress. Libor worked well until regulators mandated its elimination in 2023 due to charges of fraud in its calculation. The transition out of Libor and into SOFR[1] as the reference rate for fixed-income securities and derivatives is proceeding smoothly with virtually all new agreements now tied to SOFR. Since they were launched in 2021, SOFR rates have fallen between Libor and T-bill rates. An overview of SOFR is provided in this chapter because SOFR is not well understood even though it plays a critical role in private debt.

Two transition changes from Libor to SOFR are noteworthy. First, because SOFR is an overnight-only borrowing rate while most Libor-based agreements use 1-, 3-, 6-, and 12-month maturities, a fix was needed to secure equivalent SOFR maturities. A futures-based methodology published by CME Group[2] has been accepted by regulators as a solution. Therefore, expect to see references to CME Term SOFR Rates.

Second, Libor embedded a small incremental yield attributable to bank credit risk that is not present in SOFR where Treasuries are used as collateral. The market is now addressing this potential lost spread by (1) adding an explicit and separate credit spread adjustment (CSA) to SOFR or

---

[1]Secured overnight financing rate.

[2]The CME Group is the world's leading and most diverse derivatives marketplace and was born from the combination of the Chicago Mercantile Exchange and the Chicago Board of Trade. Today CME operates the following exchanges: CME, CBOT, NYMEX, and COMEX.

(2) implicitly including it in the credit spread charged to the borrower. Year-to-date, approximately two-thirds of SOFR-based agreements have used option (1), but the trend is toward option (2).

While the Libor/SOFR transition has proven uneventful to date, there are certain conventions and practices that are still in flux.

- In late 2020, global regulators formally announced that after December 31, 2021, substantially all global Libor rates will either cease publication or lack representativeness, thus removing any uncertainty surrounding the discontinuation of Libor.
- While many competing Libor replacements were contemplated, the industry has settled on SOFR as the accepted successor rate for US dollar-based contracts. SOFR is the volume-weighted median rate for overnight cash borrowings collateralized by US Treasury securities, as transacted in the repurchase agreement (i.e., repo) market.
- ARRC[3] and market participants coalesced around SOFR because (1) it is derived from an active and well-defined market with sufficient depth that makes it extraordinarily difficult to manipulate or influence ($1 trillion-plus in daily volume); (2) it is produced in a transparent, direct manner and is based on observable transactions rather than being dependent on estimates, like Libor, or derived through models; and (3) it is derived from a market that is, and promises to remain, active enough to reliably produce a rate during a wide range of market conditions, including time of stress.
- Treasury rates, which meet similar criteria, are not good reference rates because they are countercyclical. When the market experiences stress, risk-off demand bids Treasury security prices up and rates fall. SOFR is instead procyclical. When the market experiences stress, lenders demand a higher rate to give up cash, and borrowers pay a higher rate to access cash. This procyclicality comports with the proper intuition in the market between lenders and borrowers broadly.
- The two main issues with SOFR as a Libor replacement are that it is a rate representative of overnight, secured lending between market

---

[3]The Alternative Reference Rate Committee is a group of private-market participants—banks, asset managers, and regulators bodies—convened by the Federal Reserve Board and the New York Federal Reserve to help ensure a successful transition from USD LIBOR to an alternative reference rate.

participants while Libor is a rate representative of term, unsecured lending between banks.

- Because SOFR is an overnight rate and lacks a term structure, ARRC recommends the use of CME Term SOFR Rates,[4] which are published daily and are a series of forward-looking SOFR term rates derived by compounding projected overnight SOFR rates implied from futures contracts.[5] A term structure is important because lenders and borrowers prefer to have (1) a forward-looking rate that reflects the expectation of rates over the actual interest period and (2) a rate that is known and can be locked in at the beginning of the interest period, as opposed to in arrears calculations that are unknown until the end of the interest period.[6]

- Because SOFR lacks a counterparty credit risk spread (Libor was essentially an AA bank-to-bank risk spread), some lenders and borrowers are negotiating a credit spread adjustment (CSA) over term SOFR. Sometimes the CSA is flat over the term SOFR curve and sometimes it steps up over the term SOFR curve (commonly referencing a 10/15/25 spread over one-month/three-month/six-month maturities).

- It remains to be seen whether all-in lending rates include a CSA permanently (i.e., a two-part construct—term SOFR + spread + CSA) or if explicit CSAs are dropped in favor of building any compensating CSA into the overall spread (i.e., a one-part construct—term SOFR + spread).

- Note that references to CSAs are made in two different contexts: either a prospective spread (a spread that is dynamic and determined by the market of borrowers and lenders for new debt issues), or a fallback spread, which is a fixed spread ARCC recommends as fallback language for those documents that had not prior contemplated a transition away from Libor. The fallback rate recommended by the ARRC is based on

---

[4]The most commonly used US dollar Libor settings (overnight, one-month, three-month, six-month, and one-year) will cease publishing after June 30, 2023.

[5]"Inferring Term Rates from SOFR Futures Prices," Finance and Economics Discussion Series, Federal Reserve Board 2019, https://www.federalreserve.gov/econres/feds/files/2019014pap.pdf; https://www.cmegroup.com/market-data/files/cme-term-sofr-reference-rates-benchmark-methodology.pdf

[6]"Term SOFR is Here – The ARRC Recommends CME Group's Term SOFR Rates for Use," August 23, 2021, https://www.dechert.com/knowledge/onpoint/2021/8/term-sofr-is-here---the-arrc-recommends-cme-group-s-term-sofr-ra.html

the historical five-year median spread between USD Libor and compounded average of SOFR at the time of the recommendation.[7]

EARLY OBSERVATIONS

■ Of BSLs, 81% priced over SOFR instead of Libor in January 2022, and 90% in February. This compares to only 15% during the entire fourth quarter of 2021.

Base Rate	January	February
LIBOR	19%	10%
SOFR + spread (one-part construct)	22%	34%
SOFR + spread + Flat CSA 10 bps (two-part construct)	9%	9%
SOFR + spread + CSA 10/15/25 bps (two-part construct)	49%	43%
SOFR + spread + CSA "other" (two-part construct)	3%	3%

EXHIBIT 24.1   SOFR adoption rates in 2022.
Source: Refinitiv, "2022 Broadly Syndicated New Issue Loans."

■ While 60% of loans priced with some form of CSA in January 2022, 55% priced with a CSA in February 2022. Loans pricing as a one-part construct (SOFR + spread) grew from 22% of total new issues in January to 34% of new issues in February.
■ New CLO formation referencing SOFR totaled $4.9 billion during January 2022, plus $4.0 billion of SOFR-linked deal resets and refinancings,

---

[7]"Summary of the ARRC's Fallback Recommendations," October 6, 2021, https://www.newyorkfed.org/medialibrary/Microsites/arrc/files/2021/spread-adjustments-narrative-oct-6-2021

Fallback Spread Adjustments	
LIBOR tenor being replaced	Spread applied to SOFR base rate (bps)
1-month USD LIBOR	11.448
3-month USD LIBOR	26.161
6-month USD LIBOR	42.826
12-month USD LIBOR	75.513

which compares to only \$0.1 billion that priced with SOFR-linked tranches in all of 2021. Almost all SOFR-linked CLOs have priced with no explicit CSA but did price with a spread 15 to 20 bps higher than the equivalent Libor spread, effectively embedding the CSA into the spread.[8]

The Libor/SOFR transition has proven uneventful. Adopting SOFR, as well as use of the CME Group's term *SOFR curve*, has proven acceptable with broad market acceptance. Use of an explicit CSA in the corporate loan market has proven more mixed, however. While still early, the trend points to the market dropping a Libor-equivalent credit spread adjustment in favor of embedding the risk premium into a higher SOFR + spread construct.

---

[8]"CLO Libor/SOFR Transition Report," J. P. Morgan Securitized Products Research, February 2, 2022.

CHAPTER 25

European Middle Market Direct Lending

The European corporate direct lending market has grown rapidly since the early 2010s, following a similar pattern in the United States. On both sides of the Atlantic, alternative lenders are competing with commercial banks to provide leveraged financing to middle market companies and their financial sponsors.

However, important differences exist between the US and European direct lending markets. Chief among them is the slower development of private direct lenders in Europe due to a still significant regional and local banking system in Europe. European corporate sponsors value banks' lower cost of capital, relationships, prior deal history, and reliability. The European banking system is estimated to represent roughly one-third of the market, down from approximately half of the market in 2019 as direct lenders have gained market share.

Based on research into roughly 60 European direct lenders and conversations with more than 20 European middle market buyout sponsors, European private direct lenders are likely to continue increasing market share, but considerable time may pass until they achieve the level of institutional success and market share enjoyed by nonbank corporate direct lenders in the United States.

European direct lending historically exhibited a modest return premium over US direct lending, but that gap has since disappeared as spread compression has affected both markets over the last few years. In the current market, spreads are marginally wider and up-front fees approximately 1% higher for European direct loans, but when accounting for the difference in base rates, all-in expected yields are modestly higher for US direct loans. US investors seeking geographic diversification by adding a European component to their domestic direct lending portfolios should be cognizant of the risks inherent in European exposure, including the younger and smaller nature of the European market, unequal levels of experience among European direct lenders, differing creditors' rights regimes across countries, and potential currency exposure.

KEY CHARACTERISTICS OF THE EUROPEAN DIRECT LENDING MARKET

As in the US, direct lending in Europe (or *alternative lending*, as some market participants have labeled the market) represents a growing portion of the middle market–leveraged finance universe. These loans are provided by private lenders as an alternative to traditional bank finance for leveraged buyouts, debt recapitalizations, growth finance, and general corporate purposes. Borrowers are typically privately held companies controlled by a private equity sponsor, although borrowers may also be family-owned or even publicly traded. The businesses are, overall, smaller enterprises, with annual EBITDA, or operating cash flow, of less than €100 million. Occasionally, larger European direct lenders have financed upper middle market borrowers that otherwise would have been financed by the capital markets, a prominent trend seen in the US. These borrowers and/or their private equity sponsors source debt financing directly from prospective lenders as opposed to raising debt via a public issuance or a syndicated bank group. Oftentimes, the debt package is structured with the help of a financial advisor, who maintains lender relationships. By contrast, the US sponsor-lending market typically does not involve intermediaries and instead is managed directly by the direct lender and the sponsor, or often through the sponsor's internal capital markets function. In Europe, loans are provided by one or a limited number of lenders, with a plan to hold the loans to maturity. Given the relatively small size of the loan packages, usually less than €500 million in size and often less than €250 million, there is essentially no trading market.

Direct loans for the most part represent senior secured claims on the borrower's assets and are structured typically with five-year maturities. However, they can also be second lien loans, which have junior priority to senior secured loans in the event of a default, or mezzanine loans, which are subordinated to senior debt and may be secured or unsecured. An increasingly popular structure is the unitranche loan, which is a single loan facility that takes the place of a traditional senior debt-plus-mezzanine package. Unitranche loans have recently been offered at up to five times EBITDA, representing half of the enterprise value of a middle market–leveraged buyout.

European direct loans, like their US counterparts, usually carry floating rates of interest and are priced at a spread over Libor or Euribor. In today's market, unitranche loan pricing is in the range of 6–7.5% per annum over the benchmark rate. The lender's return is further enhanced by meaningful closing fees and/or an original issue discount, which can range from 1–4% of the loan commitment amount and usually average approximately 3%. Further, lenders may also negotiate to receive additional fees for loan prepayment and covenant waivers. These loan rates are comparable to those seen in similar US transactions, although the closing fees tend to be higher in Europe.

From an essentially standing start in the early 2010s, direct lending has grown across Europe in the wake of the GFC, as banks have curtailed some lending activities and new lenders have emerged to fill the gap. However, direct lenders tend to be more expensive than commercial banks, who continue to work to retain local customer relationships. While in the United States direct lenders have grown to represent approximately 85% of the middle market–leveraged lending,[1] in Europe commercial banks have represented more than one-third of the market. Banks in general offer more attractive rates than the direct lenders but are also seen as being less creative in terms of deal structuring. The UK has traditionally been the largest market for direct lending in Europe, followed by France and Germany. While new participants have emerged across Western Europe, the market remains to some degree segregated geographically, due largely to the strength of local relationships, as well as lenders being unaccustomed to creditors' rights laws outside of their local countries.

EVOLUTION OF THE EUROPEAN DIRECT LENDING MARKET

The European private debt market has existed since about 2000 in different forms, but it has more recently evolved following the 2008 GFC and implementation of Basel III risk capital and liquidity requirements. The market development occurred earlier in the US, where senior secured direct lending funds had developed during the early 2000s and emerged more definitively in 2009 and 2010 to fill the void where banks were no longer lending. By contrast, the evolution of direct lending in Europe has been more gradual, trailing the US by two to three years before the emergence of the first direct lending fund.

The banking landscape in Europe has not changed as uniformly as in the US where banks largely do not lend beyond asset-based revolvers in the US middle market. In Europe, regional banks are still very active, though their activity somewhat varies by country. Direct lending firms have gained market share by following the US model in offering unitranche products

---

[1]*S&P LCD Leveraged Lending Review.*

that compete with a traditional senior bank and private mezzanine package to meet middle market–leveraged finance needs. Buyout sponsors have accepted the unitranche solution in deals where flexibility and simplicity win over pricing. The emergence of direct lenders in Europe has also made the mezzanine product less competitive and, therefore, mezzanine providers have been forced to shift to unitranche structures or have disappeared altogether.

Though the US and Europe have similar-sized economies, the European banking system is nearly three times the size of the US market. Banks continue to be very active middle market lenders in Europe, particularly when comparing the size of the banking system as a percentage of GDP. The capital markets in the US are much more advanced, filling financing needs of upper middle market and large cap companies. In Europe, the capital markets are approximately one-quarter of the size of the US, serving an economy that is roughly the same size.

In Exhibit 25.1, European banks continue to provide a significant portion of the debt capital to middle market borrowers, based on their desire to retain local company relationships. Private equity sponsors, which generate the lion's share of leveraged loan demand in Europe, still often use local banks as they are consistent in their approach and offer financing packages that are 1–2% less expensive than those offered by alternative lenders. Private lenders have gained more acceptance by sponsors in recent years as their flexibility and speed have been sufficient to convince borrowers to move their business to the direct lenders.

US banks, by comparison, have lost most of the middle market–leveraged finance market to private direct lenders in recent years, because the banks have shrunk their balance sheets and face new regulatory constraints on leveraged loans. US borrowers and private equity sponsors have come to appreciate the speed and deal-structuring flexibility of the private lenders.

Capital structures have evolved as alternative lenders have entered the market, most notably with the introduction of the unitranche product that has started to compete with a senior bank loan plus second lien/mezzanine combination. In general, there are three types of unitranche. The first is a single loan provided by an alternative lender or club of alternative lenders, with interest rates in the current market equal to Euribor/Libor plus a spread between 6.00% and 7.50%. The second is called a bifurcated unitranche, where the loan is taken down by a partnership between a first-out senior piece typically held by a bank or other institution and a last-out piece provided by an alternative lender seeking a higher return. Both the unitranche and bifurcated unitranche provide a similar blended cost of capital to the borrower. The last structure is a combination unitranche and Holdco pay-in-kind note, which is typically unsecured and structured as a fixed-rate instrument.

	Europe	United States
Size of the corporate lending market[1]	$2.8 trillion	$10 trillion
Estimated number of alternative lenders[2]	Approx. 60 managers	Approx. 250 managers
Estimated size of private debt market[2]	$300 billion	$1.0 trillion
Fund leverage[2]	European investors prefer unlevered; managers offer dollar-levered sleeves with leverage typically up to 1.0 times investor commitments	Most managers offer unlevered and levered vehicles with leverage of 1.0 to 2.5 times investor commitments
Interest rates[3]	Typically, Libor/EURIBOR/SONIA + 600 bps to Libor/EURIBOR/SONIA + 750 bps for unitranche loans; up-front fees/OID of 1–4%	Typically, SOFR + 550 bps to SOFR + 700 bps for unitranche loans; up-front fees/OID of 0.50–2%
Average middle market leverage[4]	6.0 times debt to EBITDA	6.2 times debt to EBITDA

[1] Securities Industry and Financial Markets Association.
[2] Cliffwater Research.
[3] Based on Cliffwater Research; indicative pricing in the current market as described by managers.
[4] *S&P LCD Europe and US LBO Review Q2 2022.*

EXHIBIT 25.1 Comparison of European and US direct lending markets.

It is noteworthy in Exhibit 25.1 that direct lending terms in the current market are, for the most part, consistent between the US and European markets with the exception of the difference in base rates that is currently driving higher yields in the US. While the US market is appreciably larger than that of Europe, with more consistently experienced managers (given their longer tenures managing loan portfolios), deal structures and pricing are comparable.

Compared to the US, where there has been a structural shift of professionals leaving the leveraged finance groups of banks to form private lending firms, European banks are still active, and a similar talent exodus has not yet occurred.

The geographic distribution of European direct loans is concentrated in three countries: UK, France, and Germany. Together they represent more than two-thirds of all direct loans. Direct lenders have tended to be more focused on the UK because of strong creditor rights and high market efficiency.

CAPITAL STRUCTURE OF EUROPEAN DIRECT LOANS

As noted, most European direct lenders have made market inroads and achieved the most success with so-called unitranche structures, whereby the lender provides all of the debt finance required in a transaction under one loan facility. This structure works in place of the traditional senior bank debt–mezzanine loan combination, which has dominated middle market European leveraged lending for decades. The unitranche loan is priced at a level that essentially blends the pricing (interest rate) of the senior bank debt plus the mezzanine structure. The appeal to the borrower and deal sponsor of the unitranche model is that there is only one lender, thus obviating the need for complex inter-creditor subordination negotiations, which can help accelerate the closing process. Also, in the event of the need for future covenant waivers or debt restructurings, there is only one lender with whom the borrower needs to negotiate.

In recent years, European middle market–leveraged buyouts (the largest user of unitranche financing) have been valued at approximately 11 times EBITDA, with half of the capital being provided by the equity sponsor and the other half provided by the unitranche lender. In the European leveraged buyout market, rising purchase price multiples since 2013 have largely been addressed by higher equity contributions, which averaged 47% in the three years since 2019. Leverage levels have climbed modestly in recent years, averaging 5.7 times debt to EBITDA over the same time period.

Similarly, in the US buyout market, company valuations and debt leverage have increased since the financial crisis. In fact, average debt leverage has increased to 6.2 times EBITDA as of the second quarter of 2022, slightly higher than average leverage in Europe. Equity contributions to buyouts as a percentage of total capitalization in Europe and the US have converged in recent years to approximately 47% since 2019 after historically being higher in Europe. In any event, leverage and pricing are elevated in both markets, which bears close monitoring by direct lending investors.

RISK FACTORS

Direct lending has made significant strides in recent years in the United States and Europe, having raised and invested a meaningful amount of capital and having taken an important share of the market for middle market–leveraged finance from the commercial banks. With a multiyear head start, the US market leads Europe in terms of sophistication, depth, and experience of market participants, as they have filled a void left by banks exiting the space to a much larger degree than witnessed in Europe. However, European debt managers are expanding rapidly, especially in sponsored buyout transactions, and deal structures and pricing are largely similar across the two markets.

European direct lending market will continue to grow and gain market share, but there are several risks US investors should consider when looking at a potential allocation. The first concern is the possibility of adverse currency movements eating into euro- or sterling-based interest streams. US investors in private equity often assume the currency exposure of European investments, believing the long life and high expected returns of private equity will more than offset the impact of any currency moves. For a direct lending investor looking for a short duration, stable income investment, the risk of currency moves can be more problematic. Some European managers have instituted currency hedging procedures for their US investors, which may help alleviate the currency exposure; however, these programs do add complexity.

A second potential concern involves the inconsistency of experience of European direct lenders. While most of the US market leaders began their careers and/or firms before the GFC and have thus been through at least one severe credit downturn, some European lenders have much shorter tenures. Since the initial rise of European direct lending, credit conditions have been benign, and it remains to be seen how these newer lenders hold up during the next down cycle.

A third potential concern has to do with country risk. As noted, direct lending in Europe has been dominated by deals in the UK, France, and Germany, with those countries representing more than two-thirds of total deal flow. However, the European market remains quite fragmented, with direct lenders often focusing their efforts in specific countries, including, not surprisingly, their home markets, based on local familiarity with commercial conventions and the legal framework covering creditor's rights and insolvency. Given this home market bias, there are a number of country-specific direct lenders in Europe whose portfolios are exposed to the vagaries of those countries' economic and political developments.

While the European private debt industry continues to grow and take market share from the commercial banking system, the nonbank lending market is not as developed as it is in the US. European commercial banks continue to be active in providing middle market–leveraged finance, and sponsors value price and relationships first and foremost. Preferences are also driven by geography, as commercial banks in Europe are conscious about retaining local market share. While European direct lending provided a return premium to US direct lending structures in earlier years as the market first developed, the pricing differences have largely disappeared. Further, the direct lending market is smaller relative to the United States, and given continued active bank participation in the European middle market–leveraged finance space, it remains to be seen whether European direct lending will become as successful a market as it has become in the US.

Given the smaller size of the European market, the involvement of some less-experienced loan managers in Europe, and the similar pricing and leverage structures between the US and European buyout markets, coupled with inconsistent creditor rights regimes across European countries and the risks of adverse currency movements, US-based investors seeking geographic diversification for their direct lending portfolios should be aware of the additional issues inherent in European investments. That said, the European market continues to develop, and as the relative risk-reward balance between the two markets changes in the future, an allocation to European managers may become increasingly compelling.

CHAPTER 26

The Borrower's Perspective

US BORROWERS

A continuing concern among investors in direct loans is whether opportunities will continue to exist in the future if the tight bank regulations put in place after the GFC are somehow relaxed and commercial banks try to regain market share. With their lower cost of capital and the importance of financing costs to particularly leveraged buyout borrowers, a rewind scenario is possible but unlikely. This chapter provides narrative from US middle market private equity sponsors—the borrowers—on their decision-making process as to whether to use bank or nonbank financing. The purpose was to understand what factors other than price might influence equity sponsors on which lender—bank or nonbank—to use.

A survey of private equity firms was conducted to better understand the growth in nonbank lending in the private equity (sponsored) market. Private equity general partners (sponsors) shared that increased bank regulation, including capital requirements and limits on types of lending, has curtailed bank lending. However, sponsors cited the flexibility of nonbank lenders to structure creative deals, their ability to take on larger portions of a loan (both senior and junior), and the speed at which they can close, and their willingness to do delayed draw loans and revolvers as attractive reasons for moving business to nonbank lenders and away from traditional banks. Despite these trends, the most important consideration continues to be the relationship between the sponsor and lender, regardless of whether it is a bank or another supplier of debt financing.

The rapid post-2008 growth in nonbank middle market lending (defined as lending to companies with less than $100 million in EBITDA) has largely been attributed to increased bank regulation. Both the 2010 Dodd-Frank Act and the 2013 Inter-Agency Guidance on Leveraged Lending limited the amount of risk capital that banks can hold on their balance sheets and the amount of leverage that banks can underwrite in levered transactions.

However, research points to other important reasons for the success of nonbank lending, particularly in the middle market. To better understand the reasons for why private equity sponsors may use nonbank lenders, a broad group of 20 middle market buyout firms were surveyed and asked to share their primary considerations when looking for debt financing.

The survey showed that the most important consideration in choosing a middle market lender was the pre-existing relationship that sponsors had with their lenders, regardless of whether it was a bank or nonbank source. Every sponsor surveyed highlighted the stable, pre-existing roster of bank and nonbank lenders that they return to for financing. These relationships are built over time based on a successful history of closed deals and positive working experiences. Each sponsor placed very high importance on cultivating lenders who participate in club financing deals. Failing to make the preferred group can effectively shut a lender out of most of the sponsor's deals.

When comparing the differences in bank versus nonbank middle market lending, some recurring themes appeared. First, middle market banks have ceded market share, primarily due to a diminished ability to hold loans on their balance sheets and the need to arrange club deals. As a result, many middle and lower middle market sponsors have turned entirely to nonbank lenders to provide solutions. Nonbank lenders have become more flexible when it comes to out of the credit box transactions and tend to be a bigger participant in club deals and in junior structures. Banks still participate in clubs and can remain competitive at the senior level in terms of pricing. However, for more complex deals, middle market banks generally have tougher underwriting standards, demand a heavier amortization schedule, and require extra covenants. A full comparison is provided in Exhibit 26.1.

When sponsors were asked about the specific impact of regulation, most sponsors noted the acceleration in the share of middle and lower middle market lending toward nonbanks. Changes in bank behavior specifically attributed to regulation included the tilt toward more conservative underwriting and tighter covenants, the diminished ability to hold loans on their balance sheets and relegation to club deals, the cap on 6x leverage, and the higher principal amortization rate.

	Survey Findings
Underwriting Flexibility	Nonbank lenders tend to have more flexibility in structuring loans (leverage multiples, covenants, etc.), although for cleaner deals, banks remain competitive, particularly at senior levels of the capital structure.
Pricing	Nonbanks tend to charge a premium of 25 to 100 basis points (bps) for their flexibility. Interestingly, most sponsors have expressed low sensitivity to pricing as their higher return-on-equity requirements leads to a preference for nonbank lenders who are able to finance very attractive deals in exchange for the premium charged.
Leverage Restrictions	Most middle market sponsors noted that they do not participate in highly leveraged deals, although a few have noticed that banks are no longer participating in highly leveraged transactions. When applicable, banks tend to primarily participate in senior loans, whereas nonbank lenders are brought in for unitranche, second lien, and mezzanine structures.
Capacity and Deal Size	Middle market banks that compete for deals below $50 million in EBITDA have experienced eroding market share as their capacity to hold loans on their balance sheets has shrunk relative to the past. Additionally, nonbank lenders can accommodate add-on transactions, while banks are limited by the absolute dollar amount they can lend to any credit. Notably, investment banks that compete on deals over $50 million in EBITDA with the goal of syndication have seen only minor changes as a result of lending regulation.
Speed to Close	Almost all sponsors have noted that nonbank lenders tend to be faster due to quicker internal processes and fewer committees. Additionally, nonbanks can move quicker in refinancing and add-on transactions because of dedicated coverage that maintains closer familiarity with the credit and the sponsor.

(continued)

EXHIBIT 26.1 US sponsor survey on choosing bank versus nonbank financing.

	Survey Findings
Covenants	Banks tend to have tougher covenants than nonbank lenders. However, the differences are usually limited to one or two more covenants and are driven by the desire for nonbank lenders to be more flexible than banks. A number of sponsors also cited a requirement by banks to amortize a large amount of the deal in the loan (i.e., approximately 50% over seven years).
Reporting Requirements	Most sponsors have reported no differences, although nonbank lenders may require more detailed reporting or board observer rights (in junior structures).
Industry Expertise	Banks generally tend to have more industry expertise, but while it can be helpful, it does not seem to be high on the sponsor's wish list given that a lot of nonbank finance company professionals are former bankers with some level of industry expertise.
Access to Capital	Interestingly, a few sponsors have noted that in late 2015 and early 2016, and again during the COVID turbulence in credit markets, nonbank lenders dependent on capital markets for funding (particularly BDC platforms) lacked the ability to provide timely capital and saw reduced negotiation leverage.
Restructuring Troubled Deals	Many sponsors have not seen enough troubled deals over the past ten years to provide comments. The few that have had challenges in working out a troubled loan (and as such the importance of lender relationships in working out a troubled loan (and as such the importance of the participants in the club) as opposed to any differences in bank versus nonbank workouts. One common theme was the dislike for bank workout groups. This is a positive for nonbank finance companies, where troubled credits stay with the original coverage officer.

EXHIBIT 26.1 *(continued)*

EUROPEAN BORROWERS

The speed and certainty by which US sponsors have embraced the nonbank lending market has not been echoed consistently in Europe. Therefore, to understand the reasons why private equity sponsors utilize nonbank lenders and their possible hesitancy to embrace nonbank lending in Europe, a survey of 20 European middle market buyout firms was conducted with results presented in Exhibit 26.2. In this survey, nonbank lenders were cited by sponsors as being less reliable and more likely to retrade a negotiated deal. Nonetheless, several middle market sponsors noted that they work with nonbank lenders where they can obtain better covenants and more covenant headroom, with less equity in the deal. The spread in the cost of financing between bank lenders and alternative direct lenders for unitranche debt is approximately two to four percentage points on an all-in basis.

Perhaps the most important takeaway from both the US and European surveys is the importance of pre-existing lender-borrower relationships. This is an important finding because it puts significant value on the origination process used by direct lenders. It also highlights the similarities between private equity and private debt. Both require bespoke expertise and solutions executed by experienced professionals who understand that a major asset is the relationships they maintain.

	European Sponsor Survey Findings
Most Important Considerations	Sponsors noted that the choice of using a bank versus nonbank lender was deal specific. Banks are still active and willing to provide low-cost financing for straightforward deals and therefore remain the preferred choice. If a deal is more complicated or has a more aggressive growth plan, sponsors value nonbank lenders' ability to be flexible on leverage, sponsor equity contribution, covenants, and speed to close. However, many sponsors value existing relationships with their bank lenders and initially were reluctant to adopt the nonbank lending model.
Underwriting Flexibility	Nonbank lenders tend to have more flexibility in structuring loans (leverage multiples, covenants, etc.), although for cleaner deals, banks remain competitive, particularly at senior levels of the capital structure.
Pricing	Generally, nonbank lenders charge a premium of two to four percentage points more than bank lenders in exchange for being more flexible. Bank financing is cheaper unless there is a need for mezzanine debt, in which case a unitranche loan can provide a competitive all-in cost. However, some sponsors are seeing banks partner with mezzanine lenders to compete with nonbank lenders by providing a synthetic unitranche product.
Leverage Restrictions	Most banks are limited on leverage of up to 5.0× net debt to EBITDA. Furthermore, banks tend to primarily participate in senior loans, whereas nonbank lenders are brought in for unitranche, second lien, and mezzanine structures. Nonbank lenders are generally willing to provide leverage of up to 6.0× net debt to EBITDA or more in some situations.

EXHIBIT 26.2 European sponsor survey on choosing bank versus nonbank financing.

	European Sponsor Survey Findings
Capacity and Deal Size	Responses from sponsors were mixed on the capacity and deal size targets depending on the region. For example, banks in the Nordic region are able to take down relatively larger deals. Generally, banks and nonbank lenders have strong appetites for providing financing. Larger nonbank lenders may have an advantage when the syndicated market is less accessible. While most sponsors prefer to work with one counterparty, they will typically arrange a club when needed for larger deals.
Speed to Close	Some sponsors have noted that nonbank lenders tend to be faster due to quicker internal processes and fewer committees. Additionally, nonbanks can move quicker in refinancing and add-on transactions because of dedicated coverage that maintains closer familiarity with the credit and the sponsor. However, other sponsors noted that newer lenders were slower at times, most likely due to newly formed teams and processes.
Covenants	Covenant packages don't seem to be uniform across Europe and are dependent on size and geography. For middle market deals, nonbank lenders on average require a leverage covenant, whereas banks may require additional financial covenants such as cash flow covenants. Sponsors noted that nonbank lenders tend to provide more headroom in the covenants. Smaller deals may require additional covenants for both bank and nonbank lenders, whereas larger deals may be covenant lite. The most consistent difference between banks and nonbank lenders cited by sponsors was that banks have higher amortization requirements over the life of the loan.

EXHIBIT 26.2 (*continued*)

	European Sponsor Survey Findings
Industry Expertise	Banks generally tend to have more industry expertise relative to nonbank lenders. Some sponsors noted that a nonbank lender's lack of industry knowledge may prevent them from moving quickly on a deal or cause them to back out.
Geographic Considerations	Given different cultural and business relationships across Europe, as well as different bankruptcy and creditors' rights regimes across different European countries, there tends to be meaningful country-specific debt financing in Europe. Regional and country-specific banks want to retain their local relationships. In addition, a number of the alternative lenders also are country-specific in their lending. This dynamic is much less pronounced in the US, where the legal framework is uniform, and where lenders (both bank and nonbank) have operated across geographic markets for years.

EXHIBIT 26.2 (*continued*)

CHAPTER 27

Enhanced Lending

DIRECT VERSUS ENHANCED LENDING

In Exhibit 8.2, the private debt landscape was depicted as two hemispheres. The first represented *direct lending* and the second was called *enhanced lending*. This chapter covers ten of the enhanced lending strategies more frequently used by institutional investors in their private debt portfolios. These strategies are mostly managed by firms that specialize in them but there is a concurrent trend among larger credit managers to include multiple strategies, including direct lending.

The ten strategies can be divided into roughly two groups. The first group of four strategies includes mezzanine debt, CLOs or structured finance, venture debt, and rescue finance. What they have in common is an exposure to corporate risk, like direct lending. However, that exposure tends to be higher risk and more specialized. If direct lending is low beta, these corporate-related enhanced lending strategies are higher beta with a broader range of outcomes more dependent on the quality of the manager/lender than the strategy itself.

The second group of six enhanced lending strategies do not have explicit corporate risk exposure, but exposures to noncorporate risks. These six strategies are asset-backed lending, real estate debt, infrastructure debt, royalties (pharma and entertainment), reinsurance, and litigation finance. Other noncorporate credit strategies, such as marketplace lending (fintech), reg cap lending, fund finance, and life settlements, have generated interest but not to the same scale as the six covered in this chapter.

Investors in both enhanced lending groups generally expect to earn 10–15% net returns and understand that they are taking on more manager/lender risk and strategy risk than the 7–10% returns they expect from direct lending. In well-diversified portfolios, direct lending risk mitigation comes from having lots of loans, and enhanced lending risk mitigation comes from having multiple strategies, overseen by the best managers.

MEZZANINE DEBT AND STRUCTURED CAPITAL

Mezzanine debt and structured capital are both higher-risk corporate private debt that are sometimes used and will sit between second lien and equity in the capital structure depiction in Exhibit 1.2.

Mezzanine Debt

Mezzanine debt is one of the older forms of leveraged finance for middle market companies, having originally developed in the 1980s as a solution for companies seeking capital for growth or ownership transaction purposes that was beyond the capacity of bank lenders and that was less dilutive than equity. In the 1980s and 1990s, as the leveraged buyout market developed, mezzanine also became a popular form of financing for middle market buyouts, as it permitted private equity sponsors to further leverage the equity they were investing into buyout deals (sponsored deals)—lending to these sponsored deals became a primary focus of many specialty mezzanine lenders. More recently, with the advent of the direct lending market, including unitranche and second lien loans, mezzanine has increasingly become a niche product that represents the smallest portion of the corporate leveraged finance market.

The term *mezzanine* initially referred to the portion of the capital structure created in a mezzanine financing: below the senior secured level but above unsecured subordinated debt and equity. More recently, financings provided by mezzanine lenders can be broader, as part of a capital solutions product, encompassing parts of senior and subordinated debt, and may also include a significant portion of common and preferred equity.

Market Size and Structure

There is no reliable data on the actual size of the mezzanine market, due to the private nature of most mezzanine investment firms and deals, and the variety of deal structures. However, some market estimates do exist. As of 2021, Preqin reported that the global mezzanine market was estimated to have approximately $180 billion including invested capital and dry powder. This market size is meaningfully smaller than that of the buyout and senior direct lending markets and highlights the niche nature of the mezzanine world.

Expected Return and Risk

The long-term expected return for mezzanine strategies is 9% with an estimated risk of 11%. Returns are composed of 9–12% gross unlevered interest rates and fees plus 3–5% returns from equity co-investments. Strategies vary in their use of equity co-investments, but most strategies that include equity target 5–10% of the portfolio in common equity. Loss rates are expected to be 1–3% on an annualized basis excluding potential offsetting gains or losses from equity co-investments.

Investment Strategies

The initial providers of mezzanine were insurance companies and specialty finance companies that were willing to provide patient, subordinated capital to companies with predictable cash flows in exchange for above-market pricing. Borrowers tended to be small or middle market, often privately owned businesses that did not wish to access (or simply did not have access to) the capital markets. Many of these financing opportunities were negotiated directly between the borrower and the mezzanine debt provider, and typical uses included capital for growth initiatives such as building a new manufacturing facility or acquiring a competitor, or shareholder-related transactions such as the repurchase by the company of a minority interest holder or an ownership transfer between generations.

Today, mezzanine lenders tend to fall into two camps: smaller specialty firms financing lower middle market deals, either sponsored or unsponsored, and larger firms, including affiliates of major investment banks and diversified asset managers, which raise large pools of capital to serve as high-yield replacement during times of market dislocation.

Most mezzanine lenders are specialized firms that raise private funds. Given mezzanine's traditional focus on privately held, middle market companies, loan sizes tend to be relatively small (between $10 million and $50 million), so the fund sizes are modest size as well, generally less than $1 billion. There are also a small number of much larger funds, ranging from $3 billion to $10 billion, which focus on larger buyout and opportunistic situations, including periods of capital market dislocation and deals where speed and secrecy are valued. There are more than 300 private mezzanine firms active globally, over 200 of which are focused on the US market. Between 2020 and September 2022, these firms raised between 20 and 40 new private funds per year, aggregating between $12 billion and $30 billion.[1] Other players in the mezzanine market include insurance companies, investment bank affiliates, and diversified asset management companies.

Private mezzanine funds are typically structured similarly to private equity funds, with ten-year total lives including five- to six-year investment

---

[1]Preqin.

periods. Annual management fees are in the range of 1.5–2% of net invested capital or, less commonly, capital commitments during the investment period and 1.5–2% of net invested capital during the harvest period. Managers also receive 15–20% of fund profits as a carried interest, above a hurdle rate or preferred return of 6–8% per annum. Most mezzanine funds usually incur no leverage at the fund level, though few use modest leverage, and most managers make use of a capital commitment line of credit to streamline capital calls and to shorten the length of any J-curve period.

As noted, mezzanine debt is used in a variety of leveraged finance applications. Loan sizes are generally in the $5 million to $100 million range, although most transactions are between $10 million and $50 million. Buyout deals represent the lions' share of mezzanine use, and in these transactions, the mezzanine loan represents between one and two turns of leverage, and between 10 and 20% of the capital structure. For example, a typical buyout transaction valued at 10× EBITDA may use senior debt equal to 4–5× EBITDA, mezzanine debt of 1× EBITDA, and equity of 4–5× EBITDA.

The vast majority of mezzanine loans are directly negotiated financings between the lender and the borrower, with the introducing party either a buyout sponsor or, in the case of an unsponsored deal, an intermediary hired by the borrower to source potential capital providers. Similar to the direct lending market, sponsored buyouts are estimated to represent approximately 60–70% of total mezzanine transaction volume. Mezzanine lenders focused on unsponsored transactions often market themselves as solution providers to borrowers in that they can create bespoke capital structures tailored to a borrower's specific needs. For example, based on the borrower's cash flows, financial leverage, and equity dilution sensitivity, the lender could structure a mezzanine financing package composed of a mix of subordinated debt, cash pay, or PIK preferred stock and common stock.

STRUCTURED CAPITAL

Structured capital encompasses bespoke financing packages or solutions capital that fills the gap between traditional debt and for-control equity. Also referred to as *hybrid capital*, structured capital is both junior debt capital that is subordinate to senior, unitranche, and mezzanine debt, and equity that is structurally senior to common equity. Instruments can include term loans with warrants, convertible debt, holding company PIK notes, convertible preferred equity, preferred equity with dividends, or some other combination of junior debt securities and senior equity instruments.

Generally, financings are structured to include both contractual minimum returns via cash or PIK yield (often on a floating rate basis) and equity upside optionality. Downside protection comes in the form of contractual yield, maintenance covenants, debt incurrence limitations, call protection, amortization requirements, minimum multiple of money liquidation preference, redemption and put rights, and 40–60% LTV detachments. Sometimes packages include governance protections like board seats. Upside optionality is achieved through equity conversion features, warrants, or revenue participation.

Structured capital has become a popular form of solutions capital because for borrowers it is more flexible than traditional debt and less dilutive than traditional equity. Borrower or company profiles span the spectrum from lower middle market, nonfinancial sponsor–owned companies to upper middle market, sponsor-owned companies and even large cap public companies. Traditionally, borrowers are EBITDA positive and use proceeds for growth initiatives, acquisition financing, shareholder recapitalizations, or medium-term liquidity needs. More recently, structured capital financings are popular with the private equity sponsor community looking to acquire expensive, high-enterprise-value software and tech-focused business, because structured capital tranches allow them to limit their check size and achieve required returns despite high-entry multiples or valuations.

Market Size and Structure

As with mezzanine debt, there is no reliable data on the actual size of the structured capital market due to the private nature of most deals and the variability of the financing packages, which can range from first lien term loans with warrants to senior-equity-only instruments and thus they are difficult to categorize neatly. The market for structured capital is likely the sum of some subset of the traditional mezzanine debt market and special situation or opportunistic credit market, which totals about $500 billion in available investment capital as of June 30, 2022. Of course, structured capital financings are only a subset of that dry powder estimate, but certainly a growing fraction, as traditional mezzanine providers increasingly also offer structured capital packages, and traditional opportunistic or distressed debt providers move into the structured capital space as distress credit opportunities have abated since the GFC.

Expected Return and Risk

Contractual returns for structured capital financings range from 10–14% interest income, either part cash pay and PIK or all PIK, together with equity upside or equity options providing another 3–5% return, together totaling a 13–17% range in gross return. Net of manager fees, carried interest, and whether a manager applies fund level leverage, investors can expect a 10–15% net return.

In terms of risk, structured capital tranches will attach at about 6.5× EBITDA and detach at 8.5× EBITDA on a 14× EBITDA total enterprise value company. Of course, many companies are valued less than 14×, and many companies are valued more than 14×, so investors normalize measurements of attachment/detachment by translating to a LTV basis. As such, a 6.5× EBITDA attachment point translates to a 46% LTV on a 14× company valuation and an 8.5× detachment point translates to a 60% LTV. The median structured capital tranche thickness is 1.5–2× EBITDA, with a 60% LTV detachment or 40% (1/LTV) equity cushion beneath the structured capital tranche's last dollar at risk, often referred to as the creation point.

Investment Strategies

Structured capital providers are specialized firms that raise private, closed-end vehicles similar to private equity funds. A typical structured capital fund will feature a three- to five-year investment period and eight- to ten-year final term. Management fees average 1.5% on committed capital or net invested capital with carried interest averaging 20% of profits once a 7 or 8% preferred return hurdle is met. Some funds will incur no leverage and some funds will apply up to 0.3× through a capital call facility.

Structured capital managers are entering the market from two sides: private credit and private equity. Private credit managers, many of whom have traditionally managed second lien or mezzanine debt strategies, as well as managers who have traditionally managed distressed and rescue financing strategies, are both increasingly coming to market with standalone structured credit funds or collapsing structured capital financings into existing fund offerings, as the opportunity for strictly mezzanine financing or distressed and rescue financing has waned since the GFC. On the equity side, many private equity managers directly experience the need for structured capital tranches and recognize its long-term potential and importance to the sponsor community. As such, many private equity managers are organizing in-house teams and launching dedicated structured credit funds, which oftentimes fundraise alongside the private equity manager's flagship equity fund. This way, the economics and future growth of this tranche of financing accrues to the private equity franchise instead of leaking out to a third-party credit manager. Private equity–affiliated structured capital funds can be either fully captive or non-captive funds. Captive funds are fully committed to providing structured capital for all of a private equity sponsor's deals while non-captive funds have flexibility to choose between doing deals with the private equity parent or doing deals with other nonaffiliated private equity sponsors.

Like managers, investors and limited partners also come into the structured capital market from credit-focused or equity-focused perspectives. Many credit investors like structured capital for its contractual pay and downside protection features, with a view that the equity upside optionality balances the downside asymmetry of traditional credit investing. Private equity investors allocate to structured capital as a way to add some downside protection or dampen volatility in their private equity portfolio without sacrificing too much return.

Perhaps unsurprisingly, credit-focused investors often prefer non-affiliated structured credit funds, as they tend to believe a manager should be beholden to limited partners alone as opposed to having conflicts or perceptions of conflicts with incentives, economics, and loyalty to a parent or affiliate private equity firm. However, many private equity investors have close and long-standing relationships with private equity firms. These investors are less concerned about an affiliate fund's conflicts or perception of conflicts, and instead they focus on the plausible assumption that affiliated structured capital funds, and those teams leading them, can underwrite deals with an ownership or equity perspective and step in or influence management of a company should something go wrong with the credit story. It's worth noting that many private equity firms that raise oversubscribed private equity funds and have an affiliate structured capital fund will require or suggest that limited partners also subscribe to their structured capital fund to secure allocations to the oversubscribed flagship private equity fund.

Although structured capital financings can take many forms, prospective return expectations settle into a relatively tight range. Realized losses will, therefore, make the difference between outperformance and underperformance within the category. Structured capital as an investment category, however, is too nascent, with financing packages too diverse, performance date too disparate to neatly assess what type of style or risk factors might generate under- or overperformance—be it lower middle market versus upper middle market and large cap deals, nonsponsor- versus sponsor-owned company deals, cash flowing or negative cash flowing (high-growth) deals, or affiliated funds versus nonaffiliated funds.

Nevertheless, the use case and utility of the structured capital tranche promises that this will be a growing and important part of the private credit and private equity ecosystem. Borrowers value the flexible solutions-oriented capital, and investors value low teens returns with a balanced return/risk profile. As such, structured capital is likely to become a mainstay allocation for both private credit and private equity investors, with many forms of fund offerings spanning the style and risk spectrum.

COLLATERALIZED LOAN OBLIGATIONS

Collateralized loan obligations (CLOs) are legal structures designed to provide investors access to the economics found in a diversified portfolio of high-yield leveraged loans. However, unlike the mutual funds, ETFs, and managed accounts that invest holistically in leveraged loans, CLOs partition leveraged loan economics into multiple securities, allowing investors to select a higher or lower level of expected return and risk, rather than the pooled average. This report describes how CLOs parcel leveraged loan portfolio economics and the return and risk that can be expected from CLO securities typically offered.

Leveraged Loans

CLO economics are based on leveraged loans. A by-product of the leveraged buyouts (LBOs) begun in the 1980s, leveraged loans are non-investment grade, five- to seven-year floating rate corporate loans, syndicated and traded by major money center banks. The long-term success of LBOs and private equity generally has helped push the global leveraged loan market to approach $2 trillion. Investors have been attracted to leveraged loans because of their higher yield, floating rate, medium-term maturity, and relative liquidity. Today, leveraged loans have become an institutionalized asset class supporting investments by pensions and endowments, with management services offered by most large, fixed income advisory firms. Morningstar LSTA and Credit Suisse both support widely used leveraged loan indexes that serve as useful guides for measuring return and risk and serve as performance benchmarks.

CLO Structure

CLO assets total approximately $1 trillion, or 50% of the leveraged loan market, and were created soon after the leveraged loan market began to encourage investors with much different risk preferences to finance levered loans.

The CLO is an indenture agreement between lenders (noteholders) and a Delaware/Cayman legal entity as borrower. A portfolio manager,[2] typically also the CLO sponsor, selects a portfolio of leveraged loans that serves as the sole collateral to service notes issued by the CLO. The CLO also provides for various administrative functions including trustee, custodian,

---

[2]Also known as the collateral manager.

administrator, and underwriter. Notes and other CLO securities are generally exempt from SEC registration.

The CLO increases demand for leveraged loans by issuing a series of notes with different priorities over the cash flows and principal repayments produced by the CLO-leveraged loan collateral portfolio. Higher (lower) priority notes have lower (higher) expected risk of nonpayment and, therefore, lower (higher) yield to compensate for expected risk. Though individual CLO indentures differ, most issue first-priority senior AAA-rated notes equal to ~60% of total CLO assets, lower priority investment grade notes equal to ~20% of total CLO assets and rated AA to BBB, non-investment grade or non-rated mezzanine notes equal to ~10% of CLO assets, and last, notes entitled only to CLO asset cash flows after all other obligations have been satisfied. This last note is generally referred to as CLO equity.

CLO Return and Risk

The size and longevity of the CLO market is due to its successful matching of assets with liabilities. A mismatch in interest rate risk (duration) has undermined many fixed income structures when unexpected rate changes occur. In the case of CLOs, both assets (loans) and liabilities (notes) are a floating rate, so changes in interest rates increase assets and liabilities in the same direction and magnitude. Loan prepayments from lower credit spreads can be a challenge, but prepayment penalties and note resets help to mitigate the modest risk this presents.

CLO economics centers on the transference of interest income and principal (less potential credit losses) from a portfolio of non-investment grade loans, which serves as collateral to CLO noteholders and CLO equity.

In Exhibit 27.1, we use the Merton model[3] to illustrate how the CLO collateral asset returns should theoretically be distributed across CLO debt (notes) and CLO equity.

Given a set of assumptions, most important leveraged loan volatility,[4] Exhibit 27.1 plots the cost of debt at different levels of financing. Line 1 reflects a 2.25% Libor rate, which all CLO noteholders receive. Line 2 shows the *average cost* of financing spread across all debt (notes) up to the debt levels shown on the horizontal axis. Dashed line 3 shows the *marginal*

---

[3]Robert C. Merton, "On the Pricing of Corporate Debt: The Risk Structure of Interest Rates," *The Journal of Finance* (May 1974).

[4]Leveraged loan volatility at debt maturity primarily reflects cumulative credit losses.

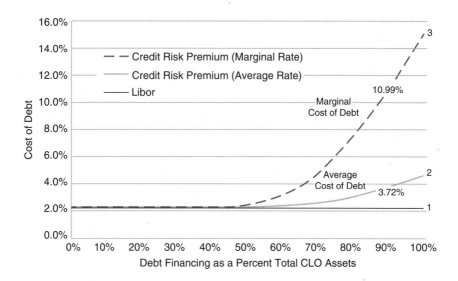

EXHIBIT 27.1 Model pricing of CLO notes and CLO equity.

cost of financing for each additional dollar of debt. For example, the Merton model with our assumptions would require an average combined cost of financing for 90% of CLO assets to equal 3.72%, or 1.47% above Libor. The marginal cost of financing at the 90% debt level equals 10.99%.

The remaining 10% of financing in Exhibit 27.1 comes from CLO equity. The required cost of financing the remaining 10% equals 13.22%, using the Merton model. This would represent the return that CLO equity would require for providing the last 10% of financing and accept first loss on loan defaults.

In our example, suppose further that the collateral assets yield Libor plus a 2.95% spread, net of management fees, or total yield of 5.20%. If 90% of the financing for that collateral can be had at an average cost of 3.72%, then the remaining 10% residual financing, representing CLO equity, will earn 18.52%.[5] Because the 18.52% CLO yield exceeds the required 13.22% financing for the last 10% of CLO assets, the CLO equity

---

[5]Collateral Yield = (Avg. Financing Cost) × (Percentage Debt Financed) + (CLO Equity Yield) × (Percentage Equity Financed), or [5.20% = (3.72% × 90%) + (18.52% × 10%)].

looks like an attractive investment. Theoretically, this imbalance between actual yield and required yield would be arbitraged away by additional CLO creation and narrowing leveraged loan spreads.

CLO Mechanics

A CLO goes through four stages. Before the CLO is created, the CLO sponsor (generally the collateral manager) and a bank create a warehouse facility to build a portfolio of leveraged loans that later will be used to launch the CLO. The sponsor contributes most of what will become the CLO equity, and the bank provides partial financing (leverage) to begin building a portfolio of leveraged loans. Expectations are that after approximately six months the warehouse has reached a size equal to approximately 70% of the final CLO structure.

If the underwriters have done their job placing the CLO notes, the CLO structure goes effective and the CLO enters a ramp-up stage of approximately three months when all assets are invested in a diversified portfolio of leveraged loans and the CLO is operating at its maximum efficiency.

The reinvestment stage is designed to be three to six years in length, long enough to give noteholders and equity holders a sufficient cash return on their investment, primarily in the form of current income. Principal proceeds from loan maturities and prepayments are reinvested during this period, keeping the size of the CLO structure constant.

When the reinvestment period ends, the amortization stage begins. All cash flow from the leveraged loan portfolio, including principal payments, is distributed to the noteholders and equity holders in priority of their claims. In the case of the equity holders, the likely outcome is only partial payment of their initial capital contribution as they absorb the first loss on all defaults.

For example, assume the CLO-leveraged loan portfolio experiences credit losses equal to 0.5% of its principal value per year, a level equal to the historical average default rate for leveraged loans. If the life of the CLO is six years, then the cumulative loss from defaults will equal 3% (6 years × 0.5%). The CLO equity holders will absorb all those losses and will receive just 70% of their initial capital back. To compensate for these losses, CLO equity holders will be receiving all the cash yield from the leveraged loan portfolio above noteholder financing costs. In our previous example, we calculated an 18.52% yield for CLO equity holders, with no defaults. If the leveraged loan portfolio experiences 0.5% in annual credit losses, then the actual return (IRR) received by the equity holders equals 14.89%. If annual credit losses are 1.0%, rather than 0.5%, then the CLO equity holders get back only 40% of their original capital but still receive an annualized return equal to 10.41%.

CLO Collateral Manager

The CLO collateral manager serves two roles. The first is to minimize the cost of financing by satisfying noteholders by reputation and portfolio construction that the manager will be a good steward of assets and meet all obligations under the indenture. The second is to maximize CLO equity returns by ongoing management of CLO assets and liabilities. This would include minimizing credit losses through strong underwriting of leveraged loans, engaging in market transactions that maximize yield over the life of the CLO without compromising covenants, and identifying opportunities to refinance or recall CLO debt.

VENTURE DEBT

Venture debt is a form of senior secured lending with equity upside opportunity, where the borrower is most likely a small, often venture capital–backed, high-growth company. These businesses may be losing money at the operating level, given their focus on investing for rapid growth, and some may even be pre-revenue. With this fact pattern, the normal rules of commercial credit, such as requiring positive cash flow to repay indebtedness, do not always apply. Therefore, the providers of venture debt base their credit facilities on a conservative estimated LTV, as well as the amount of current balance sheet cash raised by the borrower from venture capitalists and the current and projected burn rate of that cash.

Market Size and Structure

Venture debt developed in the 1980s as venture capital–backed companies sought ways to accelerate their growth without the need to launch further rounds of equity finance and/or incur additional ownership dilution. What ensued was the creation of a new type of debt financing that combined aspects of senior secured lending with mezzanine finance. Specifically, since these venture-backed companies did not have the necessary financial statistics (e.g., a history of profitability), they were traditionally capitalized solely with equity capital. If their growth slowed or their prospects weakened (or the venture market simply was not open for a further equity investment round) at the time the companies required additional growth capital, they were forced to seek alternative financing methods. Equipment leasing was an option but was limited in availability and scope. The other option was a line of credit from a venture debt provider secured by the company's balance sheet assets (which are typically composed of cash and significant intangible assets, such as technological know-how and goodwill).

To compensate themselves for the heightened credit risk of lending to small, perhaps money-losing companies, venture lenders limit their exposure to any one borrower to a conservative, perhaps 10–15%, LTV, and require equity warrants in the borrower as additional compensation. Even with the warrants, the total cost of the venture debt is still below the returns required by equity investors, so the venture debt facility is less dilutive to the existing equity investors in the company. Therefore, venture debt can be a relatively attractive temporary source of capital.

The majority of venture debt is targeted at venture capital–backed companies, although some venture debt providers will also consider non-venture-backed companies as well. It is estimated that an average of $32.2 billion of venture loans have been completed per year between 2019 and June 30, 2022.[6] However, this includes commercial banks and larger generalist lenders financing later stage growth companies. Venture-backed companies are staying private longer than ever, which has continued to expand the opportunity set for venture lenders. As with much of the venture world, relationships are critical to landing venture lending opportunities, as the venture capitalists that control potential borrowers seek to find capital partners in whom they trust and that have a reputation for serving as effective capital providers to other similar businesses. Accordingly, the universe of active, professional venture debt providers is small, perhaps less than two dozen firms. Most of these firms are structured similarly to private equity or mezzanine firms, and they raise private funds to finance their loans. As with the venture capital space, fund sizes tend to be small, generally less than $500 million. Each fund may hold between 25 and 80 loans, although the total number of positions in a lender's portfolio may be higher due to unexercised warrants of companies that have already paid off their loans. A small number of venture debt providers are structured as public or private BDCs.

---

[6]Pitchbook NVCA Venture Monitor Q2 2022.

Expected Risk and Return

Relative to other private credit strategies, the venture debt strategy has limited competition from traditional lending sources and high barriers to entry, due to the relationships needed in the venture capital space and the expertise needed to evaluate small, rapidly growing companies operating in new technology sectors. Additionally, venture debt has seniority in claim to the borrower's assets and is over-collateralized via a conservative LTV. Given the high rate of company failure, venture lending can be a risky undertaking, so venture lenders seek to compensate themselves for this added risk by requiring some form of return upside, such as equity warrants and exit fees, in addition to traditional interest rate and closing fee compensation.

The interest rate on venture debt is typically set between 8 and 12% per annum (either a fixed rate or a floating rate over SOFR, LIBOR, or prime), and the lender may also charge a closing fee (typically 1–2% of the amount of the loan) and a back-end fee of up to 10% of the loan amount, to be paid at the time the loan is repaid. In addition, the lender will seek warrants with an estimated value of between 5 and 15% of loan amount as additional compensation. All in, the lender will price the loan package to generate a gross internal rate of return of 15–25% and will target a cash yield on the loan of 10–15%.

As this strategy is limited in size and capacity, and involves lending to small, mostly private, high-risk companies with limited track records, venture debt should be considered by institutional investors as a return-enhancing, niche strategy, which should represent only a modest allocation of a diversified credit portfolio.

Investment Strategies

In a typical venture debt financing opportunity, the lender seeks a borrower who possesses a number of key characteristics: (1) a company in the information technology, life sciences, media and entertainment, and financial technology sectors; (2) the existing involvement of a strong syndicate of venture capitalists who express interest in continuing to back the company; (3) an attractive business and revenue model; (4) substantial monetizable intellectual property; and (5) a realistic business plan for future capital raising and growth. The company most likely has raised an A round, and perhaps a B round of venture equity and is seeking between $2 million and $25 million of debt capital. The company and its shareholders are typically seeking ways to continue to fund the business growth between equity rounds (extend the company's runway), while minimizing equity dilution. The lender will seek to limit its exposure to a modest, perhaps 10–15% LTV, with value based on the lender's estimate of enterprise value of the company. The enterprise value may be based on the previous venture capital round valuation, as well as company progress since the last round, current market conditions, and the valuation of comparable companies. The loan amount may also take into consideration the borrower's cash balance and burn rate if the business is not yet cash positive.

The loan structure will often be a fixed or floating rate loan of three to five years in length, perhaps beginning with an interest-only period of up to two years followed by an amortizing period. Loans are usually repaid when the borrower raises its next round of financing, or via the company's IPO or third-party sale.

Venture debt remains a modestly sized, niche strategy within private credit. Given the still-developing nature of the market, there are limited data on total fund size. That said, there are approximately 20 active institutional investment firms in the space. These firms raise fewer than five new private funds each year, with aggregate annual capital raised annually totaling less than a billion dollars.

The Cliffwater Direct Venture Lending Index (CDLI-V)

CDLI-V is composed of only venture-backed loans within the overall CDLI to investigate the comparative performance of this lesser-known type of lending against the entire universe of middle market loans represented by CDLI.

CDLI-V follows the same construction methodology as CDLI but only includes loans held by managers of BDCs that have an investment style that is determined to clearly focus on venture lending. The same quarterly performance and portfolio data that is available for CDLI is also available for CDLI-V, except that the beginning date is March 31, 2005, for CDLI-V compared to September 30, 2004, for CDLI. As with the CDLI, CDLI-V should not suffer from biases (backfill and survivorship) found in other databases because all source data comes from required SEC filings.

Some key differences between the CDLI and CDLI-V indexes at March 31, 2022, are shown here:

	CDLI-V	CDLI
# Loans	608	9,475
Total Assets	$5.9 billion	$223 billion
EBITDA (median)	n/a	$46 million
Nonaccrual (as % of Cost)	2.1%	1.1%
Implied Recovery Rate	36%	58%
% Sponsor	100%	79%
% Senior	91%	76%

Exhibit 27.2 reports performance for CDLI-V over its entire 17-year history with comparisons to the broader CDLI for the same time period.

Venture lending, as represented by CDLI-V, has performed well from its inception, achieving an 11.96% total return compared to 9.51% for the CDLI for the same time period. The reason for the higher return primarily lies with higher interest income, which equaled 13.02% from inception compared to 10.95% for CDLI. This higher interest income for CDLI-V, however, did not come with higher realized losses, which total –0.83% from inception for CDLI-V, compared to a –1.16% realized loss rate for CDLI for the same period.

Unfortunately, our CDLI-V return series does not include the period from 2000 to 2003 when venture capital was hardest hit from the internet bubble. We would expect much higher realized losses from venture lending for that period, which is not captured by our data.

Total Return and Components	Q1 2022	Last Four Quarters	Last Five Years*	From CDLI-V Inception March 2005
		CDLI-V Returns		
CDLI-V Total Return**	1.51%	12.30%	12.37%	11.96%
= Income	2.66%	11.96%	12.71%	13.02%
+/– Net Realized Gains (Losses)	–0.13%	0.24%	–0.93%	–0.83%
+/– Net Unrealized Gains (Losses)	–1.03%	0.06%	0.61%	–0.17%
		CDLI Returns		
CDLI Total Return**	1.76%	11.17%	8.63%	9.51%
= Income	1.93%	8.67%	9.75%	10.95%
+/– Net Realized Gains (Losses)	0.03%	0.49%	–1.23%	–1.16%
+/– Net Unrealized Gains (Losses)	–0.19%	1.85%	0.18%	–0.20%

*Annualized return.
**Return subcomponents may not add to total return due to compounding effects.

EXHIBIT 27.2   Venture direct loan performance (CDLI-Venture).

RESCUE FINANCING

Rescue financings occur when a company has a critical near-term liquidity issue that they are unable to solve through traditional channels such as the high-yield bond or loan market. Rescue financings may avoid the need to resort to bankruptcy, provide a borrower with immediate cash needs, and enable the lenders to improve the economic and collateral position of their loan. The reasons for the company's financing problems may be related to general financial stress, market conditions, or time constraints due to upcoming maturities. In certain situations, the lender may be acting as a lender of last resort and thus is able to extract more favorable terms, including higher interest rates and better call protections.

The term *rescue financing* includes a broad market of distressed opportunities that is considered a subsector of distressed investment. For the purposes of this discussion, we focus on a more defined part of the market—debtor in possession, or DIP, financings. DIPs refer to financing for a company that retains control of its assets and continues to operate while under the Chapter 11 bankruptcy process. Under a Chapter 11 bankruptcy, a company files for protection from creditors while it reorganizes itself. DIP financings provide capital for companies to turn themselves around as they work through a restructuring.

DIP financing provides a company that is seeking bankruptcy court protection with funds to operate its business while it develops and implements a plan of reorganization. As an incentive to lenders to provide funding, the US Bankruptcy Code provides DIP lenders strong creditor protections. Under Chapter 11 of the US Bankruptcy Code, DIP lenders receive super-priority creditor status that grants them the right to be repaid from collateral proceeds before any pre-petition creditors, including existing senior secured lenders.

Companies file for bankruptcy for many reasons, and each company takes a different path through this process. Most large companies that enter bankruptcy are able to reorganize and emerge, in which case the DIP loan is repaid. However, some companies' reorganizations fail, resulting in a liquidation scenario, which may increase potential losses for DIP creditors.

DIP loan maturities can range from six months to two years, but most maturities are less than 12 months. The loans are typically shorter duration relative to corporate bond and loan issuance, as the financings provide a specific function: enable the debtors with enough time to reorganize.

A typical exit for rescue financings involves the company refinancing the debt once the no-call period expires or after the call premiums expire, unless a strong market emerges for the debt that enables the lender to exit through a secondary sale. Some DIP financings have included the option to convert to outstanding amounts on the DIP loan to equity, providing the lenders potential upside.

Market Size and Structure

The market size for DIP loans and rescue financings is highly dependent on the distressed cycle and the amount of total debt outstanding in the market. Rising default rates on corporate debt are likely to increase the need for DIP financing and rescue financings for corporate entities. It is important to note that DIP financings are a subset of the broader rescue financing market. Given the broad definition of rescue financings, it is a difficult market to define. Consequently, we used market data on the size of the DIP financing market as an estimation of the rescue financing market.

The demand for DIPs will generally peak following a distressed cycle when the amount of companies in distress peak. The demand for DIP financings peaked in 2009 following the financial crisis but has since decreased as default rates have remained low relative to historical standards. From 2000 to 2009, the DIP market's annual volume ranged from $5 billion to $15 billion. In 2009, it was estimated that the total DIP financing market exceeded $55 billion. Post the financial crisis, the DIP financing market was heavily affected by several large capital structures that defaulted, including GM, Lyondell, and Chrysler. Since 2009, the DIP market's annual volume has ranged from a low of less than $4 billion in 2010 and 2011 to a high of $16 billion in 2016, following the energy crisis, and $27.8 billion following the onset of the COVID-19 pandemic.[7] Notable companies driving the surge in 2020 include those in industries heavily affected by shutdowns such as Hertz and LATAM Airlines Group. DIP financings in 2021 dropped dramatically to $2.4 billion as the economy quickly rebounded and adapted to the post-COVID environment. However, in 2022 year to date through August, DIP financings have started to trend upward totaling $5.8 billion as stress created by inflation and supply chain issues affect companies.

Expected Return and Risk

Most investors require double-digit returns on DIP financings, depending on the level of SOFR/LIBOR rates. At the peak of a distressed cycle, DIP

---

[7]Reorg Research, Inc. (September 2022).

financings can range from SOFR/LIBOR plus 600 bps to SOFR/LIBOR plus 2,100 bps. However, in more benign credit default environments, DIP financings typically range from SOFR/LIBOR plus 600 bps to SOFR/LIBOR plus 1,000 bps. DIP financings also include significant up-front, and, less frequently, exit fees, each often ranging from 2–4% of the loan amount. Up-front fees recently have been closer to 2%. As noted, DIP lenders are often able to extract above-market terms for their loan packages, including no-call periods and laddered call premiums, original issue discounts (OIDs), equity warrants, and structural features including blocking rights that allow the lender to control the company's ability to restructure its balance sheet. Such opportunities are more market cycle dependent and may be shorter in duration.

Under the bankruptcy code, DIP financings are granted super-priority creditor status and therefore have a first lien on company assets. According to Moody's, the default risk of DIPs for large public companies has been historically low, which translates into low loss ratios for these loans.

Investment Strategies

Historically, commercial banks were a major provider of DIP financings. However, commercial banks have retreated from this market since the financial crisis. The biggest providers of capital in this space include major debt lenders, hedge funds, private equity funds, and other distressed managers. In many cases, the major debt lenders who do not want to be involved in a restructuring situation may sell their position in the secondary market ahead of a bankruptcy filing, typically to distressed managers (hedge fund or private equity fund, for example). These types of investors are typically involved in stressed/distressed companies prior to a bankruptcy filing, which gives them a seat at the table during restructuring negotiations. Many DIP lenders are already interested parties in the distressed company financing, seeking to protect their position in the capital structure. In general, only 20% of DIP financing comes from third-party lenders.

There is not generally pooled capital raised specifically for DIP financings. Rather, DIP financings are managed as part of a broader distressed investment strategy. There are hundreds of managers that employ some type of distressed strategy, which may include DIP financings. The number of DIP financings per year peaked at over 160 following both the financial crisis and the COVID-19 pandemic but has remained fewer than 100 in years following both events. Total DIP financings in recent years have ranged from approximately $2 billion to $28 billion, while peak volume reached $58 billion in 2009.

ASSET-BASED LENDING

Asset-based lending (ABL) encompasses a variety of corporate- and consumer-oriented finance strategies where the credit is backed, either directly or indirectly, by tangible or financial assets. Unlike traditional leveraged finance strategies, such as direct or mezzanine lending, where the loan is supported predominantly by the general creditworthiness and enterprise value of the borrower, asset-based loans are backed predominantly by the value of specific assets that serve as collateral for the loan.

Market Size and Structure

As with other types of private credit, there is no reliable data on the actual size of the asset-based lending market, due to myriad different sub-specialties and the private nature of most ABL providers. However, some broad market estimates do exist. The Federal Reserve Economic Data of June 2022 reports that there was $733 billion of US consumer credit outstanding owned and managed by finance companies. There is also reported to be $347 billion of small business financing outstanding including $193 million of equipment loans and leases as well as $79 billion of other receivables including loans on commercial accounts receivable and factored commercial accounts. Of course, these figures include assets held by the major consumer and commercial card companies and lenders, so the opportunity set for the specialist ABL participants is likely a very small subset.

Asset-based finance is a broad category of private credit. Some of the more prevalent sub-strategies include the following:

1. *Working capital finance:* a large subset of ABL includes revolving lines of credit provided to small and midsized companies seeking to finance the growth of their inventory and accounts receivable. Historically this type of ABL was provided primarily by local and regional banks. However, in recent years increased bank regulation and heightened bank capital adequacy requirements have led to reductions in the quantity of bank lending targeting this borrower universe, and private lenders have entered the field. In a working capital line of credit facility, the lender will advance to the borrower a percentage of the value of inventory and receivables on the borrower's books.
2. *Equipment finance:* this broad category of ABL encompasses loans and lines of credit made against hard assets. Sub-categories include small business finance, such as equipment leasing and retailer point of purchase equipment finance; transportation finance, including aircraft and aircraft equipment, rolling stock, trailer and shipping containers,

and cargo vessels; and floorplan finance, such as warehouse lines for auto retailers. Similar to working capital finance, this type of business lending was once largely the purview of commercial banks, as well as commercial finance companies. In the wake of the GFC, many commercial banks have pulled back from this type of finance, while a number of the larger commercial finance companies have gone out of business. Private lenders have begun to fill the void on an opportunistic basis, seeking out more complex situations with enhanced expected returns.

3. *Financial asset lending and rediscounting:* a third major category of ABL involves a specialty lender providing portfolio-based loans or lines of credit to other consumer or commercial finance companies to support the growth of those lenders' portfolios. Examples of portfolios financed include (1) for consumer lenders: credit card receivables, installment loans, auto loans, and small ticket leases; and (2) for commercial lenders: merchant cash advances (purchases of future receivables), small business loans, and rediscount facilities (a note purchase facility for other finance companies such as factoring providers). In each case, the lender provides a credit facility collateralized by the underlying loans or leases, which may themselves be secured or unsecured obligations of the ultimate borrower. These credit facilities are often highly structured, to protect the lender against cash leakage and fraud.

Expected Return and Risk

Asset-based lending has varied levels of competition from traditional lending sources, based on the specific strategy employed. Additionally, ABL strategies have seniority in claim to the assets being financed and have an income component that is commensurate with the liquidity and quality of the asset and the complexity of the financing structure.

For example, working capital finance is offered by a variety of lender types, including commercial banks, commercial finance companies, and private investment funds. This strategy is the most traditional of ABL strategies and has the lowest barriers to entry, and thus the most competitive pricing. Such loans are almost always floating rate, such as a spread over SOFR or LIBOR. In today's market, spreads range from 300 to 600 bps. The lender may also charge a modest (25- to 50-bp) fee on undrawn commitments. Unlevered gross annual returns are therefore in the mid- to upper-single digit percentages. Given the short-term nature of the assets being financed, these ABL loans turn over multiple times per year. So, the loan facility may only run for one year, with cleanups of line outstandings on seasonal borrowings.

Alternatively, financial asset lending and rediscounting is a very specialized niche that requires significant investment in monitoring systems and operational controls. Accordingly, lenders offering this strategy enjoy significant competitive advantages, which can lead to the opportunity for premium returns. These financing packages typically carry a floating rate of interest, such as SOFR/LIBOR + 800 basis points to SOFR/LIBOR + 1200 bps per annum. The lender may also charge structuring and unused commitment fees and will target a gross annualized return of 12–15%.

Fixed asset finance tends to fall somewhere in the middle of these two extremes. These loans and leases typically have a tenor that approximates the useful life of the asset being financed, which may range from 2 years to over 20 years. Interest rates can be fixed or floating, and spreads vary with the quality, secondary market value, and relative liquidity of the asset.

Because of the small company and/or asset-specific risk of asset-based lending, investors should consider the strategy to be a satellite position in a diversified private credit portfolio, which would be a smaller allocation than core strategies, such as direct lending or real estate lending.

Investment Strategies

Most ABLs are specialized firms that raise private funds or are finance companies with balance sheets owned by BDCs and asset managers. Given ABLs' focus on privately held, small market and middle market borrowers, loan sizes tend to be relatively small (between $10 million and $50 million), so the fund sizes are modestly sized as well, generally less than $1 billion. Parts of the corporate ABL market have expanded in recent years as upper middle market companies, particularly in the retail sector, look to ABL funds as a source of liquidity. Due to the still-developing institutional investor interest in the sector, market size details are limited, but there are approximately 40 active private lenders in the space, which collectively raise multiple billions of dollars per year of new private vehicles with a focus on ABL. As noted, other players in the ABL market include local and regional banks.

Private ABL funds are typically structured similarly to private equity funds, although they frequently employ shorter funds lives, for example, a five- to eight-year total fund life with a two- to three-year investment period. The primary reason for the shorter fund life is the self-liquidating nature of the assets being financed, such that investment hold periods in ABL are on the whole meaningfully shorter than those of typical private equity investments.

ABL fee structures, however, are largely analogous to those seen in private equity, although lower in absolute level. Annual management fees are typically charged on invested capital. In general, annual management fees are in the range of 1–2% of gross invested assets, which may include leverage applied to investor contributions. Managers may also receive 10–20% of fund profits as a carried interest, above a hurdle rate or preferred return of 6–8% per annum. Use of leverage at the fund level varies based on the underlying sub-strategy: while financial asset lending often does not use leverage, other more straightforward strategies may employ leverage.

As noted, ABL is used in a variety of corporate and asset finance applications. Loan sizes are generally in the $5 million to $200 million range, although the majority of transactions are between $10 million and $75 million. Portfolio finance transactions involving large numbers of underlying assets can be larger.

REAL ESTATE DEBT

Real estate debt is a large, multifaceted market that encompasses a wide range of participants and loan and investment structures covering the entire universe of commercial property types around the globe. Real estate debt is used by property owners and developers to finance the acquisition or development of a property or construction project and to leverage the equity invested. Loan sizes and structures vary widely, with loans ranging from less than $1 million to hundreds of millions of dollars, and structures that include senior secured first mortgages, whole loan packages composed of a senior loan and mezzanine loan, syndicated loans, and loan tranches created and sold to structured product vehicles such as commercial mortgage-backed securities (CMBS).

Historically, traditional lenders like banks and life insurance companies supplied the majority of real estate debt capital to property owners. The real estate debt landscape began to evolve in the 1990s. The CMBS market developed following the savings and loan crisis, allowing nonbank institutions and investors to access real estate debt through the securitized market. The real estate debt market underwent further evolution following the 2008 GFC. As bank lenders pulled back from real estate lending as a result of the post-2008 banking regulations, private real estate managers and mortgage REITs emerged to fill the commercial real estate financing gap left by banks.

Private real estate debt has emerged as a well-developed market for institutional investors. There are more than 200 active private fund managers operating in the space, with most of them operating in the US. Over the past five years, these managers have raised between 40 and 50 new private funds per year, generally aggregating over $30 billion per year.

Current Market Environment

The market for real estate debt is large and deep, both in the US and globally. Average annual real estate loan origination in the US has ranged between $450 billion and $600 billion since 2016. After a slowdown in 2020 as a result of COVID, the real estate debt market recovered quickly. The total volume of real estate loans closed in 2021 was $578 billion. There is a projected $400 billion in average annual loan maturities through 2026. A large proportion of the underlying properties for these maturing loans will likely require private real estate debt solutions resulting from the properties falling out of stabilization during the previous loan term. Equity sponsors are expected to continue to seek higher leverage and more flexible structures through private loans to execute their business plans.

Private real estate debt as an asset class is particularly well-suited for an inflationary environment. Since about 2010, approximately 78% of private real estate loans have been structured with floating-rate coupons.

Private Real Estate Debt Funds

Private real estate debt funds are typically structured similarly to private equity real estate funds, with eight- to ten-year fund terms including three- to five-year investment periods. Annual management fees range between 1.00 and 1.50% on invested capital. Mezzanine loan managers may charge management fees on committed capital. Managers also receive 10–15% of fund profits as a carried interest, above a hurdle rate or preferred return of 7–8% per annum. Fund managers may use leverage at the fund level, depending on the strategy and relative security of the cash flows supporting the loan investments. Leverage on individual loans or total portfolios of loans can range up to four times invested capital for first lien strategies, with lower amounts of leverage (or no leverage at all) for mezzanine strategies. Managers may also make use of capital commitment lines of credit to streamline capital calls and to shorten the length of the J-curve period.

Investors should consider real estate debt to be a core holding in their private credit portfolios, since the market is significant and well established, with many experienced managers. Furthermore, real estate is subject to a different set of risk factors than corporate direct lending, so an allocation to real estate debt provides a degree of portfolio diversification. Senior secured debt exposure is the most core of the real estate debt strategies and merits a permanent allocation. Mezzanine real estate debt, like corporate mezzanine, should be viewed as a more opportunistic strategy. Mezzanine should perform better (and offer outsized returns) when the real estate market is coming out of a downturn, and there is less senior real estate available to finance properties. Alternatively, mezzanine exposure should be reduced toward the peak of a real estate cycle, when creditor protections have weakened, LTV levels are elevated, and credit spreads have narrowed.

Real Estate Loan Uses, Characteristics, and Structures

Real estate loans are used for the refinancing, acquisition, or construction of real estate properties. Loan sizes vary widely between $5 million and $1 billion, although the majority of transactions are between $10 million and $100 million. Senior first lien mortgage debt is typically provided up to 55–65% loan to value, while mezzanine loans may go as high as 85–90% LTV. Whole loan lenders will finance the entire debt portion of the capital structure and split the loan into senior and mezzanine tranches post-close. These whole loan lenders then sell off the senior loan portion of the loan to third-party debt investors seeking that level of risk exposure, retaining the mezzanine tranche for their own portfolio. As an example, a whole loan may be $65 million, representing a loan to value of 65% on a property valued at $100 million. The whole loan lender may repackage the loan into a $50 million first lien mortgage loan with an LTV of 50% and a $15 million mezzanine loan with an attachment point LTV of 50% and a detachment point LTV of 65%. In today's market, the whole loan may have been priced at an interest rate of SOFR + 700 basis points, while the new senior loan is priced at SOFR + 300 basis points and the new mezzanine loan at SOFR + 900 basis points. Loan maturities will vary depending on the use of the loan. For instance, construction loans will typically have short maturities of 12–24 months. Permanent loans feature longer maturities (five or more years), depending on property and lease type.

The vast majority of real estate debt represents directly negotiated financings between the lender (or group of lenders) and the borrower, with the introducing party either the equity sponsor of the property or an intermediary hired by the borrower to source potential capital providers.

Expected Return and Risk Profiles

Expected returns on real estate debt depend on a variety of factors including the seniority or loan type and the LTV of the loan. Senior secured debt is typically structured as a floating rate loan, with interest at a spread over SOFR. In the current market, senior loans are priced at SOFR + 300 to 500 bps, and these loans also include a closing fee of 1.0–1.5% of the loan principal. Mezzanine loans (and other subordinated debt types), by comparison, are priced at SOFR + 700 to 1000 bps, also with an up-front fee.

Broadly, lower-risk strategies (e.g., senior secured loans with low underlying leverage, on institutional-quality real estate properties) typically generate a 5–7% yield. Higher-risk strategies (e.g., subordinated debt or more highly levered senior loans) typically generate an 8–10% yield. Opportunistic strategies that include higher LTVs, noncore real estate sectors or geographic markets, or loans on construction or heavy redevelopment properties may generate 10%+.

In addition to loan seniority and LTV, the most significant determination of risk in real estate debt is the nature of the underlying real estate itself. There are three key real estate factors to consider when determining risk: property sectors, geographic focus, and property cash flow profile (outlined next).

Property Sector

Property Sector	Benefits	Risks/Challenges
Office: subsectors include core CBD and trophy assets, suburban and creative office	■ Properties with longer weighted average lease terms (WALT) to credit tenants offer stable cash flow streams ■ Higher liquidity for quality, well-located assets	■ Higher capex requirements for renovations and lease-up costs (tenant improvements and leasing commissions) ■ Less liquidity for larger properties in periods of market uncertainty
Industrial: subsectors include flex, warehouse, logistics/distribution, logistics fleet parking, and manufacturing	■ Logistics, distribution, and warehouse properties require minimal releasing capital compared to other sectors ■ Market fundamentals driving low vacancy rate and high rent growth	■ Tenant-specific specifications and buildouts for custom properties may present higher costs in a releasing scenario ■ E-commerce tailwinds have driven demand, and capital-seeking industrial exposure has resulted in rate compression
Multifamily: subsectors include urban high-rise, suburban mid-rise and garden communities, and single-family rentals	■ Properties with WALT to credit tenants offer stable cash flow streams ■ Higher liquidity for quality, well-located assets	■ High capex requirements for renovations and lease-up costs (tenant improvements and leasing commissions) ■ Less liquidity for larger properties in periods of market uncertainty

Property Sector	Benefits	Risks/Challenges
Retail: subsectors include high street retail, grocery-anchored shopping center, lifestyle center, regional power centers, enclosed malls	■ Higher coupon rate and lower leverage commanded in the credit markets due to sector risk ■ Some subsectors insulated from e-commerce trends (e.g., grocery-anchored and daily needs centers) and remain stable	■ Broad sector challenges related to the rise of e-commerce ■ Constantly changing consumer trends and fluctuating tenant credit ■ Capital-intensive repositioning and releasing
Hospitality/Leisure: subsectors include limited and select service, full service, luxury resorts	■ Higher coupon rate and lower leverage commanded in the credit markets due to sector risk ■ Leisure and luxury resorts benefiting from pent-up consumer demand following COVID-19 impact	■ Urban properties and those dependent on business travel remain challenged due to COVID-19 impact ■ Capital-intensive refurbishment required to maintain market position
Specialty: examples include medical office, student housing, seniors housing, data centers, and entertainment venues	■ Subsectors less familiar to traditional real estate lenders provide an opportunity for sophisticated managers ■ Lower correlation to macroeconomic dynamics (e.g., medical office, student housing)	■ Idiosyncratic risks require sector expertise ■ Sector-specific risks include university enrollment growth for student housing, technology obsolescence for data centers, and hospital system consolidation for medical office

Geography

Market Type	Characteristics	Examples	
Primary	■ Globally recognized urban metros with diversified economies and significant infrastructure	■ New York ■ Los Angeles ■ Boston ■ San Francisco ■ Houston	■ London ■ Sydney ■ Paris ■ Tokyo

(continued)

(continued)

Market Type	Characteristics	Examples	
Secondary	▪ Sizable regional commercial hubs and population centers ▪ Includes distinct cities in proximity to larger primary markets	▪ Indianapolis, IN ▪ Sacramento, CA ▪ Salt Lake City, UT ▪ Oklahoma City, OK ▪ Milwaukee, WI	▪ Columbus, OH ▪ Manchester, UK ▪ Lisbon, Portugal
Tertiary	▪ Smaller markets outside of the sphere of major metros ▪ Potentially high-growth markets but with more concentrated economies or singular growth drivers	▪ Boise, ID ▪ Greenville, SC ▪ Colorado Springs, CO	▪ Tucson, AZ ▪ Tallahassee, FL

Property Cash Flow Profile

- *Stabilized:* The property is substantially leased with significant in-place cash flow and limited near-term tenant rollover. There is minimal repositioning or lease-up risk. Typically financed through banks, bank syndication, or securitization given the stability of the cash flow profile.
- *Light transitional:* The property may have moderate vacancy or face near-term tenant expirations, but there is material in-place cash flow supporting debt service. Modest refurbishment or releasing is required to maximize value, presenting execution risk and potential lease-up risk.
- *Heavy transitional or redevelopment:* The property is largely vacant or facing significant near-term tenant expiration. The property may also face physical obsolescence. There is minimal in-place cash flow and significant near-term risk to any existing cash flow. A major redevelopment or value-add program is subject to execution risk or lease-up risk.
- *Construction:* No in-place cash flow and subject to significant execution, budget, timing, and lease-up risk.
- *Unentitled land:* No in-place cash flow and subject to entitlement and zoning risk. Binary outcomes and lack of cash flow is not conducive to typical debt fund profile.

Market Outlook

The amount of capital raised for real estate debt funds in 2021 recovered from the COVID-related decrease in 2020 but was still less than peak amount raised in 2017. Fewer managers are raising capital, indicating a less crowded field of competitors. Larger managers are raising the majority of capital for private real estate credit funds, and those larger managers are also able to command more accretive leverage and borrower-friendly structures from senior bank lenders, delivering stronger levered yields. The historical lower-volatility profile of real estate credit and the inherent inflation-defensive nature of floating rate loans coupled with the volume of near-term commercial real estate loan maturities results in an optimistic outlook for private real estate credit strategies going forward.

INFRASTRUCTURE DEBT

Infrastructure is essential, capital-intensive assets with high barriers to entry that generate stable, long-term cash flows, often under long-term contracts and/or regulatory frameworks. Infrastructure debt consists of debt financing relating to the development, expansion, and maintenance of infrastructure assets and is distinguished by strong downside protection and capital preservation when compared to debt in other asset classes. Municipalities, government authorities, and private entities (operating companies and projects) borrow money to develop, construct, and operate infrastructure projects.

Target financing opportunities within several infrastructure sectors include transport (rail, mass transit, ports, toll roads, airports, etc.), renewable power (hydro, wind, solar, distributed generation, storage), utilities (electricity, natural gas connections, smart meters, water and wastewater, district energy), midstream (transmission pipelines, natural gas storage/processing), data (communication towers, fiber networks, data centers, etc.), and social (public services such as education, courthouses, health care, etc.). The amount of capital required to achieve the buildout of these key sectors, as well as ongoing refinancing needs, will contribute to a significant investment opportunity within the infrastructure debt space. In addition, debt investments in infrastructure assets exhibit the following characteristics:

- *Monopolistic features:* Infrastructure assets often exhibit monopolistic features of the services they provide through regulatory-based controls and/or high barriers to entry.

- *High barriers to entry:* Due to high capital costs, geographic location advantages, and contractual and regulatory frameworks, infrastructure assets typically have high barriers to entry and often face little or no competition.
- *Predictable and stable cash flows:* The underlying infrastructure assets generally comprise long-life assets and benefit from stable cash generation profiles driven by regulatory regimes and/or medium to long-term contracts.
- *Inflation-linked revenues:* Cash flows produced by the underlying infrastructure assets are generally linked to measures of economic growth such as inflation, in which, in some cases, revenue increases due to inflation are embedded in concession agreements, licenses, and contracts.
- *Default and recovery rates:* Moody's Default and Recovery Rates study shows that infrastructure debt has a relatively lower probability of default and high recovery rates versus comparably rated corporate credits.

Historically, commercial banks were the principal source of debt for infrastructure assets. While banks and insurance companies continue to play a primary role in larger, investment-grade deals, post-financial crisis bank regulation and stricter lending criteria have limited the universe of infrastructure companies and projects that can access commercial banks. Banks typically limit themselves to investment-grade transactions and avoid transactions with structural subordination. As a result, this has created an opportunity for structured or nonbank financing specializing in infrastructure assets to fill the gap by expanding into bespoke direct lending. Cliffwater tracks approximately 60 private infrastructure funds totaling more than $37 billion of commitments.

Market Environment

The infrastructure debt market has expanded significantly since the early 2010s. Specifically, the exponential increase in data consumption globally, the universal push toward decarbonization of the economy, and an acceleration toward e-commerce are emerging amid other longer-term trends, such as aging utility and telecom assets, requiring significant capital for upgrades and governments and corporations seeking private sector capital solutions to ever-increasing debt loads as borrowing costs normalize from historic lows. These factors are also driving increased complexity and risk for infrastructure investors, especially as highly leveraged governments are increasingly seeking private sector solutions to their more complex infrastructure needs. With budgetary constraints prevailing globally, governments are actively seeking private investors to provide the necessary capital and delivery expertise needed to maintain and develop critical infrastructure. Infrastructure borrowers are seeking capital providers who understand their businesses and are able to provide customized bridge capital to scale and de-risk their businesses. Once stabilized, these infrastructure businesses will be able to attract cheaper, permanent capital from banks and capital markets investors.

Overall, there is a compelling market need for structured or nonbank financing by infrastructure asset owners. The demand for financing for infrastructure assets is supported by the following drivers of borrower demand:

- *Acquisition financing:* In asset acquisition scenarios, subordinated debt can decrease a bidder's cost of capital by reducing the amount of equity needed—enhancing the bidder's competitiveness.
- *Sponsor recapitalization:* For existing infrastructure asset owners, the introduction of a subordinated debt tranche can release capital for distributions and/or reinvestment toward new projects without a loss of ownership or control.
- *Refinancing transactions:* Subordinated debt can be used to refinance existing debt approaching maturity or restore senior leverage to investment-grade levels.
- *Funding capital expenditures:* For new projects, the addition of a subordinated debt tranche can help optimize a sponsor's cost of capital, enhancing project viability and/or the sponsor's overall competitiveness.

Within infrastructure more broadly, through the pandemic, unlisted equity infrastructure demonstrated resilience during 2020. Despite some infrastructure sectors being particularly hard hit (e.g., airports and toll roads), infrastructure generally rebounded strongly in 2021. Demand with some of the infrastructure sectors reached an even higher level than pre-pandemic levels, with the pandemic exposing the importance of robust health care, digital infrastructure, and energy transition. Overall, infrastructure investing is a long duration strategy that provides stable and reliable returns (much like credit-oriented investments), which served well during the volatility of the pandemic. In addition, infrastructure assets are an effective hedge against inflation.

The Preqin 2022 investor survey found inflation hedging was the third most influential reason to invest in infrastructure, behind diversification and reliable income streams. Pension plans, for example, have long-dated liabilities that are sometimes directly linked to inflation; therefore, to fund these liabilities, pensions look for assets where income is indexed to inflation measures. Moreover, rising rates accompanied by inflation will also have little impact on infrastructure valuations in the medium to long term as most current infrastructure assets have strong contractual protections with fixed rate debt, and with new infrastructure projects, most assets will also include strong contractual agreements with pass-through protections.

Market Size and Structure

Infrastructure debt financing has become much more prevalent in recent years. In 2021, Moody's rated approximately $3.1 trillion of infrastructure securities globally, including $1.2 trillion of North America infrastructure and project finance transactions and $739 billion of US municipal bond transactions. Utilities, both regulated and unregulated, comprise the vast majority (73%) of new issuance by volume, a sector that includes energy, power, and water-related utilities. Transportation sectors, including airports, roads, ports, and rail, account for most of the remainder (27%).

Infrastructure debt carries investment-grade and below-investment-grade ratings. According to Moody's, 92% of the infrastructure securities are investment grade. More specifically, when excluding municipal securities, which are nearly all investment grade, more than 80% of corporate infrastructure and project finance issues carry an investment grade rating, compared with about 40% for nonfinancial corporate issuers.

Banks have traditionally been the primary originators of project finance loans, but nonbank finance companies are now entering the origination market as banks have reduced their activity, in particular as relates to the origination of below-investment grade and unrated loans. Nonbank lenders focus primarily on below-investment grade or unrated securities. Standard & Poor's finds similarly strong default avoidance for non-investment grade infrastructure debt, along with high recovery rates of near 90%. This is not surprising, given the long-term stable cash flows provided by infrastructure assets, the value of their collateral, and their critical role in the operation of the economy.

Expected Return and Risk

Infrastructure debt is distinguished by strong downside protection and capital preservation when compared to debt in other fixed income asset classes. For example, in aggregate, according to Moody's, infrastructure debt has been less likely than nonfinancial corporate issuers to incur credit losses, especially over longer time horizons. On average, infrastructure debt strategies raised for institutional investors have an expected gross return of 7–10%, depending on seniority, structure, and leverage. The bulk of infrastructure debt return is in the form of current yield, as infrastructure debt does not typically trade at distressed levels or offer non-coupon economics. Senior secured infrastructure debt, which typically has an LTV of 50–70%, carries interest rates of 4–6%, while subordinated/mezzanine deals have higher coupon rates in the range of 7–10%. The incremental coupon compensates for the additional downside risk based on the mezzanine debt being subordinated to senior obligations. Volatility for the sector is dampened by the consistent long-term, contracted cash flows of many infrastructure assets, low default rates, and high recovery rates. Overall, within infrastructure debt strategies, returns are primarily generated through the following key components:

- *Cash interest:* current income received from coupon payments
- *Original issue discount (OID):* a discount in price from a loan's face value that is treated as interest because the lender is repaid the face value at maturity
- *Up-front fees:* origination fees that may be generated as part of a transaction and are considered fee income
- *Prepayment/exit fees:* the lender generally seeking to incorporate structural protections against prepayment risks, such as no-call periods, and various prepayment penalties, such as a make-whole premium
- *Amendment/waiver fees:* at times, borrowers seeking amendments or waivers under the terms of the loan agreement, which may generate fee income

Since expected returns and risk are on the low end of private credit, investors typically allocate to infrastructure debt as a lower-risk option within a broader private credit portfolio or as a diversifier and volatility dampener within an infrastructure portfolio.

Investment Strategies

Managers that offer infrastructure debt strategies to institutional investors are typically large, globally diversified infrastructure investors. These firms have traditionally focused on equity infrastructure strategies but have begun offering credit strategies to capture additional management fee revenue. These strategies typically focus on the non-investment grade and non-rated portion of the market since the investment-grade portion does not offer high enough returns to overcome private fund management fees and still offer an attractive return. Investors of infrastructure debt funds focused on investment-grade transactions are typically insurance companies that accept lower returns from rated debt.

There are approximately 100 investment firms involved in private infrastructure debt globally. Between 2014 and 2021, these managers have collectively raised between five and ten new infrastructure debt funds per year, aggregating between $4 billion and $7 billion of new capital. More specifically, since the COVID-19 pandemic, 34 investment firms have closed a dedicated infrastructure debt fund, totaling over $14.5 billion in aggregate capital commitments. Moreover, there are currently more than 60 investment firms raising a dedicated infrastructure debt fund, seeking over $30 billion in aggregate capital commitments.

Infrastructure debt strategies are generally global and multisector in scope, though some have a primary focus on a particular sector, such as energy. Infrastructure debt is typically not a portion of other corporate credit managers' portfolios given the sector expertise and presence required to source infrastructure deals and underwrite assets prudently. As noted, managers may focus on senior secured debt or mezzanine debt strategies. Mezzanine loans can be achieved through a variety of structures, including second lien secured loans, first lien loans made to a holding company (instead of the operating company, which has direct ownership of the infrastructure assets), or preferred equity with debt-like features.

Infrastructure debt funds are typically structured similarly to private equity funds, with a 10- to 12-year term, including a four- to five-year investment period, though there are some open-ended structures. Fee structures vary depending on the target return of the strategy (higher target return leads to higher management and performance fees) and whether leverage is employed. Annual management fees are in the range of 1.0–1.5% and, like most private credit strategies, are charged on invested capital. Managers also receive 10–20% of fund profits as a carried interest above a hurdle rate or preferred return of 5–8% per annum. Infrastructure debt funds may use leverage at the fund level.

ROYALTIES

Royalties strategies invest in cash flow streams generated by intellectual property (IP). IP represents an idea, invention, or process used in making product and services. Inventors and entrepreneurs are rewarded for developing valuable IP by capturing economic rents; in most developed countries these rents are protected by patents. Patents provide patent owners with the exclusive right to market patented products and services for a prespecifed period of time. The patent owner might be the original developer of the patent or it may be an entity that purchased the patent. The value of patents are monetized through royalty payments made by companies that, in turn, license a product or service to sell to businesses and consumers. This stream of royalty payments can be sold to free up capital to invest in the development of new products or services, to fund growth of existing products or services, to retire existing debt, or as collateral for new loans.

The three main areas in which royalties strategies typically invest are as follows:

- Health care, including drugs, treatments, and medical devices
- Media/entertainment, including films, TV shows, games, music, and other media
- Consumer brands, including apparel, accessories, housewares, electronics, and food/beverage

The largest and most popular of these sectors is health care royalties, which includes both traditional and structured royalties strategies.

Market Size and Structure

The health care royalty opportunity is supported by the increasing medical demands of the growing and aging population globally, and the development of new medicines and medical device advancement requires a significant amount of capital. Small health care companies are unable to access traditional bank financing and do not want to accept dilutive equity.

The inventory for traditional royalty investments are a derivative of the global life science revenues generated from biopharma, medtech, and diagnostic companies. Global life science revenues have steadily increased from $1.1 trillion in 2009 to $1.6 trillion in 2021.[8] It is estimated that 1–2% of the annual global life sciences revenue is sold through a licensing agreement. Assuming that global life science revenues average $1 trillion for the next ten years, the size of the market opportunity for traditional health care royalties is between $100 billion and $200 billion.

The size of the structured royalty market opportunity is harder to ascertain than the traditional royalty opportunity. The best way to estimate the size of the opportunity is based on the number of commercial-stage health care companies and the revenues they generate. Neuberger Berman estimates there are approximately 7,000 commercial-stage health care companies with revenues between $15 million and $500 million.

---

[8]CapitalIQ public companies with industry classifications pharmaceuticals, biotechnology, and health care equipment as of September 16, 2021.

The global media and entertainment market is estimated at over $2.5 trillion, and growing at over 8% annually.[9] The proliferation of new internet-based media platforms, such as YouTube, Disney+, Netflix, Amazon, Spotify, and so on, has increased demand for content, creating more opportunities for new royalty streams. For consumer brands, global retail sales from the top 88 licensors totaled $261 billion in 2021 alone.[10]

Expected Return and Risk

Relative to other private credit strategies, the structured royalty strategy has limited competition from traditional lending sources and higher barriers to entry. Additionally, structured royalty strategies have seniority in claim to underlying company assets, are over-collateralized, and have a high-income component with upside potential through options and warrants.

The traditional royalty investment strategy is dominated by a small number of large institutional investors and asset management firms. Unlevered traditional royalty investments are passive and yield an 8.0–10.0% gross return. Investors in the traditional space typically use leverage of 1.0–2.5 times equity to achieve an all-in net return in the low to mid-teens. The downside of traditional royalty investments is that the investment is passive and returns are highly dependent on product-level revenue projections.

Structured royalty returns have a significant yield component due to contracted rights associated with direct revenue participation and interest payments. Revenue participation and interest payments each represent half of the mid-teens yield when fully invested. Additionally, structured royalty returns are enhanced by fees generated from origination and exit, or covenant breach, and upside participation through options and warrants. Structured royalties typically have a five-year loan term; however, on average they are paid back in three to four years. The prepayment of the loan increases the overall internal rate of return and allows for the recycling of capital. In aggregate, the repayment of principal, yield, fees, and equity upside result in a total net return target for structured royalties of about 20%. The reasons structured royalty investments have the potential to generate outsized returns are (1) these companies are too small to access the public debt markets, (2) borrowers may be unattractive to traditional lenders as they may be cash flow negative, and (3) the structured royalty space has

---

[9]PricewaterhouseCoopers, *Entertainment & Media Outlook 2022–2026*. Global revenues of media & entertainment companies.

[10]License Global, *The Top Global Licensors Report* (July 2022). Total revenue reported by 83 participating consumer brands for FY2021.

relatively high barriers to entry—managers need to have experience creating flexible financing structures, have insight into patent protection and patent competition, and be able to value the intellectual property.

Expected returns for the other major royalties categories, media/entertainment and consumer brands, are similar, with a net return of about 8–12%.

Since expected returns are broadly in line with corporate private credit, investors typically allocate to consumer finance strategies as a diversifier within a broader private credit or opportunistic credit portfolio, as they provide exposure outside of the corporate credit sector.

Investment Strategies

Health care royalties can be categorized as traditional or structured. Traditional royalties include the purchase of a long-term royalty stream from an inventor of a patented technology for a discount to the net present value of future royalty payments. Typical sellers of traditional royalties are universities, hospitals, or large public and private life science companies that want to divest mature royalty streams. These organizations will use the proceeds to fund capital projects or increase research and development capabilities.

Structured royalties investments allow public and private companies with commercial health care products or services to borrow against their future revenue or royalty income. The typical company that uses a structured solution tends to be owned by entrepreneurs who do not want their ownership to be diluted. These small companies use the capital to expand their salesforce and to fund product launches and expansion, research and development acceleration, acquisition financing, and balance sheet management. Structured royalty investments are typically senior in the capital structure of a borrower and possess substantial underlying asset value coverage to protect against capital loss.

Royalty streams are typically purchased at a market multiple. For health care royalties this typically ranges between 5–7x annual royalties.

Royalty funds are typically structured similarly to private equity funds, with a four- to six-year investment period and 8- to 12-year fund term. Annual management fees are in the range of 1.5–2.0% of committed capital during the investment period, which may drop during the harvest period. While less common in this strategy, some funds charge on invested capital rather than committed capital. Managers typically also receive 20% of fund profits as a carried interest above a hurdle rate or preferred return of 6–8% per annum. Royalty funds typically do not use leverage at the fund level, except for traditional health care royalties strategies.

Media/entertainment royalties can be acquired from a variety of firms involved in production or distribution, including talent agencies, production companies, and artists and their estates. Consumer brand royalties are based on licensing agreements acquired from product manufacturers and retailers.

REINSURANCE

Reinsurance is insurance provided to an insurer to cover losses from a catastrophe event, such as a natural disaster. Reinsurance allows for one insurer to transfer a specific set of event-linked risks to another insurance provider. Purchasers of reinsurance, or sponsors, include primary underwriters or reinsurers, public and governmental insurance and reinsurance entities, and corporations that choose to self-insure. Sponsors seek to reinsure to reduce capital requirements and to reduce outsized risk exposures. Providers of reinsurance are mainly reinsurance companies and investors.

Sponsors pay a series of predetermined premiums in exchange for protection against losses from uncertain catastrophes. Reinsurance providers pay claims in exchange for a fixed dollar amount of known premiums. The maximum amount of claims liability that a reinsurance provider is obligated to pay is the principal amount of the reinsurance contract or bond. Any losses that occur on the reinsurance contract are paid out of the principal amount, which is typically held in a high-quality, liquid collateral account during the term of the contract. Reinsurance providers (investors) earn a reinsurance spread, equal to the reinsurance premium divided by principal. This is similar to the yield on a bond and is often referred to as the reinsurance risk premium, or yield.

Market Size and Structure

The reinsurance market has been rapidly evolving since the new millennium. Historically, the providers of reinsurance were traditional reinsurance companies, such as Munich RE, Renaissance RE, and Lloyds of London, which assumed the catastrophe risk and kept it on their balance sheets. With the advent of nontraditional reinsurance (or alternative reinsurance), these risks have become increasingly transferred to capital market investors. As a result, a wide range of investors have been able to enter the reinsurance market—from asset management firms to public companies.

Today the reinsurance market is divided between traditional reinsurance and alternative reinsurance. A series of private contracts and securities have been developed for the alternative reinsurance market, commonly referred to as insurance linked securities (ILSs). The most well-known of these ILS are catastrophe bonds (cat bonds), which are listed and traded securities. Many of the ILS are private contracts negotiated between a sponsor and investor to cover losses from specific events over a defined time frame.

Examples of ILS securities include the following:

- *Reinsurance* involves the transfer of insurance risk directly from sponsors. These are private contracts that may be collateralized and are sometimes independently rated. The contracts are sourced from brokers or direct relationships and are individually structured to cover specific events and dollar levels of loss above which the reinsurance provider has claims responsibility. The term of reinsurance contracts is generally one year. The estimated size of this market is $35 billion.
- *Catastrophe bonds* are 144A (unregistered) securities that are traded on a secondary market and generally have a short duration (one to three years). Cat bonds are typically focused on lower reinsurance risks, as they cover low probability events. They are structured as floating rate notes whose principal is tied to specified trigger conditions that need to be met before accumulating losses. The estimated size of this market is $26 billion.
- *Retrocessional contracts* transfer reinsurance directly from sponsors. A retrocession contract will bundle exposures from many reinsurance layers across different companies into a single entity. Due to the complex nature of the contract, transparency is extremely limited. These contracts have a one-year duration. The estimated size of this market is $10 billion.
- *Industry loss warranties (ILWs)* are option-like contracts, or swaps, where the payout is triggered based on industry-wide claims that are in excess of a predetermined trigger amount. These provide investors with the ability to be long or short risk and can be used as hedges. These contracts have a one-year duration. The estimated size of this market is $4 billion.
- *Sidecars, also known as quota shares*, involve property risk that is sourced and transferred directly from sponsors, where the investor takes a slice of the sponsor's entire exposure. This allows an investor to take on the full portfolio of an insurer or reinsurer and earn the risk and return of that business. Investors will pay additional fees to the company to access its portfolio. The estimated size of this market is $7 billion.

Insurance-linked investments come in tradable and nontradable form. Liquid, tradable instruments include catastrophe bonds. Illiquid, nontradable instruments include collateralized reinsurance, retrocessional, ILWs, and sidecars. Private reinsurance and retrocessional contracts typically run for one year, while cat bonds have a one- to three-year term. The contracts are mostly underwritten biannually (in January and June/July) and tend to be both short duration and offer a floating rate.

Catastrophe events, or perils, covered by reinsurance include both natural and human-made perils. Natural perils are hurricanes, earthquakes, wind, tornado and hail, flood, typhoon, and wildfire. Human-made perils include marine, terrorism, energy, cyber, aviation, and space/satellite. Generally, reinsurers will have the most exposure to peak perils, which include US wind, US earthquake, European wind, Japan wind, and Japan earthquake.

Reinsurers diversify across geographic regions and perils. Contracts and bonds are structured to provide coverage at different attachment points, which are dollar levels of loss above which the reinsurance provider has claims responsibility. The higher the attachment point, the lower the likelihood that the reinsurance provider will be responsible for paying a claim. Most reinsurance underwriting takes place twice a year. January 1 is the key renewal date for most reinsurance and retrocessional contracts. In the middle of the year, US wind contracts are underwritten, just before the start of the hurricane season in the Atlantic and Caribbean.

Expected Return and Risk

The universe of reinsurance investments can provide a very wide range of returns. Returns are highly dependent on the type of ILS held in the portfolio and the attachment points of the reinsurance contracts. Investors receive a reinsurance return that is equal to the insurance premiums plus the collateral return less any insured losses. Investors typically do not use leverage.

For lower risk strategies, a portfolio primarily composed of cat bonds will generate expected annualized returns between 5.0% and 7.0%. For a diversified portfolio of ILS, expected annualized returns range between 7.0% and 8.5%.

Historically, yields on reinsurance investments have been comparable to high-yield securities, although with less volatility. The coupon paid by the Swiss RE Cat Bond Index has averaged 8.4% since 2007, compared to 8.1% for the Bloomberg High Yield Index. The Swiss RE Cat Bond Index reflects the returns of the catastrophe bond market and is the industry's key point of reference for cat bond sector returns.

Reinsurance returns tend to decline after periods with limited or no insured losses. However, an active hurricane season in the Atlantic or other catastrophe events that lead to above-average insured losses can result in losses for reinsurance securities. Periods following catastrophe events typically see higher returns resulting from higher premiums. For example, in 2005, the reinsurance industry experienced more than $125 billion in losses after Hurricanes Katrina, Rita, and Wilma, which hit the US mainland. The following year, reinsurance spreads increased by 35%, to 8.8% per annum. In 2011, there were a series of global natural disasters (tornadoes in the United States, floods in Australia and Thailand, and a major earthquake in Japan) that caused in excess of $134 billion in insured losses. Reinsurance spreads jumped from 7.7% in 2011 to 10.2% in 2012. However, from 2012 to 2016 there was a lack of notable storm activity and annual insured losses were less than $50 billion. As a result, reinsurance spreads compressed during this period.

Reinsurance returns are primarily driven by losses from natural perils that are not related to economic or financial conditions. Therefore, reinsurance returns have a low correlation with financial markets. The correlation of the Swiss RE Cat Bond Index with major equity and fixed income market indexes has been very low. Since its inception in 2002 to 2018, the Swiss RE Cat Bond Index has had a correlation of 0.13 to the S&P 500 Index and 0.18 to the Bloomberg Barclays Aggregate Bond Index. For investors, the low correlation with public securities makes reinsurance attractive as a portfolio diversifier.

Since expected returns and risk are on the low end of private credit, investors typically allocate to reinsurance as a differentiated source of yield and a diversifier that is uncorrelated to other investments in their portfolios, rather than as a return-enhancing strategy.

Investment Strategies

Managers offer reinsurance strategies to investors in several different vehicles, including institutional separate accounts, traditional hedge fund structures, and liquid mutual funds. Managers generally accept subscriptions near the underwriting cycle at the end of December and June but may take in smaller amounts of capital throughout the year. Managers also offer a wide range of funds that have different return and risk objectives, which dictate the types and mix of ILS in which they invest. These can range from funds that primarily invest in cat bonds, and therefore have lower return and risk objectives, to funds that are primarily focused on the higher-returning (and riskier) segments of the collateralized reinsurance and retrocessional markets. Managers further differentiate themselves in their origination, structuring, and modeling capabilities.

There are several different ways investors can access reinsurance, including separate accounts, where terms are negotiated directly between the fund manager and investor; a hedge fund structure, which typically includes an initial lock-up period of one year, with interim subscription periods; and open-end funds, which typically accept monthly subscriptions and offer quarterly redemption windows, with quarterly or semiannual payouts. Management fees range from 1–1.5%; in cases when performance fees are in place there is often a hurdle rate.

Cliffwater believes there are approximately 50 investment firms involved in reinsurance globally. Collectively, these managers raise between 10 and 20 new reinsurance funds per year (mostly opportunistic/contingent vehicles), aggregating between $10 billion and $15 billion of new capital.

LITIGATION FINANCE

Litigation finance is a relatively nascent but growing specialty finance strategy whereby returns are dependent on the outcome of individual legal cases or portfolios of cases. Although litigation finance in its modern form had begun to develop in the 1990s in Australia and the United Kingdom and in the mid-2000s in the United States with respect to commercial litigation finance, the industry had begun to ramp in the 2010s. Borrowers and capital recipients are primarily law firms and corporate entities that are plaintiffs in legal matters but may also include government entities and even individuals. Litigation finance firms may provide capital to corporate entities to cover litigation expenses associated with specific cases, including attorneys' fees, or general operating expenses or to monetize future awards and to law firms to cover operating expenses, to grow their businesses or to monetize legal fee receivables.

The market for litigation finance exists for claimant financing because claimants either lack the internal funding available to pursue litigation and cannot secure funding from traditional sources like banks, need to free up working capital to pursue other projects, or wish to distribute some of the risk tied to highly uncertain litigation outcomes. Many litigations can be very costly and protracted, often taking several years to resolve. Plaintiff law firms that borrow from litigation funders are typically engaged by their clients on a contingency basis, and, therefore, obtain payments only after the plaintiff receives an award or settlement, which can create operating cash flow challenges for the law firms. Therefore, plaintiff law firms typically borrow from litigation funders to cover operating expenses as well as to grow their businesses. Specifically, for mass tort or personal injury plaintiff law firms, they may borrow to fund their marketing budgets for case acquisitions. In addition, for participating in a less efficient market than traditional capital market, litigation finance providers are typically compensated with a higher return than financiers in more traditional asset classes for taking on litigation risks.

Market Size and Structure

The size of the litigation finance market is not readily available as it is a private market with limited aggregated data on total activity. What is clear is that the addressable market is potentially very large, and the receptivity of claimants and law firms seeking third-party capital is growing. Each year, hundreds of billions of dollars are spent globally on legal fees (one study estimated the total legal spend in the United States at $437 billion in 2016[11]) and an estimated commercial litigation spend of $170 billion in the United States in 2018.[12] Furthermore, the total addressable market would be even larger when including contingency fees from mass tort and personal injury claims.[13] A 2020 survey of law firms and in-house legal departments across the US, UK, and Australia conducted by Burford provides insights into the recent growth trajectory of litigation funding.[14] Of the respondents, 76% indicated their organizations have used legal finance, which was increased from 37% in 2017. In a 2021 survey conducted by Bloomberg, 69% of the respondents indicated they are more likely to use litigation funding now than they were five years ago.[15]

The size of funding amounts sought varies significantly, from less than $100,000 to $50 million or more. Typically, for single case fundings, a funder would target an advance rate of 10%, meaning the target claim value coverage to funded amount is 10 to 1. The small size of the funding sought relative to other credit strategies and claim value indicates that this is a very bifurcated market and that putting significant amounts of capital to work takes time and patience.

---

[11]Thompson Reuters. (2016). "How Big is the U.S. Legal Services Market?" The Legal Executive Institute.

[12]*IMF Bentham Annual Report 2019.*

[13]In 2016, total compensation of the US tort system exceeded $429 billion according to US Chamber Institute for Legal and Compensation of the *U.S. Tort* report dated October 2018. Assuming a 35% contingency fee rate, plaintiff law firms would have been entitled to approximately $150 billion of fees. Further, assuming a loan to value ratio of 25%, funders could have lent approximately $30 billion collateralized by such fees.

[14]*Burford Capital—2020 Legal Finance Report: A Survey of In-house and Law Firm Lawyers.*

[15]*Bloomberg Law—Litigation Finance Survey 2021.*

The small size of most litigation funding also helps explain why legal finance funders largely comprise relatively small, private funds. Most legal finance providers' balance sheets are sized in the hundreds of millions of dollars or less. As in other sectors of specialty finance, technology is starting to reshape the litigation finance market, specifically in how capital recipients and funders interact. For example, Legalist, founded by two Harvard dropouts, uses proprietary software to scrape court dockets in search of claimants that may need fundings. Using technology can help funders scale their investment strategies.

Another reason for the relatively small number of financiers in the legal finance space is that relative to other investment strategies, there is limited competition from traditional financing sources given a higher barrier to entry. In most instances, due diligence requires both legal expertise as well as structuring expertise, and the lack of a steady income stream increases operational risks for credit providers. In addition, sourcing is largely relationship based,[16] and with the legal community only in the last decade or so beginning to adopt the use of third-party capital, existing firms have a decided advantage in giving comfort to law firms and claimants who are new to the space. Finally, banks may also be reluctant to finance claimants or law firms due to their fear of indirectly financing a lawsuit against their other banking clients.

Expected Return and Risk

The economic terms attached to the capital provided can vary widely, but the most common transaction involves the capital provider securing a senior claim on the proceeds of litigation for funding claimants, which would include any awarded judgments or settlement amounts accruing to the claimants or on legal fee receivables for funding law firms. The capital providers may receive only a fixed interest rate, a preferred rate of return in addition to a percentage of the proceeds above the preferred return, only a percentage of proceeds, or a multiple on their invested capital. Interest payments are typically paid in kind, and cash payments ultimately depend

---

[16]Auctions are uncommon in legal finance as clients would unlikely be willing to pay law firms by the hour to work through due diligence with multiple potential funders, and attorney-client privilege may limit law firms from disclosing sensitive information to multiple potential funders. With respect to law firms obtaining fundings for their own businesses, they typically would not be willing to dedicate the time or the effort to seek out many bids as their time is best spent to work on cases, and the cost of capital is typically a small fraction of the law firm's return on investments when using the funds to grow their case inventories.

on the availability of proceeds from settlement or award amounts or attorney fees as they are collected. Litigation funding is typically structured on a nonrecourse basis, meaning the capital provider is fully exposed to the risk of loss from unsuccessful litigation or a collection failure. There is, however, a meaningful segment of the market that includes loans to law firms that have recourse against the law firms and in certain transactions, even personal guarantees from the law firm partners.

The return and risk profile of litigation funding strategies can vary widely depending on the type of financing that is involved. The highest return and risk is associated with risk-sharing with plaintiffs in single cases. In such arrangements, the financing provider is subject to a complete loss in the instance that the litigation fails. The capital provider is compensated for this binary risk through equity-like upside potential measured in multiples of invested capital, which they may target a return of 3–5x their invested capital. However, the lowest return and risk is associated with loans to law firms secured by or a purchase of fee or award receivables from law firms or claimants stemmed from settled cases. Because the return from these investments is generated from settled cases, litigation risk would have been eliminated, and on occasion credit risk with respect to the defendants would have been reduced if there were a funded escrow account. For such investments, the primary risk considerations are fraud risk and duration risk. However, the return would also be commensurately lower for such investments as funders would typically target a gross return in the low-teens IRR.

A fast-growing segment of the market is portfolio financing, whereby capital providers provide capital to claimants secured by the collective outcome of a cross-collateralized portfolio of cases or law firms secured by contingency fee receivables from a cross-collateralized portfolio of cases. For the capital providers, portfolio financings have the benefit of reducing the binary risk of single case financing and allowing them to deploy more capital in a single investment than a single case financing would. For the capital recipients, portfolio financings would lower the cost of capital. Though portfolio financing is decidedly less risky, it can still carry higher interest rates relative traditional debt investments. In such funding arrangements, a gross interest rate of mid-teens to low-twenties with additional servicing fees of 1.5–3% is not uncommon for financings secured by a portfolio of pre-settlement cases that still carry litigation risks and a gross interest rate in the low-teens for financings secured by a portfolio of settled cases that do not carry litigation risks. While loan maturities are typically about two to four years, the expected payoff time can be shorter subject to the duration of the underlying cases, though prepayment penalties can help the lender achieve its desired multiple on invested capital even when the time line shrinks.

Risk is entirely dependent on the mix of funding arrangements in a litigation finance portfolio. The reported investment results reasonably diversified portfolios by type of loans or equity-like investments provide a sense of the potential variation in returns. Gross of operating expenses, for non-loss concluded cases by vintage year from 2010 through 2021, the IRRs have ranged from 10% to 1,125%, and the returns on invested capital have ranged from 1% to 3,278%.

In a broad credit portfolio context, the risk profile of litigation financing has more merits. The return outcome of each litigation finance investment is idiosyncratic and uncorrelated to other debt or equity investments and has minimum influence from economic cycles. Thus, investors typically allocate to litigation finance as a diversifier within a broader opportunistic credit portfolio.

Investment Strategies

Litigation finance is still relatively early in its development as an institutional asset class. While there are a few dozen firms that offer funds in the sector, the bulk of the assets are managed by a handful of small to mid-size firms. Fund sizes range from $50 million to $750 million. According to Westfleet Advisors, in 2021, there were 47 active funders in the commercial litigation finance space (not including those that focus on mass tort and other personal injury claims) with $12.4 billion in assets under management, increasing from $11.3 billion in 2020.[17] These funders committed $2.8 billion to new investments from July 2020 through June 2021, increasing from $2.5 billion from the prior 12 months.

Litigation finance funding can be broadly categorized as equity-like or credit-like investments and be bifurcated into pre-settlement or post-settlement financings. As discussed previously, equity-like investments are generally made in connection with financing the cost of prosecuting a single case where the funder is typically targeting a return of multiple of their invested capital and on average with longer duration than credit-like investments. Credit-like investments are generally made in the form of a loan with an interest rate secured directly or indirectly by future proceeds from multiple cases or a single case with the litigation risk eliminated.

---

[17] *Westfleet Insider—2021 Litigation Finance Market Report.*

- Pre-settlement investments involve providing capital in active litigation where the cost of capital is largely driven by idiosyncratic litigation risks. Capital is used by companies or law firms in all types of claims and deployed at various stages of the legal process prior to the settlement of the case or cases. In addition to considering the merits of a case, funders will also need to consider the potential duration risks, collection risks (credit profile of the defendants and, in the case of foreign defendants, the ability to enforce a judgment or settlement), the quality of the attorneys, and the commercial reasonableness of the claimants. Pre-settlement investments can be structured as an equity-like investment or a credit-like investment.
- Post-settlement investments are more akin to credit opportunities where the investments are made in or secured by post-judgment or settled cases. Event risk for these investments is low, and funders generally target a low-teens IRR for these investments. Law firms seek to monetize legal fees and claimants seek to monetize judgment or settlement awards after litigation is largely resolved and risk has shifted from legal to credit and duration risks. The investments can be made in the form of a loan collateralized by or a forward purchase of one or more judgment or settlement awards to be received by a claimant or fee receivables of a law firm from settled cases.

Litigation finance funds are structured similarly to private equity and private lending funds, with a two- to three-year investment period and a four- to seven-year fund term. In general, annual management fees are in the range of 1.0–2.5% of invested capital or commitments with a 15–25% carried interest, above a hurdle rate or preferred return of 6–8% per annum. Litigation finance funds typically do not use leverage. Funds may focus on single case funding or multiple case (portfolio) funding or pursue both strategies. In either case, funds will diversify by duration, counterparty, industry, type of claims, and geography to reduce total risk.

Conclusion

The United States has witnessed and supported tremendous growth in financial assets since the middle of the 20th century with a significant fraction smartly warehoused in pension plans, insurance companies, endowments, and foundations to provide for the future needs of the old, the young, and the needy. Few places elsewhere in the world have established the institutions and policies that grow, house, and protect this type of capital.

The 2008 GFC placed a severe strain on these institutions, not only creating historic losses in the value of assets held but also causing interest rates to fall to near zero. As a result, asset growth suffered, further jeopardizing the future obligations of these institutions. A recovering economy and stock market has helped, but fiduciaries know all too well that it is too risky to rely on stocks alone for their institutions' well-being. As a result, a search for yield megatrend has manifested to find safe assets that throw off a steady stream of cash flow of at least mid-single-digit percentage levels that can help maintain institutional status quo.

During the same time, regulation and stepped-up capital requirements forced commercial banks to step back from their leadership role of financing middle market companies. Private asset managers replaced them and in so doing introduced a new asset class called corporate direct lending. Its growing acceptance is helping fill the yield demands of investors.

Institutional investors seldom buy on yield alone, so in constructing this book, the intent was to examine the asset class from the many perspectives institutions find important. In so doing, several unique contributions were presented.

- First is the CDLI as a useful benchmark for measuring return and risk in an objective, unbiased way. Institutionally, asset classes seldom exist without an agreed-on benchmark, and the CDLI has the potential to serve that role. The CDLI is also important in defining realized credit losses as the source of return that largely defines the value added that managers contribute. Ultimately, manager alpha is represented by the track record for credit losses. Yield reflects risk taken, or beta, rather than manager skill. This second edition introduced two additional CDLI subindexes: a senior-only direct loan index called CDLI-S and a venture-only direct loan index called CDLI-V. The senior-only direct loan index is particularly valuable to investors that look to allocation to only senior secured loans. Chapter 9 showed that while senior-only loan yields are lower, they have offsetting advantages in lower loss rates and easier financing terms.

- Second is the identification of systematic risk factors in direct corporate loans and the measurement of risk premiums that compensate lenders for taking those risks. In so doing, investors will better understand what risks they are engaging when they buy yield. New data were presented in Chapter 11 showing the persistence of premiums for the four major risk factors over time. Unlike the public markets, where risk factors are seemingly inconsistent and tend toward zero, the risk factors for private debt appear increasingly consistent and of meaningful value.

- Third is a methodology for cataloging direct lending managers by their risk factor exposures that is useful in differentiating managers and putting them together in a multi-lender portfolio. The importance of diversification can't be stressed enough, and the ability of most single lenders to achieve a sufficient number of credits in a portfolio can be a challenge, particularly in a more competitive environment. Diversification places challenges on investors as well, particularly those without resources to engage in the administrative and legal challenges of multiple private funds. Chapters 15 and 16 showed how private BDCs, interval funds, and tender funds have emerged to help those investors that need convenience as well as performance.

- Fourth is the application of early models of credit risk to explain and differentiate yields and risks across the firm capital structure and, importantly, place a value on covenants that are so important to lenders in protecting principal.

- Fifth is applying the all-weather label to private debt and direct lending in particular. High inflation combined with economic stagnation, has been dormant since the 1980s but has now re-emerged as a major future risk factor. Chapters 7 and 23 were added to support the thesis that private debt should perform well in such an environment, primarily due to the floating rate nature of direct loans and their safety through senior positioning in the borrower capital structure and the presence of covenants.

Looking ahead, direct lending to US middle market companies will only grow. Bank regulation may become more lenient, but risk-taking by banks is very unlikely to reach pre-GFC levels. The evidence presented from surveys of sponsored borrowers speaks to their willingness to pay a little more for execution size, convenience, speed, flexibility, and reliability. These are more the characteristics of unregulated private sector direct lenders than they are of today's commercial banks.

Growth can have risks, and for direct lending, like other asset classes, it is too much money chasing too few opportunities. In the past, the loan middle market has been immune to the credit cycle that governs the traded and broadly syndicated loan and bond markets. But as institutional investors increasingly penetrate the middle market, risk may increase and spreads narrow. Offsetting this is the increasing acceptance of nonbank lenders among borrowers among sponsor-linked borrowers. Evidence provided in these chapters shows little degradation in the return opportunity for private debt. In fact, prospects for private debt look strong as the entire private market ecosystem continues to outpace the public markets.

Size does beget attention, and private debt is now seeing arrows thrown its way. Some in Washington are concerned with an unregulated market sector supplying capital to borrowers that banks can no longer serve. Are alternative lenders creating risks for investors and a monetary system that will need new supervision and controls? Hopefully the answer is an emphatic no. Excesses will always appear in isolation. That seems inevitable. But the existence of broader systemic risks of the type that brought on the GFC does not exist with private debt. Diversification, transparency, safety, and innovation are key characteristics of the private debt market today that should ensure that growth continues.

The motivation for this second edition was to give new readers an updated history on the progress private debt has made. That it proved to be a safe asset during the COVID crisis and thus far in 2022 during the Russian invasion of Ukraine. That its cash yield remained robust in the face of near-zero interest rates and now as rates rise, private debt yields are rising with them. That innovation in private debt is at work helping individual investors access the best that private debt offers through new structures that deliver both attractive risk-adjusted returns and convenience.

Finally, we come back to the equation underlying private debt economics described in the Introduction:

$$Private\ Debt\ Return = Income - Realized\ Gains(Losses)$$
$$\pm\ Unrealized\ Gains(Losses) - Fees$$

It is just not that difficult. Income is fairly certain and much higher than anything publicly traded. Realized losses are small compared to interest earned and almost insignificant if better lenders are used. Unrealized gains (losses) cancel each other out definitionally over a short three-year window so they don't really matter. So that leaves the investor with assessing fees against the quality of lender. Above all, surprises are to the downside so add diversification to high-quality lenders and reasonable fees and resulting investment outcomes should be rewarding to the investor.

Glossary

'40 Act The 1940 Investment Companies Act, an act of the US Congress that regulates the oversight of investment companies and their product offerings.

AFFE Acquired fund fees and expenses are fees charged by BDCs that mutual funds and other registered funds must aggregate with their own fees when reporting expense ratios.

Alpha That portion of total investment return attributable to manager skill and not market return.

Alternative risk premia That portion of total investment return attributable to common factors (value, growth, momentum) that are thought to potentially provide long-term incremental return due to investor behavioral biases.

ASC 820 The generally accepted accounting principal (GAAP) standard that dictates how the fair value of assets is determined, breaking up the process of valuation into three levels (*see also* Level 3 assets).

Asset weighted An index or portfolio whose security holdings and returns are weighted by the asset value, as opposed to equal weighting.

Base rate A short-term, typically floating, interest rate (e.g., Libor, SOFR, Prime, T-bill, Fed Funds), which, in addition to a constant spread to compensate for credit risk, determines the amount of interest periodically paid to the lender by the borrower; also called the reference rate.

BDCs '40 Act investment vehicles called business development corporations that invest in securities, mostly loans, to middle market US companies.

Benchmark return The return of an index, known as the benchmark index, that serves as a comparative measure to assess portfolio composition and gauge relative performance.

Benchmark risk The degree to which the return of a portfolio deviates from that of its benchmark; also known as tracking error.

Beta The measure of an asset's price volatility relative to a market index. For example, a security with an equity beta measured at 0.80 moves up or down 0.80 multiplied by the market index return.

Black-Cox model A formulation for valuing covenants using option pricing theory.

Black-Scholes model A formulation for valuing security options based on price, exercise price, the risk-free interest rate, and time to expiration.

Bloomberg Barclays High Yield Bond Index A commonly used index of publicly traded non-investment grade, or junk, bonds.

Broadly syndicated loans (BSLs) Larger secured and unsecured corporate loans originated by banks and nonbank lenders, with smaller shares then sold (syndicated) to other investors (*see also* Leveraged loans).

Broker quote A price representing what a broker would pay for a specified security at a point in time. Used to value broadly syndicated loans that trade among broker dealers.

C&l loans A commercial bank classification for commercial and industrial loans made primarily to the bank's corporate borrowers.

Cambridge U.S. Buyout Index An index based on financial information of US buyout funds. Source: Cambridge Associates LLC; data provided "as is" and at no cost to Cliffwater LLC.

Capital International Index The earliest index of non-US stock performance that is now Morgan Stanley Capital International.

CAPM The capital asset pricing model, a framework developed by Nobel Laureate William Sharpe for separating the idiosyncratic (diversifiable) and systematic (undiversifiable) risk of an asset and how exposure to these risks affect expected returns.

CDLI The Cliffwater Direct Lending Index, an asset-weighted index of direct US middle market loans originated by private and public BDCs.

CDLI-S The Cliffwater Senior Direct Lending Index, an asset-weighted index of senior-only direct US middle market loans and a subset of CDLI.

CDLI-V The Cliffwater Venture Direct Lending Index, an asset-weighted index of venture-only direct US middle market loans and a subset of CDLI.

Collateralized loan obligation (CLO) A structured investment vehicle composed of loans and other fixed income securities. CLO cash flows are pooled into tranches and packaged as securities, with a separate credit rating for each, and sold to investors. The most junior security, which is last in receiving coupon and principal payments, is referred to as CLO Equity. The purpose of the CLO is to allow loan originators to offload their exposure to these loans and also to obtain a lower cost of capital for making new loans.

Common factor risk Risks related to prespecified systematic (non-diversifiable) factors, such as price momentum, carry, and earnings quality, that are expected to generate above-market returns under certain conditions. Certain investment strategies such as Risk Premia rely on quantitative models to identify and assign weightings to common factor risks.

Convexity The degree to which asset returns are affected by the change in, as opposed to the level of, a systematic risk factor, such as beta or duration. For example, assets with positive convexity to equity beta will perform better during down markets, as their convexity offsets the negative impact on returns of equity beta.

Correlation The degree to which the prices of assets move in relation to each other. Portfolio diversification is improved when adding assets with low correlation to a legacy portfolio.

Cost value The initial amount paid for an asset, which is compared with the fair value of the asset to measure its realized or unrealized gain or loss.

Covenant Part of a loan or bond issue requiring the borrower to fulfill certain conditions on an ongoing basis. A covenant violation can lead to the lender declaring the borrower to be in default of their loan. Covenants may include taking on additional debt or maintaining a certain level of interest coverage.

Covenant lite A loan agreement or bond issue with a relatively small number of covenants, or where covenants are less stringent. These make it easier for a borrower to avoid default.

Credit premium The additional yield of a fixed income security to compensate the lender or investor for credit risk. Higher credit risk leads to a higher credit premium.

COVID crisis The period beginning February 2020 and ending June 2020 when the COVID pandemic caused a drawdown in risky assets, including stocks and credit securities.

Credit rating agency A firm that assigns credit ratings to securities, enabling investors to assess their credit risk; the big three rating agencies are S&P Global, Moody's, and Fitch Group.

Credit risk The probability of a borrower defaulting on their loan.

CRSP The Center for Research in Security Prices, part of the University of Chicago Booth School of Business, was launched in 1960 to provide objective, accurate, and comprehensive data on listed stocks.

Current yield The annual coupon payments of a bond or loan divided by its current price.

Default The failure of a borrower to make scheduled coupon and/or principal payments. When a borrower defaults, the lender(s) have certain remedies, including foreclosure on collateral used to back the loan.

Delayed draw loan A loan whose principal can be increased at the option of the borrower, subject to size and time limitations.

Dispersion The spread of returns or prices within a group of securities or portfolios. For example, a higher dispersion of prices among related securities, or wider spread between the high and low observations, can indicate the market is less efficient, providing more opportunity to generate alpha.

Dodd-Frank Act The Dodd-Frank Wall Street Reform and Consumer Protection Act, or Dodd-Frank Act, signed into law by President Obama in 2010, which created new, and amended existing, regulations to improve the stability of the US financial system and protect consumers against abusive lending practices. The law was a consequence of the 2008–2009 global financial crisis.

Down-and-in option A type of option that becomes active when the price of an underlying security falls below a certain level, called the barrier price; once this occurs the option behaves like a normal put or call option.

Duration A measure of how changes in interest rates inversely affect the price of an asset. For example, an asset with a five-year duration would decrease in price by 5% with a 1% increase in interest rates.

EBITDA Earnings before interest, taxes, depreciation, and amortization is an adjusted measure of the net income of a business that enables better comparability across companies.

Effective life A measure of how long a depreciating asset will generate cash flow.

Effectively connected income Income generated in the US by commercial or investment activity of a foreign person or business.

Equity The residual value of a company after deducting debt and other liabilities; investors purchase equity in a company through common or preferred stock.

Euribor Euro Interbank offered rate is a daily reference rate based on several money market rates at which eurozone banks lend to one another for uncollateralized loans (*see also* Libor).

Euro Crisis The European debt crisis, which effectively began in 2009 and has continued to the present day, refers to the inability of certain members of the eurozone to maintain the total debt of their countries within the initial guidelines set when the euro was originally created; this affects the perceived creditworthiness of their sovereign debt. The adoption of a single currency creates less flexibility for member countries in refinancing debt.

Fair value An estimate of the market value of an asset, typically provided by an auditor during the appraisal process.

Fair value accounting An accounting industry approach to establish an estimate of the market value of an asset, using independently observable inputs in lieu of a market transaction.

Fiduciary A person or legal entity holding assets, or making business or investment decisions, as an agent-in-trust on behalf of a principal, such as a stockholder or trust beneficiary.

First-out loan The senior component of a unitranche loan where first-out lenders, in exchange for a lower coupon rate, are the first to receive interest payments and have a more senior repayment position if the loan is paid off or refinanced, as opposed to last-out loans.

Floating rate Loans whereby the coupon payment is not fixed but adjusted with the level of a reference rate, such as US T-bills, Libor, or SOFR.

Global financial crisis (GFC) (2007–2009) A reference to the period 2007–2009, generally considered the worst global financial crisis since the Great Depression in the 1930s. The GFC was sparked by aggressive mortgage lending practices, which enabled unqualified borrowers to obtain mortgage loans, on which they subsequently defaulted. Exposure to these loans spread throughout the global financial system through structured securities, worsened by excessive leverage taken by banks and other financial institutions. These dislocations led to failures and government bailouts of many banks and investment firms worldwide, including most notably Lehman Brothers in September 2008.

Gordon model, or Gordon Growth model A method of estimating the intrinsic value of a security, whereby the value of the security equals the present value of future dividends, measured by the sum of current cash yield plus cash flow growth. Also known as the Dividend Discount model (DDM).

Illiquidity premium The incremental return of an asset resulting from it being priced and traded infrequently, compared with a more liquid asset having otherwise similar characteristics; it represents the return required by an investor to hold an illiquid asset.

Impairment A permanent reduction in the fair value of a loan to below its cost basis, due to the increased probability that the interest and/or principal of a loan will not be repaid.

Income return The portion of an asset's total return from interest or dividend income, rather than capital gains.

Incurrence covenant Part of a loan agreement or bond issue whereby the borrower is not allowed to take certain affirmative actions, such as incurring additional debt, an additional dividend payment or share repurchase, or acquiring or divesting a business (see also Maintenance covenant).

Intercept The constant in a model regression, or the number that results if the variable equals zero.

IPO Initial public offering, whereby a company or subsidiary is first listed on a stock exchange.

J-curve The initial period of a private investment whereby returns are low or negative due to the payment of management fees and expenses before investment gains are captured. Being out of the J-curve means investment gains more than offset cumulative fees and expenses.

Junk bonds Bonds rated below investment grade; also known as high-yield bonds.

Last-out loan The junior component of a unitranche loan where last-out lenders, in exchange for a higher coupon rate, are the last to receive interest payments and have a more junior repayment position if the loan is paid off or refinanced (as opposed to first-out loans).

Level 3 assets Assets whose fair value cannot be determined using broker quotations or observable inputs or measures; this is part of an accounting classification system used for valuing assets introduced by FASB 157 as ASC 820.

Leverage Obtaining debt to increase investment capital for purchasing assets or originating loans.

Leveraged buyout The acquisition of another company using a high level of debt financing.

Leveraged loans Secured and unsecured loans originated by banks or nonbank lenders that are then syndicated to a group of investors; also known as broadly syndicated loans.

Libor London Interbank Offered Rate is a widely used reference rate set daily among the main UK banks, at which banks around the world lend to one another for uncollateralized loans. Libor is being phased out in 2023 and replaced by SOFR in the US.

Liquidity premium The incremental value of an asset resulting from it being priced and traded frequently, compared with an illiquid asset having otherwise similar characteristics. For example, public companies generally trade at higher price-to-earnings multiples than similar private companies.

Loan-to-value ratio The amount of aggregate debt compared with the total value of an asset, including equity and debt, typically used in the real estate industry. It is frequently cited as a measure of financial leverage and risk.

Log scale A logarithmic scale is a nonlinear scale used when the y-axis represents a percentage change or multiplicative factor, such as a compounded rate of return.

Lower middle market Typically represents companies with annual EBITDA of less than $25 million.

Maintenance covenant Part of a loan agreement or bond issue whereby the borrower must maintain certain financial tests, such as net interest coverage or profitability (*see also* Incurrence covenant).

Marginal yield The change in yield relating to increased leverage, used to measure the relationship between increased leverage and higher borrowing costs.

Maximum drawdown The maximum historical drop in the market value of an asset or portfolio from peak to trough.

Mean-variance analysis An analytical framework first posited by Nobel Laureate Harry Markowitz that compares the expected risk of an asset or portfolio, typically measured by the standard deviation of returns, with its expected return.

Merton model A model proposed by Robert Merton that uses an options pricing model to value a company's equity, with equity as a call option on its assets.

Mezzanine The layer of a company's financing, or capital structure, that falls between senior secured and asset-backed debt and equity. Mezzanine financing often covers multiple capital structure segments, including subordinated debt, and may include equity warrants.

Middle market direct loans Loans originated by banks or nonbank lenders directly to middle market corporate borrowers (defined as having annual EBITDA between $10 million and $100 million). These loans are typically bilateral (not broadly syndicated) or may be syndicated to a small group of lenders. The companies may be sponsor-backed (controlled by a private equity firm) or nonsponsored (often family-owned businesses).

Morningstar LSTA US Leveraged Loan Index An index designed to reflect the performance of the largest facilities in the leveraged loan market.

Morningstar LSTA US Leveraged Loan 100 Index An index designed to measure the performance of the largest 100 loan facilities in the US leveraged loan market.

NCREIF National Council of Real Estate Investment Fiduciaries, an industry association serving real estate investors in the US that seeks to collect, aggregate, and disseminate real estate industry data.

NCREIF Property Index (NPI) A market-value-weighted index sponsored by NCREIF that is composed of commercial real estate properties in the US used to measure the performance of private real estate funds. Returns are reported gross-of-fees and unlevered.

Net annualized returns Annual returns from an investment inclusive of market value gains and losses, and net of all fees and expenses.

Net asset value The market value of a fund's assets minus its liabilities, divided by the number of shares outstanding.

Non-investment grade loans Loans rated below investment grade by one or more of the major credit rating agencies; direct loans are typically non-investment grade.

Nonsponsored borrower A company borrowing from a direct lender that is not controlled by a private equity firm or investor.

Oil crisis (2015–2016) The period during which oil and natural gas prices fell precipitously due to a rapid increase in production by the US, paired with decreased demand from China and a refusal by OPEC to slow production. This led to distress among energy producers refinancing outstanding debt.

Original issue discount A form of loan origination fee, typically 2–4% of the loan balance, structured so that the loan amount received by the borrower is slightly less than the par value of the loan.

Origination The sourcing and structuring of a loan.

Pari passu A financing arrangement that gives multiple lenders equal claim to assets used to secure a loan.

PIK income, or payment-in-kind A bond interest payment in the form of additional securities of the same bond issue rather than cash.

Prepayment The settlement of bonds or loans before maturity; bond issues often have terms or penalties limiting prepayment to mitigate reinvestment risk for the lender.

Prepayment penalties Fees charged to the borrower for settling a loan or bond before maturity.

Principal The notional amount of a bond or loan, representing the amount borrowed, on which coupon payments are calculated.

Private equity The ownership and/or control of companies that are not listed on public exchanges; can also represent private partnerships formed for the purpose of raising investment capital.

Random walk Refers to price changes that do not follow a discernable pattern or trend.

Realized gains The profit resulting from selling an asset at a higher price than its cost basis.

Recovery The collection of a portion of the remaining amount due on a defaulted loan.

Reference rate A short-term, typically floating, interest rate (e.g., Libor, SOFR, Prime, T-bill, Fed Funds), which, in addition to a constant spread to compensate for credit risk, determines the amount of interest periodically paid to the lender by the borrower.

Reinsurance Insurance purchased by insurance companies to reduce the risk of catastrophic events.

REIT Real estate investment trust, a type of regulated investment company (RIC) that owns real estate assets and is required to pass through at least 90% of related income to the shareholders.

Revolver A secured credit line, typically provided by a commercial bank, for a company's short-term funding needs; revolvers are senior in the capital structure to other debt and equity; also called revolving credit facility.

RIC Regulated investment company, a legal entity regulated by the SEC that is publicly traded, like common or preferred stock. RICs are required to pass through at least 90% of capital gains, dividends, or net interest earned to maintain their tax-exempt status.

Risk premium A yield or return in excess of the risk-free rate, compensating the lender or investor for the various sources of risk relating to the investment.

Risk-off A capital shift by investors to limit or reduce exposure to riskier investments in favor of those perceived as being less risky.

R-squared A statistical measure representing the proportion of variance for a dependent variable explained by an independent variable; a higher R-squared suggests a stronger relationship between two variables and a more powerful regression model.

Rule 17d The rule prohibits first- and second-tier affiliates of a fund acting as principal or engaging in a joint arrangement with the fund; what this means in practice for direct lending is that investment managers cannot allocate participation interests in loans they buy or originate to both private and registered funds without a 17d exemptive order.

Russell 3000 Index A market capitalization weighted index maintained by FTSE Russell designed to represent the broad investible US equity universe. It includes approximately the 3,000 largest stocks listed in the US.

Russell 2000 Index A small-cap stock market index including approximately the 2,000 smallest stocks in the Russell 3000 Index.

Senior debt, or senior secured debt A priority claim over subordinated debt, mezzanine, and equity in a company's capital structure, typically secured with collateral such as property, plant and equipment, and receivables.

Senior first lien A senior secured claim to second lien and other subordinated and junior debt, mezzanine, and equity in a company's capital structure, and is typically junior only to bank revolvers, accounts payable, and other short-term secured financing.

Senior second lien A junior secured claim to first lien debt in a company's capital structure, which is senior to subordinated debt, mezzanine, and equity.

Serial correlation The degree to which the value of a variable at a given time (t) is related to its value in the immediately preceding period (t–1), measured over various time periods.

Shadow rating An unofficial credit rating given by a credit rating agency to a bond that is not publicly announced.

Short volatility An investment strategy designed to profit from a decrease in market volatility.

Skew A measure of the asymmetry of a probability distribution.

Smoothing of asset values When the fair values of assets don't change significantly over time due to their being appraisal-based rather than marked to market.

SOFR Secured Overnight Financing Rate, the new reference rate for loans and derivatives that has replaced Libor for most new financial agreements in the US.

Sponsored borrower A company borrowing from a direct lender that is controlled by a private equity firm or investor; the direct lender typically works directly with the private equity sponsor to negotiate the size and terms of the loan.

Standard deviation A measure of risk or volatility of an asset's prices and returns, it is the degree to which individual observations within a statistical set vary from their mean.

Stretch senior A type of hybrid loan structure that combines senior debt and junior debt; the senior debt stretches to include junior parts of the capital structure.

Subordinated debt Unsecured debt that is junior to more senior secured debt; subordinated claims are paid out only after senior claims are satisfied.

Syndicate A group of investors and lenders that contribute capital to participate in a loan; syndicate members acquire their loan interests from the loan originator or underwriter.

Tracking error The degree to which the return of a portfolio deviates from that of its benchmark; also known as benchmark risk.

Unitranche loan A flexible hybrid loan that combines senior secured debt and subordinated debt at a single blended interest rate.

Unrealized gains The profit on an investment that remains unsold.

Unrelated business taxable income Income generated by a tax-exempt entity for investment and business activities outside the main function of the entity.

Unsmoothing A technique to more accurately reflect the degree to which an appraised asset's fair value changes over time based on market conditions.

Upper middle market Typically represents companies with annual EBITDA of more than $75 million.

Valuation agent An agent or entity responsible for determining the value of an asset.

Variance The square of the standard deviation.

Vintage weighting A measure of business cycle diversification of an investment portfolio.

Vintage year The year in which capital is first called for a private partnership.

VIX Shorthand for an index created by the Chicago Board Options Exchange that measures the stock market's expected volatility based on the pricing of S&P 500 Index options, formally known as the CBOE Volatility Index.

Warrants A derivative security that entitles the holder to purchase an underlying security at a fixed price up to an expiry date.

Yield Interest income plus fee income, divided by fair value.

Yield-to-three-year takeout The equivalent of yield-to-maturity for a loan, reflecting that middle market corporate loans are typically refinanced within about three years, rather than their five-year stated maturity.

Yield-to-maturity The estimated rate of return based on the assumption that it will be held until its maturity date and not prepaid or called.

About the Author

Stephen L. Nesbitt is chief executive officer and chief investment officer of Cliffwater LLC, an investment management and advisory firm specializing in alternative investments including private equity, private debt, real assets, and hedge funds. At Cliffwater, Steve manages more than $13 billion in assets and advises institutional clients on another $55 billion in alternatives.

Index Citations

Bloomberg U.S. Aggregate (Bloomberg US Agg Total Return Value Unhedged USD Index)

Source: Bloomberg Index Services Limited. BLOOMBERG® is a trademark and service mark of Bloomberg Finance L.P. and its affiliates (collectively "Bloomberg"). Bloomberg or Bloomberg's licensors own all proprietary rights in the Bloomberg Indices. Bloomberg does not approve or endorse this material or guarantee the accuracy or completeness of any information herein, nor does Bloomberg make any warranty, express or implied, as to the results to be obtained therefrom, and, to the maximum extent allowed by law, Bloomberg shall not have any liability or responsibility for injury or damages arising in connection therewith.

Bloomberg High Yield (Bloomberg US Corporate High Yield Total Return Index Value Unhedged USD Index)

Source: Bloomberg Index Services Limited. BLOOMBERG® is a trademark and service mark of Bloomberg Finance L.P. and its affiliates (collectively "Bloomberg"). Bloomberg or Bloomberg's licensors own all proprietary rights in the Bloomberg Indices. Bloomberg does not approve or endorse this material or guarantee the accuracy or completeness of any information herein, nor does Bloomberg make any warranty, express or implied, as to the results to be obtained therefrom, and, to the maximum extent allowed by law, Bloomberg shall not have any liability or responsibility for injury or damages arising in connection therewith.

Cambridge (CIA) US Buyout (Cambridge Associates US Buyout Benchmark)

Source: Cambridge Associates US Buyout Benchmark by S&P Dow Jones Indices. S&P® is a registered trademark of Standard & Poor's Financial Services LLC and Dow Jones® is a registered trademark of Dow Jones Trademark Holdings LLC. © 2022 S&P Dow Jones Indices LLC, its affiliates and/or its licensors. All rights reserved.

Cambridge Private Equity (Cambridge Associates Global Private Equity and Venture Capital Benchmark)

Source: Cambridge Associates Global Private Equity and Venture Capital Benchmark by S&P Dow Jones Indices. S&P® is a registered trademark of Standard & Poor's Financial Services LLC and Dow Jones® is a registered trademark of Dow Jones Trademark Holdings LLC. © 2022 S&P Dow Jones Indices LLC, its affiliates and/or its licensors. All rights reserved.

Cliffwater Direct Lending Index (Cliffwater Direct Lending Index – Total Return)

Source: Cliffwater LLC. Cliffwater Direct Lending Index is sponsored by Cliffwater LLC. Copyright © 2004 - 2022 Cliffwater LLC. All rights reserved.

HFRI Fund Weighted (HFRI Fund Weighted Composite Index)

Source: HFR Inc., www.hfr.com, © 2022 HFR, Inc. All rights reserved.

Merrill Lynch 0-3 Month T-Bill (ICE BofA US 3-Month Treasury Bill Index)

Source: ICE Data Indices, LLC ("ICE DATA"), is used with permission. ICE® IS A REGISTERED TRADEMARK OF ICE DATA OR ITS AFFILIATES, AND BOFA® IS A REGISTERED TRADEMARK OF BANK OF AMERICA CORPORATION LICENSED BY BANK OF AMERICA CORPORATION AND ITS AFFILIATES ("BOFA") AND MAY NOT BE USED WITHOUT BOFA'S PRIOR WRITTEN APPROVAL. ICE DATA, ITS AFFILIATES AND THEIR RESPECTIVE THIRD PARTY SUPPLIERS DISCLAIM ANY AND ALL WARRANTIES AND REPRESENTATIONS, EXPRESS AND/OR IMPLIED, INCLUDING ANY WARRANTIES OF MERCHANTABILITY OR FITNESS FOR A PARTICULAR PURPOSE OR USE, INCLUDING THE INDICES, INDEX DATA AND ANY DATA INCLUDED IN, RELATED TO, OR DERIVED THEREFROM. NEITHER ICE DATA, ITS AFFILIATES NOR THEIR RESPECTIVE THIRD PARTY SUPPLIERS SHALL BE SUBJECT TO ANY DAMAGES OR LIABILITY WITH RESPECT TO THE ADEQUACY, ACCURACY, TIMELINESS OR COMPLETENESS OF THE INDICES OR THE INDEX DATA OR ANY COMPONENT THEREOF, AND THE INDICES AND INDEX DATA AND ALL COMPONENTS THEREOF ARE PROVIDED ON AN "AS IS" BASIS AND YOUR USE IS AT YOUR OWN RISK. ICE DATA, ITS AFFILIATES AND THEIR RESPECTIVE THIRD PARTY SUPPLIERS DO NOT SPONSOR, ENDORSE, OR RECOMMEND ANY PART OF THIS PUBLICATION.

Morningstar LSTA US Leveraged Loan 100 (Morningstar LSTA US Leveraged Loan 100 Total Return USD Index)

Source: © 2022 Morningstar, Inc. All rights reserved. Reproduced with permission. The information contained herein: (1) is proprietary to Morningstar and/or its content providers; (2) may not be copied or distributed; (3) does not constitute investment advice offered by Morningstar; and (4) is not warranted to be accurate, complete or timely. Neither Morningstar nor its content providers are responsible for any damages or losses arising from any use of this information. Past performance is no guarantee of future results. Use of information from Morningstar does not necessarily constitute agreement by Morningstar, Inc. of any investment philosophy or strategy presented in this publication.

NCREIF Property (Real Estate) (NCREIF Property Total Return Index)

Source: US commercial real estate indices: the NCREIF property index. All rights reserved.

Russell 3000 (Russell 3000 Total Return Index)

Source: London Stock Exchange Group plc and its group undertakings (collectively, the "LSE Group"). © LSE Group 2022. FTSE Russell is a trading name of certain of the LSE Group companies. FTSE® and Russell® are trademarks of the relevant LSE Group companies and are used by any other LSE Group company under license. All rights in the FTSE Russell indexes or data vest in the relevant LSE Group company which owns the index or the data. Neither LSE Group nor its licensors accept any liability for any errors or omissions in the indexes or data and no party may rely on any indexes or data contained in this communication. No further distribution of data from the LSE Group is permitted without the relevant LSE Group company's express written consent. The LSE Group does not promote, sponsor or endorse the content of this communication. This book is not in any way connected to or sponsored, endorsed, sold or promoted by the London Stock Exchange Group plc and its group undertakings (collectively, the "LSE Group"). The LSE Group does not accept any liability whatsoever to any person arising out of the use of this book or the underlying data.

Index